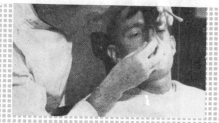

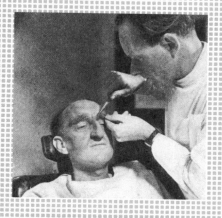

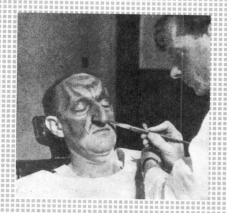

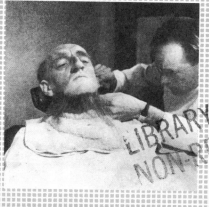

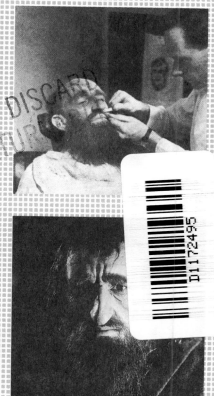

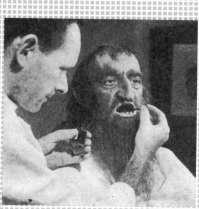

ALEC GUINNESS
Master of Disguise

ALEC GUINNESS
Master of Disguise

Garry O'Connor

"He is always a joy, the intelligence acute, malice serene, sense of absurdity alert when game's about."

Gore Vidal

Hodder & Stoughton
LONDON SYDNEY AUCKLAND

British Library Cataloguing in Publication Data

O'Connor, Garry
Alec Guinness: Master of Disguise
I. Title
792.028092

ISBN 0 340 48562 0

Typeset by Hewer Text Composition Services, Edinburgh
Printed and bound in Great Britain by
Mackays of Chatham, Chatham, Kent

Hodder and Stoughton,
A division of Hodder Headline PLC
338 Euston Road
London NW1 3BH

To Emilie, Fred, Joe and Tobias

Foreword

In 1958, when he was forty-four, Alec Guinness was called the "hottest box-office property since Rudolph Valentino". Yet the process of writing about him has been described as trying to find a fingerhold on a smooth and gently shining piece of plastic. J.B. Priestley felt that his distinctive quality as an actor was continually undervalued both by critics and by the public: "They tend to respond to publicity, fuss, showmanship," he wrote, "and these are not what this modest but dedicated man is offering them."

Alec Guinness *is* a difficult subject. He is almost the complete opposite of Laurence Olivier, who can fruitfully be examined in the light of Congreve's couplet from *The Double Dealer*:

> No mask like open truth to cover lies
> As to go naked is the best disguise.

Guinness has, very deliberately, never gone naked, yet he has dressed himself in closeness and intimacy and he covers what he wants to hide with a truth that partly satisfies him and deflects the curious. His reaction against truth, against revealing himself, is deep, instinctive and should be respected. But while respected, this can also be questioned and not followed in blind subservience. The important question to be asked perhaps is, "Would his instinct for non-disclosure ultimately prove to be a limitation?" Some people have argued that it has.

Guinness has frequently defended his privacy: "It was Disraeli, I think, who said, 'Something unpleasant is coming when men are anxious to speak the truth'," he wrote in the *Spectator* in 1993. Yet Disraeli, whom Guinness once played on film in *The Mudlark*, was, according to recent accounts, a man who cherished privacy not necessarily for its own sake, but for the ulterior motive of wanting to keep something hidden. But we know what Guinness means.

Guinness has also complained that some of his contemporaries have become, in their seventies, "unexpectedly and brutally frank". Is this a warning as well as a fear? There is surely only one way to safeguard one's private life, and that is not to become a public figure. Paul Scofield, another great actor, has done just this, truly denying himself the attention that should have been his due. So have other, younger actors, such as Michael Kitchen, who refuse all interviews. Guinness, on the other hand, has enjoyed the limelight while claiming not to; but he has enjoyed fame very much on his own terms, which have not necessarily made him happy. Fame has, to some extent, become identified with that sense of shame he has most wanted to avoid. He has felt as trapped as he was when a child.

This book was begun as long ago as 1988, and although it is perhaps needless to say this, Guinness has not cooperated with it or helped with it, much to my disappointment. The reason he has given is that there have been already too many books written about him. He mentioned the number as five.

It had always been my intention to send the completed manuscript to him. These were his words on the subject:

> A.E. Housman wrote, in 1936, to a would-be-biographer – "Do not send me your manuscript. Worse than the practice of writing books about living men is the conduct of living men supervising such books". Would you please accept that as being my own sentiment and possibly make it clear to your publisher.
>
> Yours sincerely
> Alec Guinness

In spite of his reluctance to help, I have found it endlessly challenging to try and catch his mysterious quality, and portray his unique anonymity. As Peter Ustinov wrote in 1994, "His elusive nature sees to it that however well one knows him, one is never without an ardent desire to know him better." The paradoxes are many and varied. For instance, his film and stage acting have enjoyed large financial rewards and great prestige in America, which has no mystique of evasiveness, yet Guinness has never shied away from working there. Or take the case of Sir Sydney Cockerell, the art historian, and Guinness's most admired mentor during his formative years: Cockerell was about as public a person as it was possible to be. "In your account of me," he instructed Wilfrid

Blunt, his biographer, "I wish my faults and shortcomings to be emphasised and not suppressed . . ." Perhaps I am flattering my subject by believing that might also be his feeling and that it might just prove to be the final paradox.

Contents

Contents

Illustrations

Acknowledgements

1 Mander and Mitchinson
2 *Dear Alec*, Hodder and Stoughton
3 Original drawing by D.W. Hawksley, 1952
4 National Portrait Gallery
5 Hulton/Deutsch (also front cover)
6 John Vickers Archive (also back cover below left and right)
7 *Daily Mail*
8 Lumière Films Ltd
9 MGM
10 Sands Films Ltd (also back cover top left)
11 Alistair Muir and *Daily Telegraph*
12 EMI
13 Yvonne Arnaud Theatre, Guildford
14 Lucasfilms Ltd and 20th Century Fox
15 *Punch*
16 *Guardian*
17 Production Design Company and Thames Television
18 Paul Grover and *Daily Telegraph*
19 Rank Film Distributors

The author and publishers also gratefully acknowledge the BBC (back cover centre left), the British Film Institute, the Kobal Collection, Anne-Marie Ehrlich Picture Research, and the *Picturegoer's Guide* (Sweden). Every effort has been made to clear copyrights and permissions where necessary, and any omission is regretted and will be rectified in future editions.

PART ONE

Getting Nowhere for a Start

But seriously, I wonder whether for a person like myself whose most intense moments were those of depression, a cure that destroys the depression may not destroy the intensity – a *desperate* remedy.

Edward Thomas

1

The Geddesses of Peeblesshire

Is Alec Guinness, as Richard Burton once said of Elizabeth Taylor, "a secret wrapped in an enigma, inside a mystery", or is he that far more elusive thing, something quite simple that evades definition? Either way we can be sure that Guinness dislikes explanations. The door would seem to be firmly closed on the past. Yet perhaps not altogether so, because one has the feeling that occasionally, and when no-one is looking, Guinness likes to steal along the corridors at the back of his past, terrify or tantalise himself by opening a door, and then shut it again smartly. What exactly has he had a glimpse of? A skeleton? Possibly, but also possibly an unexpected joy which might free him from a lot of constricting taboos and uncomfortable feelings.

Tolstoy once wrote that people were like rivers who all contained the same water, yet each river could at times be narrow, swift, broad, smooth-flowing, clear, muddy or warm: "So it is with people, each man carries within himself the germ of all human qualities."

This applies especially to an actor. Guinness has shown, in the extraordinarily wide range of parts he has acted on film and stage, that he possesses the germ of most human qualities. Yet if challenged he would point out how useless it was trying to swim backwards. Wanting to remain in, and be part of, his personal river he has no desire to know what the river is composed of. That is someone else's job. As he said in an interview in 1985, "I wouldn't go to a psychoanalyst in case he unravelled something and said, 'And that is the springboard of such talents as you have'. I would feel, it was just that, was it? – instead of something you can't explain, something tucked inside."

Yet rivers have a source, just as the strands of biological programming in someone's personality pass to and fro through the structure of his or her being. Contemplating the work of a complex actor and man in relation to his life is often like being in a hall of mirrors or a corridor of echoes. One thinks of a John le Carré novel, perhaps *A Perfect Spy*, in which the hero, Magnus Pym, is continually trying to unravel the past, while the present closes in on him. Inevitably one is drawn to the idea of uncovering, inside one person, another self: the clergyman beyond the spy, say, the sinner behind the saint, the arrogant upstart behind the diffident prude. But, then, why all these disguises? Actors in their parts, like authors in their fictions, play out unrealised possibilities of their nature.

The paternal source of Guinness was mysterious. Although named Guinness the subject of this book believes he is probably the illegitimate son of one Andrew Geddes, a Scottish banker and friend of the Guinness family, from one of whom Geddes asked permission to lend his name to an unwanted child. The name Guinness is on his birth certificate. It was Edwardian practice for a best friend to give his name to a love child. This is the Guinness version, as revealed at the very end of Guinness's autobiography, *Blessings in Disguise*. One of these blessings is, by ironic or humorous implication, Guinness himself.

Agnes de Cuffe, Guinness's mother (and the bearer of an equally mysterious name) would not – or could not – clear up the mystery for him, but he did see the man called Andrew Geddes several times during his childhood. He also found himself the possessor of a small allowance which suggested some provision made for him by a wealthy father.

Guinness also revealed in his autobiography that the last time he saw his father he was eight years old. Guinness, if such he was, came to visit his father. The cynical smile Geddes wore when he handed him half-a-crown may well have reflected the link of guilt and financial support. Guinness himself commented, identifying strongly with the possibility that Geddes *was* his father, that from the cynical smile this was the Geddes personality he remembered and which he had, through the years, seen in himself: "Something very similar when I have felt hurt or taken advantage of". Guinness added swiftly, coveringly, "He died when I was sixteen."

If we add this to a statement Guinness made about his father – "My father generated me in his 64th year. He was a bank director.

Quite wealthy. His name was Andrew" – we have a father who was eighty years old when he died.*

Everything Guinness has said points to the possibility that his father, if called Geddes, was a well-connected Geddes, in other words "a Geddes" and part of the code of the British class system. The most famous member of this family, Sir Eric Geddes, was a businessman and politician who served in Lloyd George's coalition cabinet of 1919 as Minister of Transport and later wielded the famous "Geddes Axe" of post-First-World-War economic planning. Another Geddes, Sir Auckland, also reached cabinet rank and was created Baron in 1942.

Later Guinness was constantly subject to the misunderstanding of being assumed to be one of the famous Guinness family. Possibly his mother liked the name because it conferred on him a bit of class, and might help to give him a start in life. Perhaps this became part of the drive which resulted in him becoming "Alec Guinness", ultimately "Sir Alec Guinness", a one-man institution outweighing by far his confused family "lettres de crédit".

One day in November 1986, at King's Cross Station bookstall, the present Lord Geddes picked up a copy of *Blessing in Disguise*, then no. 1 on the paperback bestseller lists, and read it with great amusement and interest until page 308 when suddenly the name "Andrew Geddes" – a regular name in his family – sprang out at him. Beginning on that page Guinness spent six pages talking about his ancestry during which he says that since earliest childhood and from the time he first recognised he was illegitimate he believed, although "without any good reason", that his father was Andrew Geddes, "a Managing Director of the Anglo-South American Bank, who had been born, I discovered later, in 1860".

Lord Geddes became fascinated. The Geddesses were a large clan and, as he wrote to a close relation, it would be quite fun to "find a benighted illegitimate relation". Taking his cue from Guinness's assertion that the search for his father had been a "constant, though fairly minor speculation for fifty years" he wrote to Guinness that he had become intrigued by his supposition that his father might have been an Andrew Geddes born in 1860. He then went on to say that he himself had long had an interest in Geddes genealogy

---

* There is no record of any Andrew Geddes dying in England or Wales or Scotland in 1930. Agnes de Cuffe was born Agnes Cuffe in 1887. Her father, Edward Charles Cuffe, was a captain in the Royal Navy.

and for that reason was occasionally referred to by members of his family as "Head of the Family".

But there was no Andrew Geddes in their direct descent, although a son of one of the four brothers of his great grandfather Acland Geddes (1831–1908), might have been an Andrew Geddes. However, he went on, so curious was he in exploring this possibility that he wondered whether Guinness might care to join him for a drink or lunch. Guinness replied that he would. He now realised that the date he had given for the birth of his father, 1860, was more likely to have been 1850, but this too did not fit in with any possible connection with the Geddes family. He had also found out that there was a Catholic bishop called Geddes who lived in New Zealand in the last half of the nineteenth century, but that he obviously could not be laid at his door. He had heard when small that the Geddes who may have been his father came from Dumfriesshire, or Ayrshire. He was sure that there was no Andrew Geddes.

Geddes replied that the different dates did not help establish any connections with his family, and while there was a strong branch of the family who were in shipping and trading, based in Rachan, Peeblesshire, none of these fitted what Guinness knew. Although they arranged to meet for a drink, somehow this fell through so that, yet again, the remotest chance that Guinness might find out more about his father than he already knew, came to nothing.

But were there any other, non-factual connections between Guinness and the Geddes family that might be worthy of note? Hardly, although it must be said that Alexander Geddes, father of a present-day Andrew Geddes (born 1943) who is a distinguished barrister, had a distinct resemblance to Guinness in certain features of the face, that physically the Geddesses were quite small, stocky men with big heads (Guinness is similar here), and that the existence of a famous cabinet minister and a tradition of public speaking suggested certain talents that might have been shared.

But the most significant aspect about the contact that Lord Geddes made with Guinness was that, for all the protestations of interest on Guinness's part and the warm tactful interest on Geddes's part, the elaborate courtesies, the prestigious suggestions of places where they should meet – the Connaught Hotel, "my too expensive hideaway", the Guests Bar of the House of Lords – the meeting between them did not ever happen. It was as if, without either of them noticing quite how or why, Guinness slipped away and was seen no more. What might have been remained – in the words of T.S. Eliot, a favourite poet of the actor – a possibility only in a world of speculation. After seventy-odd years of not knowing exactly who was his father, did Guinness really want to know? Would you, or I? Probably not.

Yet why not? Guinness has a ceaseless, restless mind. He is, without any doubt, the outstanding intellectual actor of the age, with a range of interests and a quickness of mind suggestive of the higher reaches of diplomacy or academia. One has the sense that, in all areas of his life, he has liked the idea of uncertainty and of mystery; it was provoking, stimulating, it kept one alive and on one's toes. In all his speculation there was a lot of toing and froing. His life has been one long balancing act, and here again, of course, one cannot help thinking of the "pushme-pullyou" nature of the le Carré double-agent. About his father, about his mother, and ultimately about himself there were facts that will never be conclusively proven one way or another. This uncertainty has been to him a main source of energy. Who else but Guinness has portrayed so many heroes, villains, saints or men of genius – in order both to work himself out and to find out who he is, as well as to take something from them to add to himself?

Guinness did not know the circumstances in which Geddes came to accept his paternity. The cynical smile which he gave Guinness could be interpreted in a different way. It may even have been a reflection of complicity in a deception. He was not to know how much or how little Guinness believed he was his father.

But in spite of Guinness's assertion to the contrary, Andrew Geddes had been born in 1860. Guinness may have changed the date to 1850 to put Lord Geddes off the scent. Geddes had not, as Guinness told *Time* magazine in 1958, generated him in his sixty-fourth year, but in his fifty-sixth year or thereabouts. Guinness wrote further in *Blessings in Disguise* that he died, "when I was sixteen. *The Times* printed a fairly long, dull obituary, representing him, if I remember correctly, as an industrious and conscientious man". But there was no obituary in *The Times*, and no mention of his qualities. There was only a brief report of his will and of his age at death in *The Times* of 26 June 1928 (when Guinness was fourteen). Presumably this is what Guinness had seen:

Andrew Geddes (68) of Meadside, Northumberland-road New Barnet, late of the Anglo-South American Bank, Limited, and lately also a director of the Allanza Company, Limited, and of the Pan de Azucar Nitrate Company, Limited (net personalty £51,468) – £53,460.

This was a considerable fortune at that time. According to the certificate issued in Barnet, Geddes died at home on 18 March 1928 from pneumonia and mental degeneration. In his will – which described him as "formerly known as Gaddes" – Geddes had directed that his money and estate should for the most part be left to his four daughters and put in trust for his only son, Andrew, who was in permanent care as a mental invalid. There is no mention of his wife or of Guinness. "Catherine Weldon", who many years later introduced herself to Guinness after a performance in Brighton as the youngest daughter of Geddes, was left three thousand, three hundred pounds. She told Guinness nothing about her father or herself.

But what if a Guinness from the banking and brewery family was his father? From what we know of Andrew Geddes (or "Gaddes"), it seems most unlikely that he was a Guinness family friend and therefore on the family yacht in the summer of 1913, at the place and time when the subject of this book was conceived.

Some members of the Guinness family still strongly believe that the Hon. Anthony Ernest Guinness, or "Uncle" Ernest (1876–1959), was Guinness's father. Ernest, who became Vice-Chairman of the brewery firm, had married into the English aristocracy in 1903 and had three daughters. They believe he met Guinness's mother Agnes when the family yacht was moored in Cowes, and she was working as a waitress or chamber-maid in an hotel. Guinness modestly distances himself from any connection with the family, although when he met Honor Guinness, Lord Iveagh's daughter, on the *Queen Mary*, in 1959, she told him he was definitely a Guinness. Perhaps the date was significant because it was the year of Ernest's death. Several Guinnesses of his generation also looked uncannily like Alec Guinness.

Thus, early on, the power and atmosphere of a hidden secret came to permeate Guinness's life. But while being his secret, it was also a secret hidden from him. The quality of unsolved mystery and its seductive, Janus-faced nature – shame and guilt, yet desire for success and artistic achievement – were to become important components of his personality.

Secrecy lies at the core of power. Secrecy and terror are a double act. Someone with something to hide arranges his or her secrets to guard each other. There is a saying in the Arabic *Book of the Crown*: "It is the privilege of kings to keep their secrets from father, mother, brothers, wives and friends."

2

In my glass I find you

But there is a second and very different kind of birth from that of a mother's womb. There is the birth of the actor which Alec Guinness himself has eloquently described as a raw and youthful Ego pursued by fiends, entering from the wings on to the public stage: "Deep in his heart," he wrote in *Blessings in Disguise*, "he hankers to be an artist of some sort, but he is only an actor."

This may be Guinness, but it also applies to a fictional character of Shakespeare who has, above all, dominated the ambition of Alec Guinness in the way that Napoleon hovers over the heroes of Stendhal's *Le Rouge et le Noir* and *La Chartreuse de Parme*. This is, of course, Hamlet. Not only did Guinness act on two separate occasions the most minor roles in the play, he twice attempted the role of Hamlet himself.*

Like Hamlet, Guinness all through his life has been a watcher, an observer – not only a scrutiniser of himself, but a commentator on others. Shakespeare showed Hamlet not only to be fascinated by acting, but an excellent clown and mimic. In terms of expressing his passion, his deepest feelings, however, he remains alienated, cut off from everything except, perhaps, disgust at his mother's behaviour with his stepfather. He, too, has a secret; his silence to others is an extreme form of defence. Because of his secret he appears more dangerous than he is. Watching the Player King mouth his rhodomontade Hamlet says,

> Is it not monstrous that this player here,
> But in a fiction, in a dream of passion
> Could force his soul so to his own conceit?

* Later in life one of the very few parts he regretted never having acted was the Ghost.

Yet something holds him back, something arrests his natural feeling of revenge. Throughout the play he changes and develops, deepens and becomes more accepting. "When the mystery of Hamlet has been solved, the mystery of human life will have been solved," wrote the critic Harold Child in 1935. Like attracts like, or so they say.

Laurence Olivier, the great power-hungry devourer of parts, played Hamlet three times: "Hamlet – Anybody can do Hamlet; nobody can do him properly, but we can all do him," he said. But Olivier was not a great Hamlet, for the core of the part never touched him. His Hamlet was the thwarted man of action, not the brooding genius or potential self-portrait of the creative spirit itself. "Hamlet is a part which can be compared to a man given a pistol, completely blindfolded and told to fire it off in a room, completely papered with targets", said Ralph Richardson, who never played the part but would have liked to. "If he goes, bang, bang, bang, he'll hit three targets."

The many-sided Guinness developed from his earliest days a kind of genius similar to that of Hamlet himself, while his own childhood had many points of contact with that of the melancholy Dane. The role, when he came to play it at the age of twenty-four in 1938, attracted him quite outside the measure and power of his own technical resources. "O shame, where is thy blush," says Hamlet to his mother, while she answers, "O Hamlet, speak no more!/Thou turn'st mine eyes into my very soul . . ." He became fascinated by the figure of Hamlet because it beckoned to him in his own search for identity; it promised a completeness, a synthesis.

3

Special providence

On the first page of his autobiography, almost as if he was being pushed reluctantly into doing the "done" thing, Guinness mentions his birth certificate. He says that he was born in Marylebone, which is not strictly true – unless, that is, his mother moved within six weeks of his birth. The certificate gives Lauderdale Mansions as her address: this is in Lauderdale Road, Maida Vale, near Warwick Avenue and Elgin Avenue, two streets away from the Paddington recreation ground. At his time it was an area associated with the *demi-monde* and prostitution, although of course many respectable people lived there.

Guinness was born in 1914, the first year of the first world war which was declared in August, a few months after his birth. His mother was twenty-seven when he was born, his father twenty-six years older than she was. They never lived together. They had met, apparently, at Cowes on the Isle of Wight, during Regatta week. To be born just before the war meant that, personal conditions of chaos and unhappiness apart, the whole of his infant and early life was steeped in an atmosphere of optimism and formal discipline. Whatever his mother may have been doing, the country before and during her pregnancy was gearing itself up for war, and there was always a sense of life larger than oneself.

Not only was this feeling of nationhood an integral part of his early life, but it must have been reinforced, although not entirely in a salutary way, by his mother's immediate post-war marriage to a demobbed "Captain", David Stiven, who had apparently served in Ireland during the war (or just after), and who kept a loaded revolver beside his bed in case members of Sinn Fein came after him.

Several millions of men were away from home, many mothers lived with their children alone during these years, so Agnes de

Cuffe's situation was hardly remarkable. But illegitimacy in those days was much less common then than it is today, and knowing this fact from an early age set Guinness apart. He guarded the knowledge as a secret, he took special pains to make himself respectable and build up for the outside world an image of himself so he could feel accepted. You might keep quiet about yourself, but you would always be suspicious that someone else knew. Guinness's exact sense of what was right, his punctiliousness and self-discipline, came from a need and a determination to show he was better than the facts of his birth. The guard was never lowered.

Captain Clipton, who observed Colonel Nicholson in *The Bridge on the River Kwai*, the most famous of the characters acted by Guinness, came to the conclusion (in the novel by Pierre Boulle on which the film was based) that the individual characteristics which contributed to Nicholson's personality – sense of duty, observance of ritual, obsession with discipline and love of the job well done – could not be better described than by the word "snobbery". Nicholson, he thought, was a perfect example of the military snob, a type "which has gradually emerged after a lengthy process of development dating from the Stone Age, the preservation of the species being guaranteed by tradition".

Boulle continues in a vein which is particularly relevant to Guinness, and which also gives the character of Nicholson his universal appeal:

> Clipton, however, was by nature objective and had the rare gift of being able to examine a problem from every angle. The conclusion he had reached having somewhat calmed the brainstorm which certain aspects of the Colonel's behaviour caused him, he would suddenly feel well disposed and recognize, almost with affection, the excellence of the CO's qualities. If these were typically snobbish, he reasoned, then the argument needed to be carried only one stage further for the noblest sentiments to be classified as such, until even a mother's love would eventually come to be regarded as the most blatant sign of snobbery imaginable.

Snobbery, an almost princely sense of being set apart, became part of Guinness's early determination that no-one should know who he was. The pressure on him to conceal must often have been greater than any other feeling he knew. At the same time he would cherish and nurture any sense of virtue, of being in the right, to gain self-respect.

But there was another side. In him also was that component which had made his mother what she was: not only the potentiality, as in everyone, but the actual ability to sell herself cheap. His outlet for this was to become very attached to those tawdry music-hall figures who sported themselves, tarted their talents on the stage; he developed a "wicked" side to himself, a sense of subversive fun, a lavatorial humour – that kind of "don't-leave-your-fan-on-the-seat" smart remarks that were the catch phrases of his adolescence, and which also became a deliberately outrageous side of his personality in later life – a way of living out an exhibitionist streak in his nature.

In April 1954, just after his conversion to Roman Catholicism, Guinness took the leading role of the Cardinal in *The Prisoner* by Bridget Boland who, in her portrait of the Cardinal, supplied parallels for Guinness's own early life. The play was dedicated to Guinness, and in it he achieved a quality of identification and spiritual conviction which has rarely been surpassed on stage or film. The secret weakness of this prince of the Church is the truth about his background which he has concealed. How had Bridget Boland picked on this? Did she work it out unconsciously from being a close friend and near neighbour of the Guinnesses? Possibly she did. The powerful impact which *The Prisoner* had on those who saw it, or saw the film of the play made later, was that Guinness seemed to be "confessing", at one level removed and in emotionally safe circumstances, the shameful background of his own life (and if not the actual truth, then the feelings he had about it). The Interrogator asks:

What were you hiding? Why were you ashamed?
Prisoner. Unclean flesh.
Interrogator. Yes. Yes?
Prisoner. My body of her flesh and blood.
Interrogator. Your mother.
Prisoner. Filth of her filth, me at the root of it, her lust.
Interrogator. Behind the Fish Market. A prostitute?
Prisoner. Not even for money. A whore. Not even for money, for lust ... Remembering the smell of the women who bent over you to try and kiss you good night. Where, before I was born or after it, would I find a heart?

Later the Prisoner is even more explicit when he says what should go into his confession: "That I am the son of my mother, and my whole life a fantasy to hide me . . . I prayed for forgiveness, but I knew I had no heart."

Guinness's birth, on 2 April 1914, had not been registered at once. It was held up until the absolute legal limit of six weeks before his mother, reluctantly or so one imagines, went along from Flat 155, Lauderdale Mansions to the nearest registration office which was Paddington North. The certificate is enigmatic for it contains his name ("if any" in the words of the form) "Alec Guinness", his mother's name, Agnes de Cuffe, the date of his registration, one calendar month and sixteen days after his birth. The name of the father and his occupation have both been left blank. Long delay over the registering of the birth was quite a common occurrence with an unwanted or illegitimate child. Guinness later told someone that, whenever he talked over with his mother the question of his father, she went into a catatonic state.

4

Few intimations of immortality

If all childhood is but a fantasy and a dream, as Charlotte Brontë
describes it in her novel *Shirley*, and at eighteen one confronts the
dawn of experience and the dim perception of reality arrives as
distant mountains in a mist, then Guinness's childhood was a
nightmare. It was only illusion, i.e. the theatre, which provided
fairyland vistas of happiness, or as least comic relief. He recalled his
first visit to the London theatre as that of seeing *Chu Chin Chow* at
the Coliseum, when he was four. It made on him, he said in a radio
interview in 1975, a "huge impression". Two years later he was
taken to one or two shows, "which I hated, a pantomine which I
was scared by. I think the kind of dressing-up and pretending to
be someone else probably happens to all children. And I think as
my particular background wasn't a very happy one I probably did
console myself with make-believe a lot."

His upbringing was a mixture of privilege and deprivation. He
was sent to private boarding schools, but when his mother arrived
she would borrow ten pounds off a master. Guinness has hardly
spoken publicly of her more than five times, and what he said
was less than warm: basically she was unhelpful; even less helpful
was the solicitor who channelled the money into his schooling and
abruptly turned off the dribble of funds when he ceased being a
drama student.

When Guinness began to recall all this he found the experience
alarming: the effect was powerful and Proustian, as a smell of some
other memory would fill him. He had so much hidden recall. "I
only had to say I went to pre-prep-school at Bexhill at six, and
suddenly a vision of a master picking off the tree a diseased crab
apple, crawling with maggots, haunted my days. Something with
a shiny outside that hid the corruption."

The most upsetting of his memories was his violent stepfather, whom his mother married in 1919 when he was five.* David Daniel Stiven, recently demobbed, had not become truly detached from the habits of military life. He may not even have been demobbed at all, but still a serving officer, for he gave his address to the marriage registrar as the Ordnance Depot, Didcot. The "captain", also like Geddes a Scot,† was to Guinness a threatening and exploitative type. In truth he was a Royal Army Service Corps lieutenant, a master gas engineer, like his father before him. He was twenty-eight years old and was divorced from his first wife Winifred. Stiven not only kept a loaded service revolver but once menaced Guinness with it, saying he would kill both of them to get whatever he wanted out of his mother. On another occasion he held his young charge upside down from a bridge, ready to drop him into the river below.

Much later, however, Guinness felt, or so he said, he may have provoked the "captain" to behave in the way he did. Reluctant as he was to speak ill of his mother after she died,‡ there was an undercurrent of resentment at the way he was treated which coloured his relationship with certain of the opposite sex and may have made him contained, even very shy, towards feminine sexual attraction. This became evident later on in his acting: the last thing he could ever convey was passionate attraction towards women, although this of course is not to say he did not feel it. His refusal, when rehearsing, to kiss when it was called for is well-known, for he would save this only for the performance.

The marriage lasted three years, during which time Guinness said he lived in a depressing three-roomed top-floor flat in St John's Wood, not far from the Victorian block in Lauderdale Road where he had started life. But Agnes gave her address when she and Stiven married as 31 Upper Bedford Place, Bloomsbury. The personal, family complexity or muddle gave Guinness an early drive towards becoming an actor, while the schools he attended did not provide much by way of stimulus or academic achievement, except perhaps that most important element of all, curiosity.

The first of these, Normandale boarding school in Collington

---

* At the St Giles Register Office on 9 August.
† "'Why are Scots so attracted to the secret world?' wonders Smiley in *Smiley's People*, not for the first time in his career. 'Ship engineers, colonial administrator, spies . . . Their heretical Scottish history drew them to distant churches,' he decided."
‡ She died, apparently, in 1985 when, according to Guinness, she was ninety-six, but possibly older. I have not been able to find records of either her birth or her death in any of the years which would seem to have been likely.

Avenue, Bexhill, had a headmaster named Mr Salmon. Bexhill was a flourishing area for preparatory schools because it was quiet and respectable, the air was healthy, while it possessed two railway lines to London. His second school, Pembroke Lodge, Southbourne-on-sea, which he attended from the age of seven to thirteen, had the same qualities; a "School for Young Gentlemen", preparatory for Public School and the Royal Navy, it was a stone's throw from the Dorset beach. His third, Roborough School in Bournemouth, saw him through to the age of eighteen, establishing a lasting basis of discipline in him, mostly by means of a series of prohibitions which, if broken, threatened dire punishments.

His doubt about who he really was, and the loneliness of his position, developed his imagination more than that of other children. "If I look back now I can see traces from being very, very small and escaping into something of a fantasy world," he said in that 1975 radio interview. His anecdotal eye developed, the observing side of his personality also became important to him. At the same time he found, perhaps as a reaction to the pain that had been inflicted on him, that he could easily merge "with the background when he wants to", as Michael Noakes, who painted Guinness's portrait over a two-year period, noted. "When I was young," said Guinness himself, "I used to follow people for miles sometimes, women as well as men, just studying them. It was a kind of obsession."

In 1928 Guinness was told, presumably by his mother, that his real name was Guinness, which it was not, although this was the name on his birth certificate, and that de Cuffe and Stiven no longer applied. Yet by this time he and his mother had moved thirty times (so Guinness said) while in the hotels and lodgings where they lived they left behind them, as in a paper chase, a wake of unpaid bills. While there is no proof of a shady profession, one does suspect the means by which his mother came by her money. You do not ever get a sense that Guinness trusted his mother or that she ever made him the centre of her attention. Later, when he became an actor, he did not see her for long periods. But what she clearly did do was to stimulate his aspiration to have a family, to "belong" in a wider sense, for which he developed an extraordinary capacity – an appetite which he has been fulfilling meticulously and conscientiously ever since. He became incredibly precise in his attachment to form, and in details of life such as dress, and even hand-writing.

In his childhood and youth Guinness always had to keep quiet, gain respectability and good report by the calm quality of his behaviour. But inwardly this little boy was seething with a guilt and resentment that was often near to boiling point. As le Carré said to Frank Delaney in 1982 of an upbringing in some ways similar, "I was scrupulously well-behaved, appallingly polite, a little butler, not able to do anything naughty". It was a dangerous condition, akin to that "of a liar or a spy". To amuse himself Guinness used to do plays in a little cardboard puppet theatre. He wrote them himself and they were very sophisticated pieces, or so he said, about titled people.

"I must have been struck in the holiday time by something I'd seen." Escaping into a fantasy world had developed at about the age of eight, and he used to tell stories in his dormitory and rather overdramatised them. "I acted my head off . . . Other boys were fast asleep when I was still droning on." And of course there were the school plays. Once he scored a "great hit" in *Macbeth* because, as the Act V Messenger, he ran round the soccer field for exactly six minutes before he made his entrance to deliver his news in a convincing state of exhaustion. At another time, when he was nine, a conjuror came to school and he joined in his act, sitting on a chair and then getting up. Guinness felt an instinctive need to underplay: "He wanted me to scream and shout. I knew it was phoney."

During his schooldays or after Guinness expressed or described no awakening of sexual feeling or attraction to girls or young women. The extreme, bizarre antics of middle-aged female music-hall stars engaged his attention more, as did some odd notions about male procreative equipment, discussed in the dormitory after lights-out where the headmaster made an occasional visit to "tickle" the captain of the First XI. About sperm ("male seed") one school friend assured Guinness, one had to be very careful, as it was a black pip which popped out of the penis unexpectedly and had to be caught when you micturated, or you would never be a father. One suspects Guinness knew more about this subject than he was prepared to say. And his awareness of the hypocrisy of grown-ups was acute.

In the school holidays he always stayed in hotels, one in particular in the Cromwell Road in London, where he became great friends with chambermaids who brought up hot water, and had great fun working the hydraulic lifts. Again one senses something impermanent and seedy about this background, but not without its own kind of mystery and glamour. It was the world the atmosphere of which Eliot caught so forcibly in his poems of 1909–1925 which are contemporary with Guinness's early years: the evocation of the half-deserted, post-war city streets, the one-night cheap hotels, the yellow smoke outside the window panes, the smells of cheap eau-de-Cologne and cocktails in bars, the rattling breakfast plates in basement kitchens – all of this breeding an oblique, hidden, and yet insidious undercurrent of sexuality.

The emotional outlet Guinness so desperately needed was provided by the variety stage and, in later childhood, the "legitimate" stage. "I used to be always asking for bits of pocket money to get into the gallery or pit somewhere." He described with joy in the *Observer* in 1984 Nellie Wallace bending over the stage to the accompaniment of farting sounds from the orchestra: "She was an extraordinary comic, in loud tweeds and boots with a long feather in her hat. She was hideous as a parrot." He found himself leaving the Coliseum in a daze, trying to talk like her, and repeat her act of assisting a surgeon in a baroque, surreal operation. She made him want to be a clown. He caught imaginary corpses in the air, glared with wildly shocked eyes at innocent passers-by, and generally misbehaved himself.

He could never remember not wanting to be an actor, while the delight of escaping from himself came at the age of fourteen. "Somehow I had got hold of a long, straight-haired wig. One night before going to bed I put it on, then teased some wool out of my blanket and stuck on a moustache and a little beard. I looked in the mirror and thought, 'I look like Charles I'. And I began to *feel* like Charles I. It was much better than feeling like me."*

In the theatre he also experienced that formative moment which indicated his future. Ralph Richardson found it when Frank Benson as Hamlet scraped his sword across the stage after his father's ghost called for revenge and made a noise which sounded like hell. Guinness was similarly "seized" by Henry Baynton as Shylock, a "bit of an old ham", whom he saw at the Pier Theatre, Eastbourne,

---

* Later he played Charles I in the film *Cromwell*. These almost instant acts of self-transformation inside have been many times recorded by journalists, in this instance Bel Mooney, writing in the *Telegraph* Magazine in 1973.

Alan Brien observed (*Daily Mail*, 7 March 1958) that it was related to his intense self-consciousness: "When he plays a man he feels like him; when he feels like a man he finds himself playing him."

with his Shakespearean company of "mostly undergraduates he picked up on the cheap".

Baynton, said Guinness, modelled his Shylock on Henry Irving's. He made some "curious and obviously phoney gestures but they were very arresting, and a sort of strange Eastern waving of the hand . . . I remember spending the rest of that term, it was the summer term, in the cricket pavilion. I couldn't be less interested in the sports side of things, but [was] making this strange Eastern signal to my school fellows."

By the age of eighteen Guinness had severed all connection with his mother. The headmaster of Roborough School helped him to get a job as a copywriter in Ark's advertising agency in Lincoln's Inn Fields. He was paid a pound a week. Later this was increased to thirty shillings. He wrote about razor-blades, Rose's Lime Juice and radio valves. "I learnt a lot. I learnt to trim my English quite a bit." They wanted to try him out in all sides of the business. One day he took into the printers a four-foot square block instead of a four-inch square block. "They didn't sack me, of course."

But he wanted to go to the Royal Academy of Dramatic Art, and they sent him a form. He got in touch with John Gielgud whom he admired "dottily . . . I think I must have had some secret hope he'd say come round to the theatre and I'll put you through it . . . which could have been terrible". It would probably have been to his father, who was away in South America, he told a BBC interviewer in 1975, "a great shock to hear his son had gone into the theatre".

5

More Hamlet in the interim

It seemed as if Shakespeare's unfinished seeker of his own identity was part of Guinness's destiny. In the unsorted emotional darkness of his early life he may well have suffered what the psychologist Heinz Kohnt has called "disintegration anxiety", as summarised by Anthony Storr:

> The individuals whom [Kohnt] considers liable to this are those who, because of the immaturity of their parents' responses to them in childhood, or because of the absence of empathic parental understanding, have not built up a strong coherent personality ... one might compare Kohnt's conception with looking in a mirror. A clear, clean, polished mirror will repeatedly reflect the developing personality as he actually is, and thus give him a firm and true sense of his own identity. A cracked, dirty, smeared mirror will reflect an incomplete, obscured image which provides the child with an inaccurate and distorted picture of himself.

In the young Guinness, who remained strange and enigmatic, one feels there was at the centre an instinct of panic, of flight, of loss of reason and of face. Of, in a word, terror. One false move, one could well believe him saying to himself, and I shall be swallowed up by the nameless darkness, the small, shamed, and helplessly unhappy boy I was will overwhelm me again.

And then there was his appearance. He had never been deeply attractive, even as a young man. "Colossally unattractive," someone called him, "like a shrimp ... My God, he would want to be liked." He commented much later that his ears made him look "like a bat straight out of hell", but hoped they might wing him to heaven in the end. He feared ordinary people, and he conquered his fear by imitating them and laughing at them. Deep down he hungered for love and affection.

Describing the experimental nature of acting Guinness remarked much later, "We are artists playing with our bodies and voices and our whole physical and spiritual make-up." Again like John le Carré, who has stated baldly that he never liked how he looked, he found it more and more comforting to become someone else: a "cuddly package", as le Carré called Smiley. There had to be a certain vulgarity about actors, it could not be escaped. Guinness likened them to tubes of paint squeezing themselves out in full view, commenting that it was not surprising that "we like to cover up".

Yet, to play Hamlet inevitably meant to confront one's own vulnerability and helplessness.

In 1933, at Sadler's Wells, Guinness saw someone do this. The nineteen-year-old had followed in the footsteps of many who experienced their first "overwhelming theatrical experience" by watching Ernest Milton, an American actor of Jewish descent who had settled in England and become one of the greatest interpreters of Hamlet. But he was by no means universally applauded. Forty-two years of age when Guinness saw him, he was often called a classical actor who would not stick to the rules of the game: "an emotional force sometimes almost demonic", one critic called him, "speech after speech he double-charged". "Hamlet, I knew the man – you will remember that," Milton later told that same critic.

Guinness was shattered by the impact of his performance. He found that Milton and Shakespeare seemed to be of one mind, "presenting the Renaissance Prince *par excellence*, a man familiar with the ways of mankind – not unlike Montaigne – who could always see the two sides of a coin, tortured by conscience and burdened by duty, a man of sharp wit but exquisite manners . . . I returned to my bed-sitter in Bayswater, incapable of speaking for about twenty-four hours, knowing I had witnessed something I can only call both transcendental and very human."

That Guinness should have been so fascinated by the role of Hamlet is not surprising, for not only is the play a tragedy of reflection but it is also a study of genius in crisis, that crisis being one of identity. Hamlet is profoundly unsettled in his mind about a family crime; he is at the same time rebellious, obscene, choric, sublime. He hates his stepfather as Guinness had hated the "captain"; and as Guinness did, he deeply distrusts his mother's flightiness and sexuality. He passes from scorn and ironic incongruity to soul-searching meditation. The pseudo-insanity is both real and assumed; he wields, and is capable of, great comic power. Above all he is a delightful person, the model of a Renaissance prince, who finally achieves complete mental balance in the working out of the doubt and confusion into which the circumstances of his family have plunged him. By the end of the play he has begun to know where he himself ends and God, or fate, takes over. He accepts the inevitable consequences of the goodness that has emerged inside him; he acquiesces in the central feeling of reconciliation which he comes to embody:

> If it be now, 'tis not to come. If it be not to come, it will be now.
> If it be not now, yet it will come. The readiness is all.

All this, in an uncanny way, was to become true of Guinness too. *Hamlet* is above all, a test, a touchstone of change and growth; it is about its own creator's attempt to come to terms with himself. Self-confrontation and self-examination are at its core. It is the play in which, paradoxically, in depicting the character which would show the greatest spirit and nobility, Shakespeare also exhibits his affinity with the actor, his closeness to the "free" vagabond spirit, the rogue and peasant slave.

6

The great red herring

The girl with whom Guinness sat on the grass as they watched elderly gentlemen "feathering" on the boats which bumped each other on the lake in Regent's Park, drew on a cigarette "with all the sophistication of an inexperienced smoker". Guinness, now aged twenty, had just heard that his allowance of twenty-five shillings a week had stopped. He had, or so he said, only seven shillings left in the world.

"After a long silence my companion stubbed her cigarette out and said, I don't think you should be sitting about on the grass. You should be *doing* something. Why not go and see if John Gielgud can help?"

Both the girl and he had been dramatic students at the Fay Compton Studio. Guinness had not been at the studio very long. Before going there he received ten private lessons from Martita Hunt, an extravagant, Argentinian-born character actress who lived the life of a rich eccentric — she had been the suggestion of John Gielgud.

A few weeks before there had been the end-of-term performance at the school. John Gielgud was a judge of the acting. Later he could not remember who the other judges were (they were Jessie Matthews and Ronald Adam), but he did "very vividly remember being greatly struck by the evident talent of a skinny boy with a sad Pierrot face and big ears to whom we all agreed the prize should be given":

> The plot of the short play in which he appeared was about the owner of the Punch and Judy show who, in despair at losing his customers as they drifted away to some other attraction went home, and, like Mr Punch, battered his wife to death. It seems to me that there was no dialogue, and that the boy's compulsive miming impressed us all very much.

Of course, Guinness thought immediately when the girl suggested he see Gielgud, he might have voted against me for the prize for acting. The girl then offered to lend Guinness a pound "until something turns up". This really hurt Guinness who asked huffily how long it would take him to walk to Wyndham's Theatre.

When he arrived at the theatre and asked to see Gielgud, to his astonishment he was shown straight to his dressing-room:

> He had remembered my name though he looked somewhat surprised when he saw what I looked like. I was in rather dirty grey flannel trousers, a check shirt (to keep down the laundry bill) and skimpy sports jacket. Also I was very thin, large-eared and strange.
>
> He sat making-up for the evening performance of *The Maitlands*, and I told him of the absolute necessity for my finding work. This was the first time I had seen a real live star actor applying his make-up; I believe I was even more fascinated by that than by being in the presence of a man I had hero-worshipped so long.
>
> He was friendly and kind, but under the unpowdered grease-paint, which gives actors the look of china dolls, I couldn't tell whether he was really interested in my predicament and talents or not. He painted his eyebrows for a moment or two in silence and then became immensely practical.

The Maitlands, in which Gielgud appeared, opened in July 1934. Although the "real live star" encounter made a good anecdote, in fact Guinness had by this time already appeared in Edward Woolf's *Libel* as a Junior Counsel, which had opened on 2 April 1934, his twentieth birthday, and which starred Sir Nigel Playfair. So the sense of naïvety was playful, although Gielgud must have been a fascinating figure to encounter. His other first professional experiences had mostly been of failure. He had been a "walk on" for a film called *Evensong*. He had begun his career by realising what he thought of as his extreme limitations: "I was a very lightweight, thin cadaverous creature then . . . I was never a glamorous juvenile". He has never retailed exactly how many times he was turned down at this time, but Douglas Fairbanks, Jnr, recounted an incident which may have been typical of the life of the twenty-year-old Guinness. Fairbanks was playing the lead in *Moonlight is Silver*, which was based on *Othello*'s jealousy theme:

> Binkie [Beaumont] interviewed a keen and serious young actor for the job of my understudy. He was my colouring and about

my height. His name was Alec Guinness. Binkie and Winifred heard him read a scene or two and politely told him he had not yet had enough experience and let him go. Alas.

Guinness next played three tiny parts in Noël Langley's *Queer Cargo*, a month later, at the Piccadilly Theatre. As well as his three small parts in this, he understudied all six leading men. *Queer Cargo* was a tale of piracy on the China Seas, in which Franklin Dyall played a magnificent pirate. Guinness shaved his hair for one of the parts, the Chinese Coolie, and his hair never grew back on. His memory for lines was always exemplary: in 1939 he was to learn the whole of Macbeth's part in just four days. He also memorised Dubedat in *The Doctor's Dilemma* in a few days in 1938 using cold compresses on his head while Merula Salaman, an actress, heard him in the train to Richmond.

Guinness was also a sophisticated and highly observant play-goer by now. For example, in November 1933, he had been to see Schnitzler's *Fräulein Elsa* at the Independent Theatre Club in Kingsway, the daring and *risqué* production by Theodore Komisarjevsky in which, for the first time on the English stage, a serious actress briefly appeared naked. The actress was Peggy Ashcroft.

Was Gielgud really that interested in Guinness's predicament? Guinness believed that he might just have been impressed by the aristocratic name. Anyway, to begin with, Gielgud's efforts on his behalf yielded no result. Guinness did a brief audition of Mercutio's Queen Mab speech for the Director Henry Cass, not getting further, he said, than "little atomies" when Cass stopped him, told him he had no business in the theatre and "wouldn't take me as a gift". ("Howls of derision from the director in the darkened stalls . . . 'You're no actor!' he shouted. 'Get off the fucking stage,'" the later Guinness version ran.)

In the earlier version of this episode given by Guinness, he returned to Gielgud after the failed audition and Gielgud was at the end of his resourcefulness but by no means at the end of his generosity. Guinness recalled:

> All I had left was the proverbial half-crown. On the side of his make-up table was a neat pile of one-pound notes. "The next time I do a play I'll give you a part," he promised, "but you are far too thin. Here's twenty pounds – for God's sake go and eat properly." He frantically painted his eyebrows with embarrassment. I stared at the money. I had a vision of eating,

buying clothes (particularly shoes), of spending fourpence a day on park chairs for twelve hundred days. Then I saw myself being thrown into gaol for debt. "I am all right for money, thank you," I said, so foolishly that it makes me blush even twenty-two years later, and walked out of his room. (*Sunday Times*, 1956)

Much later Gielgud recounted the same incident. "He was extremely shy and diffident and refused to accept the few pounds I offered him," said Gielgud, who probably remembered nothing about it but accepted what Guinness wrote. All later accounts hinge on Guinness's refusal of the loan, but in one earlier account Gielgud simply lent him £10 and he pocketed the money gratefully, returning it as soon as he was able to. Only weeks later Gielgud had signed him up for his New Theatre Company with which he remained until July 1936.

"In spite of my fondness for him," Gielgud reported later, "Alec is not an easy man to know. He has never confided to me his ambitions, his hopes and his despairs." This conveyed that there was a resistance, a refusal, in Guinness towards Gielgud. Gielgud also regretted not working with him more – they have appeared in later life together only once, in a TV dialogue by Friedrich Dürrenmatt called *Conversation at Night* (1970) – and added, perhaps tartly, "I know I should have learnt much by studying at first hand some of the fascinating mysterious secrets which have enabled him to create so many different types of characters with so much subtlety and skill."

In *The Ages of Gielgud*, Guinness has described in great detail his first several encounters with John Gielgud. One of the fascinations in writing about Guinness is the effort it requires of one to determine how every gesture and attitude becomes, after some time and then finally, revealed as careful and studied. This is as true of everything he has written and said, as of his acting. In this respect he is the complete antithesis of the more volatile, unfixed Gielgud.

But the most revealing touch, the constant in these early encounters and in their subsequent retailing in the early 1980s, was how Guinness saw himself as inferior to Gielgud as an actor. Although time had apparently brought about humour and objectivity he remained in awe of Gielgud, overwhelmed – and yet mocking and ironic – that the great man could show such an interest in him. Why? Gielgud was interested in anybody who was somebody. When Gielgud said to him after a week's rehearsal in October

1934, "What's happened to you? I thought you were rather good. You're terrible. Oh, go away! I don't want to see you again!" Guinness was shattered. He was, after all, only playing Osric and the Third Player.

This was his first skirmish, a rather circumspect and tentative one, with *Hamlet*. Far from being the prince himself, Osric was a prodigally endowed invertebrate, who none the less had the function of releasing, as one critic said, a "significant reflex of Hamlet's temperament and state of mind".

7

Irascible, haughty, witty, endearing

Gielgud was almost exactly ten years older than Guinness. One is struck immediately by the difference between their relationship and that of Gielgud with Ralph Richardson, who was nearly two years older than Gielgud and a much more powerful, dominating personality. That Gielgud should, it seems, almost whimsically cast Guinness as the pliant gadfly courtier Osric showed that, sharply, he had perceived something about his personality. He seemed at once to become – as Guinness put it – a butt for Gielgud's unpredictability. Shortly after being cruelly dismissed Guinness was heaped with praise – he maintained he was not doing anything differently from what he had done before. "Motleys! Motleys," Gielgud then called to his designers, Sophie Harris, Margaret Harris and Elizabeth Montgomery, "you should give him a hat with a lot of feathers, like the Duchess of Devonshire!"

Hats played a major part in the early mythology of these two actors. When Guinness finally earned his first weekly salary as an actor the first thing he did was to buy himself a very cheap replica of the kind of hat Gielgud wore. It gave him as he thought, "a sort of elegance in the second class". Later, when Gielgud had given him more than his first job, he reflected that no quality could be "put on the head in the shape of someone else's hat".

When Ralph Richardson first met Gielgud he had been suspicious of him. While neither encroached temperamentally on the other, the two men could not have been more different. Richardson avoided Gielgud's acting, which used to keep him out of the theatre, while as he said, "I found his clothes extravagant, I found his conversation flippant. He was the New Young Man of his time and I didn't like him." Richardson commented that Gielgud was "a kind of brilliant sort of butterfly, while I was a *gloomy* sort of boy".

But Guinness saw Gielgud not as the butterfly which he himself was playing in *Hamlet*, but as the judge of his talent: as, moreover, a strict disciplinarian, intolerant of any slovenliness of speech, a living monument of impatience. While Richardson perceived Gielgud as a spluttering catherine-wheel sparking off in all directions which "happily have never been resolved – tongue and mind work so closely together that it is sufficient for him to think of something for it to be said" – Guinness noted his emperor-like head held "higher than high", his patrician Polish breeding – both grandparents on Gielgud's father's side were Polish – and that he lacked nothing "as far as I could see, except tact". Yet, oddly enough, tact would seem to be exactly that quality valued above all others by Guinness later.

Gielgud's Hamlet was a technical tour-de-force, beautifully scored, exalted in spirit, a prince, in no way a rogue and peasant slave; he was also, however, "swayed by a thousand subtle influences, physiological and pathological . . . sensitive and disillusioned". This was the 1930 definitive performance, perhaps in the appeasing, "sensitive" spirit of the times. The duty of revenge terrified him.

This Hamlet had mesmerised every young actor: according to Donald Sinden, who was also in the cast, Gielgud spoke Shakespeare's lines "as if he had written them himself". Sinden vividly pointed up the effect that Gielgud had when Hamlet has just seen and talked with his father's ghost. He has just pronounced that, "The time is out of joint", and he turns to Horatio and Marcellus to say, "Nay, come, let's go together". Gielgud conveyed in that simple line: "Please go with me"; "I don't want to let you out of my sight"; "It would be better if we arrived together"; "Let us leave this awesome place"; and "Don't leave me". This taught Sinden the infinite possibilities open to an actor in just one line.

Guinness was also spellbound by Gielgud's Hamlet because it showed so much of what he himself would have liked to have shown in Hamlet. But here there was the great danger of being sucked into imitation. Night after night he watched it from the wings, for ten whole months. Guinness watched the performance 155 times and knew every inflection of every line: it was "the lovable, distressed and romantic prince of all time".

But *Hamlet*, the portrait of a genius, was also seizing control at a level deeper than art. The mark of a certain kind of genius is that he is all of one piece: everything he does changes the order and balance of the rest. Guinness did not know it at the time but this first encounter with *Hamlet* was feeding a deeper quest, that would emerge increasingly as the actor grew older. He strove for unity, for integration: he wanted everything he did to be part of some greater wholeness.

Gielgud had an inkling of this deeper, stranger, integrity inherent in Guinness when he presented, "To Alec, who grows apace" an edition of his aunt Ellen Terry's letters, quoting Act Five's motto, "The readiness is all". In the context of becoming an actor, it could have meant any of a dozen different things: it could even be seen as a not highly complimentary comment on his talent – or lack of it. It could equally be construed as an admission of Guinness's independence of spirit. His refusal of Gielgud's twenty pounds possibly tells us from Guinness's point of view that there may have been something excessive about the offer and sensibly suspicious about the refusal.

Guinness was again cast as Osric in the Old Vic's 1936–7 season, this time with Olivier as Hamlet, and Tyrone Guthrie as the director. "When he swept the stage with his plumed hat he bewitched me," commented Kay Walsh. The two years spent under Gielgud's pernickety and impatient direction had somewhat unnerved him; the pages of his script were "filthy grey" with the rubbing out of conflicting directives written in "soft lead pencil and sometimes smudged with tears". He saw himself as still greatly limited: "I was never a handsome chap. I didn't think I had anything personal to offer." But he discovered he could transform his persona. "All I could offer is through my imagination." And Guthrie advocated a more creative and imaginative process than Gielgud, and rebuked him for pencilling notes in his script – "If I've given you a good move you'll remember it, if bad you'll forget it."

8

Stalking the mighty ones

Guinness was now working for £7 a week. But he was still almost beneath the notice of Lilian Baylis, the manager of the Old Vic Company, and remarked on how she only ever spoke to him twice. On the first occasion, at his audition, she said, "Let's have a look at your legs, dear," and, having looked, she said, "You'll do". On the second occasion he dropped three pennies in a corridor, just as she came round the corner. She eyed the coins, remarked, "Father, Son and Holy Ghost", and swept on.

Guinness played, as Audrey Williamson wrote, Boyet in *Love's Labour's Lost* as "a perfect and stylish cameo of the middle-aged courtier". Guinness himself called it wretched and humourless, but Michael Redgrave, who felt he had been passed over for Berowne in favour of Alec Clunes and played Ferdinand instead, commented that Guinness "had a rather tiresome part, and succeeded against the odds in bringing it to life. He had, and still has, the most valuable asset for comedy: the appearance of possessing an impenetrable secret."

Later, Guinness cleverly doubled Le Beau and the rustic William in *As You Like It*, in which Edith Evans, as Rosalind, set a standard for the times and Michael Redgrave played Orlando as a handsome well-spoken "stripling". This production was directed by Esme Church, the woman director of the Old Vic School.

If Gielgud produced something which, in the terms of so reticent an actor as Guinness approached loquacity, Olivier stimulated disapproval. When on 5 January 1937 Olivier opened as Hamlet in Guthrie's "uncut" production, Guinness, who understudied Olivier, professed himself "outraged at the gymnastic leaps and falls required by his example. I never liked the performance or Guthrie's production, but it was huge box office . . . It would have been fatal if I had had to go on. I would have fainted rather than throw myself off a twelve-foot rostrum." Later, he conceded that it had been "necessary for Olivier to do what he did – and it laid the foundations for his becoming a truly great actor."

Olivier himself admitted that his first consideration in playing the part was to seduce Vivien Leigh, who came to nearly half the performances, with what the critic Kenneth Tynan later called his "physical virility and acrobatic flash". At the time James Agate wrote, "Mr Olivier's Hamlet is the best performance of Hotspur that the present generation has seen."

Gielgud did not mince his words. According to legend, he went backstage after the opening night and said, "Larry, it's one of the finest performances I have ever seen, but it's still my part."

Guinness had perfected the impact he made as Osric, which now became the essence of Osric: his performance was by all accounts the most brilliant of the minor performances, cleverly placing the waterfly in the treachery of the duel, gaining laughter "easily without losing the hint of the courtier's craft beneath the mask". His Reynaldo also made a strong comic impact.

But in *Twelfth Night*, the next Guthrie production at the Old Vic, Guinness's career made a leap forward. In this downbeat, melancholy production, in which with bustling ebullience Olivier played Toby Belch, Guinness took the risk of underacting as Belch's foil, Sir Andrew Aguecheek, in a way which emphasised the production's haunting sense of fatality: "A wistful flaxen gull with the sad ingenuous eyes of a Dan Leno, and the same upstanding quiff of hair on the forehead. The character had a harmless, amiable silliness that was likeable as well as funny." Agate commented that he was too youthful in his capers. Guthrie himself hated the production, calling it "baddish" and "immature".

In the Guthrie production of *Henry V* which followed with Olivier as the King, Guinness's Exeter passed without comment. The play was chosen to chime in with George VI's coronation. Immediately after this he came back to *Hamlet* for the much celebrated performance at Elsinore. This was supposed to be an outdoor gala performance by the first British company to play in the turreted and flagged courtyard of Kronberg Castle since the late sixteenth century. But a cloudburst saturated the stage and the courtyard benches which should have held 2500 people. They had to move to the ballroom of the Marienlist Hotel where the company was staying.

"Be polite to Kings and Queens if they get in your way. Alec, make your entrance through the french windows," barked Guthrie. Guinness shivered on the beach, soaked to the skin, although well-fuelled with Danish liquor:

> Outside, waves were riding high in the narrow water between Denmark and Sweden, and it was plain that the storm had set in for the night, with a noise like the ride of the Valkyries. All the costumes and property had been brought over from Kronberg; hotel bedrooms became dressing-rooms; and not so long after eight o'clock the ballroom, with Danish royalty [Prince Kund and Princess Caroline Mathilde] in the front row, was filled for what, in effect, would be an improvisation. It had been left to the players, directed by Laurence Olivier whom Guthrie had put wisely in command, to get the night together with only the sketchiest idea of ways and means ...
>
> Guthrie came forward to apologise briefly for "the strangest performance of *Hamlet* on any stage," and presently Francisco and Barnardo were "on the platform before the castle," Horatio and Marcellus were on their way up through the audience, and somewhere, within a few moments, the bell was beating one.

"Never was there such a performance," commented Lady Diana Cooper, who was also in the audience.

Guinness's own small contribution was, he said, unduly affected by the schnapps with which his Danish dresser supplied him prior to his "blowing in" through the french windows. He smiled rather too much. He rested his sword on the King of Sweden's lap, and blocked the view of at least two crowned heads.

But the evening was a triumph. This was the third of Guinness's appearances in *Hamlet* and he now added the Player Queen to his repertoire. Offstage, the furtive affair between Laurence Olivier and Vivien Leigh was at its height. Jill Esmond, Olivier's wife, accompanied Olivier everywhere on the tour. In an almost gloating tone Olivier said he found himself making love to Vivien "almost within Jill's vision. This welding closeness tripped the obvious decision and two marriages were severed."

Guinness recalled more distantly and enigmatically that "many bedroom doors were locked, or slammed or opened that night". This actor who could be so loquacious in the cause of revealing the biography of others while so reticent about his own, informed one of Vivien Leigh's biographers that he was delegated to take Jill out on afternoon trips to give the lovers time to be together. Had Jill not gone to Elsinore with Olivier, said Guinness, "It might just have been an exciting new affair." But it was always more than that, while even at Elsinore Vivien fell into extreme fluctuations of mood, at one moment screaming at Olivier, then "becoming suppressed and silent and staring blankly into space".

In the meantime Gielgud had become manager of the Queen's Theatre and Guinness again joined Gielgud's "family", as he had at the New Theatre in 1935 and 1936. In those earlier seasons Guinness had "experienced", if that is the word, not only Gielgud's direction, but that of Michel Saint-Denis and Theodore Komisarjevsky. The latter, who was highly temperamental and emotional and briefly married to Peggy Ashcroft, had a high regard for Guinness as a mime. Ashcroft came back from lunch one day during rehearsals of *The Seagull* when Guinness, as the workman Yakov, had mimed pulling a rope. She said, "I've had a quarrel with Komis about you." She maintained there was no rope there; but Komis said, "Yes there was: I saw it when he was pulling."

In this second season there were four productions: *Richard II*, Sheridan's *The School for Scandal*, Chekhov's *The Three Sisters* and *The Merchant of Venice*. In *School* Guinness played Snake* – Gielgud's Joseph Surface was acclaimed as a dazzling masterpiece but the production, by Guthrie, was poor, for Gielgud and he did not see eye to eye. In *Three Sisters* Guinness played the humble Fedotik; in *The Merchant* he was the pallid lover Lorenzo to Gielgud's "challenging and unusual" Shylock. These were hardly stimulating roles but Guinness made them so; on the one hand one can imagine Gielgud dishing them out in an offhand way to this new arrival of no fixed talent and easily pliable substance. On the other hand Gielgud had an acute and generous sense of the talent of others and would surround himself only with the best. He simply was never jealous of other actors. And Guinness made each role distinctive: Peggy Ashcroft recalled Lorenzo's "grave Italian look", Snake's "sly mischief"* and Fedotik's "ingenious youth". As Lorenzo he was fitted by Motleys with a suit of white calico: he went back to the theatre saying the costume was a disaster and he looked dreadful, not realising they had still to cut and spray the calico and trim it with black velvet.

He attended classes at this time given by Michel Saint-Denis, the French director of *The Three Sisters*, who was Stanislavksy's

---

* Herbert Farjeon wrote in *The Bystander*, "From the tip of his nose to the acid in each syllable he utters Alec Guinness's Snake is as arresting as Hogarth."

apostle in the West. These opened up his imagination to realism:

> I wish I could describe something which I remember taking place
> when Michel Saint-Denis was rehearsing *The Cherry Orchard*
> ... It involved another actor who was playing Epihodov, whose
> boots squeak. Saint-Denis was so insistent on the way the actor
> *listened* to his boots squeaking ... Witnessing that altered my
> whole attitude to acting which I thought had been would-be
> romantic, admiring flourishes of various sorts – although I
> couldn't do them. And here was something very basic ...

Peter Daubeny, aged sixteen, who later became an important
impresario, met Guinness at this time. He was, he said, very
nervous, and could sense Guinness's own shyness:

> There was something curiously unemotional, inaccessible, beyond
> his gentleness. Even then he had the kind of intellectual humility
> which was described by Matthew Arnold: "You must get
> yourself out of the way to see things clearly." But he listened
> kindly and with understanding, as if in a confessional – and,
> indeed, the sort of help our meeting gave me was similar to that
> which I might have obtained by pouring myself out to a priest in
> some shadowy cathedral stall. I came away feeling relieved of a
> psychological wound ...

Guinness told him to study with Saint-Denis at the London
Theatre School. "You can't get away from Stanislavsky," he
declared buoyantly. "You'll like him."

As Richard II Gielgud was, way beyond the others, the commanding "presence". Redgrave played Bolingbroke: John, he said in his
autobiography, "even at the first reading was as near perfect as
I could wish or imagine. Ninety per cent of the beauty of his
acting was the beauty of his voice. To this day I can see no way
of improving on the dazzling virtuosity of phrasing and breathing
which was Gielgud's ..." But Gielgud saw it as otherwise,
identifying abruptly to another admirer the important elements
in acting as "*feeling* and *timing* ... I understand it's the same
in many walks of life ..."

Guinness reported an exchange between Gielgud and himself
which hardly reflected the older man's belief in his junior, who
was playing the mighty and commanding role of the Groom in
Richard II and enjoying it (he also played a delightful Aumerle).
On the morning of the first night he finally got to rehearse with

Gielgud, who told him that he wasn't as good in the role as Leslie French when Gielgud did the play before. "Try coming on from the right tonight instead of the left and see if it makes a difference." When Guinness asked, as he said, cheekily, "which right?", Gielgud replied, in a fatigued manner, "Oh, have it your own way. Do it as you've always done it. I can't be bothered."

But Gielgud was not only like this with Guinness, said Margaret Harris, he was a "strange mixture of thoughtfulness and thought-lessness". Guinness undervalued his own impact. He "always made an impression", said Margaret Harris. "I don't think he was ever better. His sense of character was amazing." Everyone saw his potential, but especially Tyrone Guthrie.

The production of greatest value to Guinness in fulfilment of his ambition to become a better actor was undoubtedly *Three Sisters*, which Peggy Ashcroft called "the particular triumph of the season". Saint-Denis had demanded seven weeks' rehearsal, which in those days was unheard of: "I think the company, under his influence, reached its climax as a wonderfully welded ensemble." Guinness said, "Lots of people flowered in *Three Sisters*: it was like going to some delightful and sad party: we couldn't wait to get back to the place every night."

Guthrie and Gielgud had always represented opposing theatrical traditions. It was now into Guthrie's camp that Guinness was drawn. It was to take more than ten years for Guinness to throw off the inhibiting influence of Gielgud on his stage activity – if throw it off he ever did – but it was Guthrie who perceived the twenty-two year old actor's acute intellect and essential ordinariness and tried to champion them long before they found their full integration into his acting. Guthrie was never much of an admirer of West End stars and in particular did not seem to like or get on well with Gielgud. Ralph Richardson thought him the most stimulating and extraordinary man of the theatre since Harley Granville-Barker; but, Richardson also commented, it was as if he were trying to take the scene away from the leading actor and give it to the man who carried the spear.

Or, in Guinness's case, the Groom: for now Guthrie, almost, it seemed, in an act of defiance to Gielgud, summoned Guinness back to the Old Vic and asked him if he would care "to give us your Hamlet . . . Think we should do it in modern dress. You could wear that nice grey suit you've got on."

Guinness nearly fainted.

PART TWO

A Bigger Stage

You are in fact enraptured with empty joys, embracing blessings that are alien to you as if they were your own.

Boethius

Perhaps the mentality of the Japanese Colonel, Saito, was essentially that of his prisoner, Colonel Nicholson.

Pierre Boulle

The crew had seen the results of misfortunes of battle; ships burning red and yellow, ships sinking, men scrambling over dripping slanted hulls, men soaked in oil, men ripped bloody, and floating dead men. They were inclined to think less of the odds than of the disagreeable possibilities.

Herman Wouk

9

Swelling a progress

Was he ready for Hamlet, and was Guthrie taking an absurd risk? Guinness could still hear the scathing words of Gielgud about his small-fry Groom: "You're not nearly as good in the part as Leslie French was . . ." And only a few months after the big roles he took in this 1938 season he met John Gielgud in Piccadilly who said to him, "I can't think why you want to play big parts. Why don't you stick to those funny little men you do so well instead of trying to be important?"*

Guinness's first instinct, as always, was to agree. His fundamental humility – not a trait Gielgud was renowned for – aligned him to the persona of T.S. Eliot's J. Alfred Prufrock:

No! I am not Prince Hamlet, nor was meant to be.
Am an attendant Lord, one that will do
To swell a progress, start a scene or two.

He was not Prince Hamlet. Politic, cautious, and meticulous, he had the mentality of a small-part player. Is this what, clearly, Guthrie found so attractive? Here, in embryo, was the personality of the anti-star, the anti-celebrity. The young actor was highly malleable and Guthrie, now nearing his fortieth year, was in full rivalry for power with the active stars of the theatre. He was impelled to succeed with Guinness where he had failed with Olivier, in a production of *Hamlet* without a star player in which, at every point, the quality of the thinking in the production and the integrity of his own vision of the play could be realised. Significantly he had chosen to do the text again in its "entirety".

But with Guthrie there was an even more daring and radical

---

* So Guinness reported in a letter to Enid Bagnold, December 1964. This came to light in a bookshop in Wiltshire (*Evening Standard*, 15 May 1991).

streak. Few productions of that time achieved in advance of their first night such heated controversy. Modern-dress productions of plays by Shakespeare were hardly ever attempted; notably, in 1925, Colin Keith-Johnson had played a quiet and colloquial Prince to fit in with the overriding country-house Englishman ethos, known as the "Hamlet in plus-fours". Semi-liberated Ophelia wore short skirts, and light stockings, while Claudius kept a siphon and a decanter in his prayer cabinet. Much the same gimmickry therefore was expected of Guthrie, but Guthrie had different plans: he sought, in Roger Furse's permanent setting of classical pillars and changing backcloths, a racy tumult of visual effects and a compelling atmosphere. "Modern dress I do not greatly care for," he had said in 1933: while he described his new approach as "a cadenza on the familiar theme of the Painted Smile and the Breaking Heart".

This was the time, during the summer break of rehearsals for *Hamlet* and for *Trelawny of the Wells*, due to open in late September 1938, that Alec Guinness married Merula Salaman, who became his lifelong partner.

He had met the actress Sylvia Merula, as she was known at the time, "otherwise Merula Sylvia" Salaman, during Michel Saint-Denis' production of André Obey's *Noah* in July 1935. Red-headed Merula was a year younger than Guinness. Her name was the ancient Italian word for the blackbird that flew into her mother's room at the birth. In *Noah*, Guinness wrote:

> I think Gielgud tried to get me a very nice part as Shem. That was the first time I ever met Saint-Denis. He obviously thought I was too inexperienced: quite rightly. And I was offered the part of the Wolf who doesn't say anything at all, just trots across the stage. I understudied someone and incidentally met my wife who was playing the Tiger.

Subsequently Merula had played small parts or attendants in *Richard II, The School for Scandal, The Three Sisters*, and *The Merchant of Venice*.

Merula, on her mother's side, was not "a Guinness" or "a Geddes" but "a Wake" (after Hereward the Wake), while on her father's side she was descended from the Saloman, a Sephardic Jew, who had brought Haydn to London in the 1790s. He was an entrepreneur as well as an impresario. Saloman emigrated to England from Livorno in 1740. One of his descendants joined the British

Navy, fighting at Trafalgar, and changed his name to Salaman to make it appear more English.

Thus Guinness joined a well-established and highly cultured family which he had never had.

The Salamans had great charm, great wealth and fine taste. Physically they were small men, and presented no threat, but they had a puckish quality.

Chattie, Merula's mother, first became engaged to Michel Salaman when they were fellow-students at the Slade School of Art. The Salamans were a large clan: Michel's father, Merula's grandfather, made a fortune with straw hats. He had fourteen children, and Michel was the youngest but one. They invested the money in property and had an office, S.M.N. Salaman Estates, in Southampton Place in London. They were a rich, leisured set, with a lot of friends, and they entertained generously. Chattie was very beautiful when young, but she was determined not to be a housewife so she occupied herself with painting and gardening.

She and Michel had five children, two sons and three daughters. The eldest, Susie, was a choreographer with the Ballets Rambert who became ill with meningitis while on Tour. She recovered, but her brain was seriously impaired and she died two and a half years later. Jill, a potter, was two years younger. The elder son was Euste, who took a degree in architecture at The Queen's College, Oxford. Michel, or "Mike" as he was known, was born two years after him – he became quite a well-known artist. Some years later, Merula, the youngest, was born. Like her mother, Merula was keen on ponies and riding, she left school to attend the Randell Phillips riding school and was scornful at first of the arty crowd.

The Salamans lived at Ruckmans, a large rambling house set in a large and beautiful garden in Ockley, ten miles south of Dorking in Surrey. They kept open house, inviting down many well-known people from the world of art and theatre. Michel was the dominant figure. They used to sit down to a large party at every meal. Michel had reddish hair, and several of Merula's aunts, who often stayed at the house, also had red hair. Two of them had studied at the Slade, and Michel used to joke in a good-natured way that they spent all day sleeping in armchairs.

Peggy Ashcroft came to Ruckmans; so did Ninette de Valois, the dancer, so did Theodore Komisarjevsky. Michel, a member of the Athenaeum Club, was fond of Michel Saint-Denis. When Merula took part in Komisarjevsky's famous production of *The Seagull* Michel gave a party for it. Elsie Fogarty, Olivier's acting teacher, he also knew well.

The Salaman family had many other artistic connections. Michel's younger brother, Clement, married Dora Tullock, the Scottish actress who had been an infant prodigy and acted with Beerbohm Tree. Clement had once taken up with Ira Nettleship, but she jilted him and went off with Augustus John, the painter, who had been a close friend of Michel's at the Slade. Both Augustus and his sister Gwen wrote to Michel frequently. Michel, who was a retired major of the Royal North Devon Hussars, a Territorial Regiment, and who "graduated from an art-student into a fox-hunting squire", lent John money, part of which he repaid by painting Michel's mother. The family owned a lot of John's paintings.

The impression Michel and Chattie gave was that of a marvellously happy and amusing pair. The golden-haired Chattie was a better painter than Michel, and, as Merula came to do, she kept a goat. Michel was a bit of a flirt and he had a wry sense of humour, to the point of telling jokes against himself, as his son-in-law would learn to do. But he would not suffer fools gladly: he liked charm *and* danger.

At first Guinness found the house alarmingly hearty. Martin Esslin, later head of BBC radio drama and a well-known writer on the theatre, was taken up by the Salamans when he arrived in April 1939, aged twenty-one, from Vienna as a refugee, and stayed with them until the outbreak of war. To some degree, he believed, they hoped he might be company for Susie. After his harrowing experiences he found it difficult to adapt to the wealth and Bloomsbury informality, the interacting strength of family emotions. There was a great deal of talk of Guinness's marriage to Merula. One night Esslin was eating dinner with them and felt upset, asking to be excused and so retired to his room. Here he shut himself in, broke down and just howled with grief. There was a knock on the door. It was Alec Guinness.

"May I come in?" He came in and they sat down on the bed. "I understand just how you feel," said Guinness ... "No, you will never be part of this ... I ... I have managed to become part of this and it has been difficult for me too."

Merula Salaman has been described as a woman with a restful

air, and a charming, enigmatic smile. Her appearance was statuesque: "Titian hair melting perfectly with her freckled skin and brilliant eyes". She was to have a strong harmonising influence in Guinness's life. They were both natural loners, attracted to the similar aspirations they found in each other. They became engaged during a late-night rehearsal of *The Merchant of Venice* at the Queen's Theatre, which Gielgud was directing and in which Guinness was playing Lorenzo. On 20 June 1938 they were married quietly at Reigate Register Office, in the presence of Juliet O'Rourke and Michel Salaman.

The affection between Michel and his son-in-law remained close. Guinness described him in old age with great warmth as "my very wise old father-in-law who died at the age of ninety-five or ninety-six, saying don't kid yourself" (about the decrease of desire):

> He said – he was a well-read man – that he used to think he would sit down and read everything he had never read, and that everything would be under control. "Not a bit of it," he said, "you revert in a strange way to your younger ways of thinking. You're not past it. And the younger and prettier the girls that go by the more you think, oh it would be lovely, you know." (*Guardian*, 7 October 1985)

10

The new school of direction

Before rehearsals of *Hamlet* started the newly married pair spent a
week in Ireland staying with the Guthries in their house in County
Monaghan, passing the time happily in a "Chekhovian atmosphere
of gaiety and decay". But it was a busman's holiday. On walks
through woods and by lakes they discussed the production. Merula
joined Judy Guthrie while Guinness and Guthrie worked at *Hamlet*
in a huge and neglected room with pitched roof and ceiling of dark
timbered beams, the so-called "concert room" at the back of the
house where, in this family home still inhabited by elderly relatives,
Guthrie as a child had performed plays. Guthrie tried to seize on
anything original Guinness had to offer, or so Guinness claimed,
which wasn't much: "I could never emulate the pyrotechnics of
Olivier, or the classic formality of Gielgud . . ." For intellectual
stimulus he read John Dover Wilson's *What Happens in Hamlet*
and Ernest Jones's Freudian interpretation, *Oedipus Complex as
an Explanation of Hamlet's Mystery* in which Jones explains that
Claudius's success in killing Hamlet's father and marrying his
mother are two things he himself unconsciously wished to do. This
also explains why his power to act against his hated stepfather is
paralysed by his own sense of guilt.

One should admire Guthrie's laid-back attitude about the
whole production, for it allowed Guinness his own pace of
self-development. He found Guthrie superior even to Michel
Saint-Denis, who had driven him mad with meticulous little
moves. He shared a quality Guinness also found in Gielgud,
Olivier and Peter Brook: the faculty of galvanising a company
into good work by sheer physical presence. Under his tutelage
Guinness learnt, gradually, and with much back-tracking and
mistakes, to make his own decisions about how his own talent
should develop. No doubt he would have loved to escape from

this burdensome process – who wouldn't? – but Guthrie saw more deeply and more wisely the need not to interfere and impose. He practised a kind of inspired indifference which strikes one as truly remarkable in what is now such a power-hungry profession, and it did not seem to bother him much if his actors made fools of themselves. His unconventionality appealed to Guinness, who yet, forever grasping uncertainty, hankered after certainty. Later he would complain that Guthrie failed to wean him away from his "pale, ersatz Gielgudry". In truth, Guthrie was just letting him grow in his own time.

Before *Hamlet* opened Guinness had the penance of acting the role of Arthur Gower, the ineffectual hero of Pinero's *Trelawny of the Wells*, which they put on to commemorate the Old Vic's first quarter-century with a sideglance at its sister theatre. The predominant note of the reviews of *Hamlet*, which opened on 11 October 1938, was a surprised interest. The settings and costumes struck the audiences as timeless and Ruritanian rather than modern: Hamlet wore sombre black and plum-coloured dress jackets, Horatio unassuming civilian tweeds, the women long and

PROGRAMME

HAMLET

(IN ITS ENTIRETY)   By WILLIAM SHAKESPEARE

Characters in the order of appearance

BERNARDO	ANTHONY COMPTON
FRANCISCO	STANLEY HILDEBRANDT
HORATIO, *friend to Hamlet*	ANDRÉ MORELL
MARCELLUS	ERNEST HARE
GHOST OF HAMLET'S FATHER	MALCOLM KEEN
CLAUDIUS, *King of Denmark*	ANDREW CRUICKSHANK
GERTRUDE, *Queen of Denmark and mother to Hamlet*	VERONICA TURLEIGH
POLONIUS, *Lord Chamberlain*	O. B. CLARENCE
VOLTEMAND	PHILIP BOWEN
CORNELIUS	WILLOUGHBY GRAY
LAERTES, *son to Polonius*	ANTHONY QUAYLE
HAMLET, *Prince of Denmark*	ALEC GUINNESS
OPHELIA, *daughter to Polonius*	HERMIONE HANNEN
REYNALDO	JOHN KIDD
ROSENCRANTZ	RICHARD WORDSWORTH
GUILDENSTERN	JAMES HOYLE
FIRST PLAYER	CRAIGHALL SHERRY
PLAYER KING	GEORGE WOOD
PLAYER QUEEN	FREDA JACKSON
SECOND PLAYER	JOHN KIDD
FORTINBRAS, *Prince of Norway*	WILLOUGHBY GRAY
CAPTAIN TO FORTINBRAS	OWEN REED
FIRST MESSENGER	ANTHONY COMPTON
FIRST SAILOR	OWEN REED
SECOND SAILOR	ROBERT CHRISTIE
SECOND MESSENGER	STANLEY HILDEBRANDT
FIRST GRAVEDIGGER	FRANK TICKLE
SECOND GRAVEDIGGER	JAMES HOYLE
PRIEST	PHILIP BOWEN
OSRIC	JOHN KIDD
FIRST ENGLISH AMBASSADOR	ROBERT CHRISTIE
SECOND ENGLISH AMBASSADOR	ANTHONY HOWARD

Court Ladies—Laura Dyas, Brenda Newbold, Meg Townsend, Lorna Whitehouse.

Lords, Soldiers, Attendants—Howard Bourgein, Miles Greenwood, Neville Mapp, Ferdinand Mayer, Siegfried Maynard, Ian Morris.

SCENE—DENMARK

The play will be presented in three parts with Two Intervals of Ten Minutes each

Produced by TYRONE GUTHRIE.

Scenery and costumes designed by ROGER FURSE

Music specially composed by HERBERT MENGES

Orchestra under the direction of HERBERT MENGES. Leader, DAVID CARL TAYLOR

Ladies' dresses by BLANCHE ARUNDELL and THEA SCOTT

Fight arranged by EVAN JOHNS.

Men's clothes by NATHANS.

Furniture by THE OLD TIMES FURNISHING CO.

Columns and balustrade by ZURIC, LTD.

Wigs by BERT

All Scenery built and painted in the OLD VIC Workshops.

While smoking is permitted, it is requested that the convenience of non-smokers and artists be considered and that it be limited to the intervals.

Members of the audience are forbidden to take photographs during the performance.

Fire Curtain. The design on the fire curtain is by Robert Medley, and won the prize in the competition organised by the Sadler's Wells Society, and judged by Winston Churchill, Sir Kenneth Clark and C. B. Cochran.

FREE SEATS—AT THE OLD VIC ONLY.

Owing to the generosity of the "Sunday Pictorial" twelve people (in a special queue) will be admitted without charge to the Vic gallery, at all except special performances, on Saturday, first or last nights. Please bring this kindness to the notice of those who could not otherwise afford to enjoy the performance.

Stage Director	GEORGE CHAMBERLAIN
Stage Manager	JAMES HOYLE
Asst. Stage Managers	BRENDA NEWBOLD
	WILLOUGHBY GRAY
Master Carpenters	JAMES R. SMITH
Property Master	FRED STUBBINGS
Electrician	WILLIAM THORNBY
Wardrobe Mistress	JACK EGAN
Wardrobe Master	MRS. NEWMAN
	REGINALD AMOS
Scenic Artists	GEORGE WIGGINS
	HELEN STEINTHAL

In accordance with the requirements of the Lord Chamberlain.
1. The public may leave at the end of the performance by all exit doors, and such doors must at that time be open.
2. All gangways, passages and staircases must be kept entirely free from chairs or any other obstruction.

3. Persons shall not in any circumstances be permitted to stand or sit in any of the gangways intersecting the seating, or to sit in any of the other gangways. If standing be permitted in the gangways at the sides and rear of the seating, it shall be strictly limited to the numbers indicated in the notices exhibited in these positions.
4. The safety curtain must be lowered and raised in the presence of each audience.

sweeping evening dresses. The production was much praised for its atmosphere.

"For the first time," wrote Audrey Williamson in *Old Vic Drama*, "one realised how a modern-dress production may give new life and reality to Shakespeare's characters without losing intellectual excitement or beauty." Everyone carried open umbrellas at Ophelia's graveside – possibly an effect touched off in Guthrie's mind by the downpour at Elsinore. Guinness entered the graveyard in sailor's jersey and thigh boots.

Guinness's Hamlet fitted admirably into Guthrie's production: "essentially sane", Williamson called it, or, in other words, lacking in emotional turmoil, as Guinness might counter. Even worse, Williamson picked up the similarity to Gielgud's early Hamlet, "a sensitive young intellectual temperamentally incapable of meeting violence with violence – an interpretation aided by Guinness's youth and fragile appearance, as well as by the curiously impotent expression with which he regarded his sword at the words "O curséd spite!" This response mortified Guinness when he read it in his press books and he was to call attention to it later.

James Agate attacked the performance for lacking power, pointing out that, as Guinness had chubby, practical hands, he attempted few rhetorical gestures. This Hamlet failed because it deliberately refused to succeed. He seemed to be adding another complex to Dr Jones's Oedipus Complex. "This young actor attempts neither play of feature nor gesture. He reflects mordancy . . . Yet this non-acting comes, in the end, to have a value of its own." In an astonishing *volte-face* Agate still found it, in spite of the performance by Guinness and in spite of the modern costumes, "the most moving performance of *Hamlet* in my experience".

Robert Speaight, the actor, went further. In *The Property Basket*, an unusually intelligent memoir, he described the performance as "sensitive and *intimiste*, spurning spectacular effects". J.C. Trewin, who saw well over a hundred different Hamlets in his lifetime, recording all of them in a single book, dubbed it the youngest and quietest of them all, above all "a thinking man". Trewin noted he was the first Hamlet sitting alone by the Players' property basket before the conscience of the King speech who found himself tapping out the rhythm upon the upturned drum: "As he would so often, he seemed to be creating a character as he moved, without previous calculation."

What was the thinking man himself thinking about his Hamlet?

He claimed originality for his wild outburst of misogyny after the "To be or not to be" soliloquy, saying he interpreted that, from Ophelia's attitude and false orisons, she was a decoy; also for the drumming, which he said came about almost by accident. Otherwise, through being over-familiar with Gielgud's manner of timing, he quoted Dr Johnson to the effect that, "almost all absurdity of conduct arises from the imitations of those we cannot resemble". Yet here he was being too hard on himself, for he did resemble Gielgud. Looking back on the production, Guinness confessed to me in 1989 that he had hardly penetrated below the surface of the part. There was no overall grasp of the complexity. "Why, it was ridiculous," he said. "It was like water off a duck's back." He marvelled that they had performed the play in its "eternity" text, nearly "five" hours of it.

But at the time Guthrie did not agree. He thought that Guinness's youth, combined with rare intelligence, humour, and pathos, realised a great deal of the part. "He had not yet quite the authority to support, as Hamlet must, a whole evening, or to give the tragedy its full stature. The performance demanded that the public reach out and take what was offered. To this demand the public is rarely equal."

Gielgud wrote to Guthrie that he was stirred and provoked. "I was deeply touched by Alec's performance," said Gielgud, "which I thought grew in distinction and quality all the time as it went on . . . I thought that the Recorder scene was fussed by the busyness of the production, and you haven't got any further than anyone else in solving the problem of the ghost. I also hated the new punctuation, but perhaps that is only my Terry blood crying out . . . I was terrifically moved by the closet scene, almost the best I have ever seen . . ."

But the public's response was depressing, at first anyway. Guthrie admitted the production wasn't doing very well, even though he declared proudly, "Alec is much *much* better in the part than Larry, but Larry with his beautiful head and athletic sexy movements and bursts of fireworks are what the public wants . . . It represents my very utmost effort. It's easily the best work I've done so far and may well be the best I shall do — in this job, as in all semi-creative work, experience tends to kill invention and it is a blow to have it fall very flat."

Guthrie understood the difficulty the part presented to Guinness. He commented in *A Life in the Theatre*:

It's been far more difficult for Alec to weather. The actor's position to success or failure is so terribly personal. The work of art is inseparable from himself. It's *him* "they" like or fail to like. And it's a very personal ordeal to have to tussle through that enormous physical effort to empty houses. Still, he's got great spirit and sense of proportion and the houses though empty are immensely enthusiastic and nearly all the people whose opinion we value have been sincerely and wholeheartedly praising him.

Something else was beginning to stalk Guinness at this time: religion. Up to now he had been almost an atheist. As a schoolboy he had sung hymns of twilight or geography, Greenland's icy mountains — either melancholy or rumbustious. When he was confirmed in Holy Trinity Church, Eastbourne, by the Bishop of Lewes, he realised with a flash that he had never believed. Later he attended a few Quaker meetings, one Buchmanite Conference on moral rearmament and considered Buddhist guru worship.

But one night a Roman Catholic priest came backstage and told him he was crossing himself in the wrong way. The next week the priest called again and told him he was still doing it.

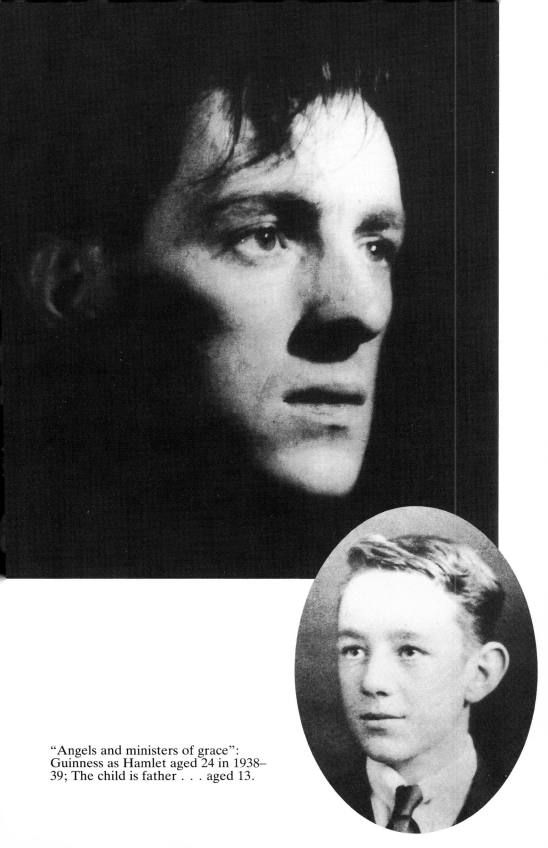

"Angels and ministers of grace":
Guinness as Hamlet aged 24 in 1938–
39; The child is father . . . aged 13.

Influences: Nellie Wallace, "as hideous as a parrot"; Sir Sydney Cockerell – "strip off the veneer of distinguished men and women . . . and what remains?"; Gielgud as Romeo, and Guinness as the Apothecary, Romeo's poison in his pocket (1935).

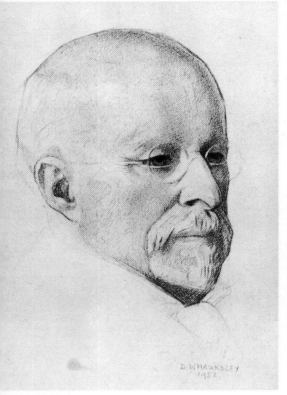

More Hamlet "in its entirety": Guinness (left) with Andrew Cruickshank as Claudius, Veronica Turleigh as Gertrude, Anthony Quayle as Laertes; "Quite chopfallen" with Yorick's skull.

No. 7 St Peter's Square:
Guinness with Merula; "a
hit, a palpable hit" – with
Matthew in the garden.

11

Thursday was black tie night

But who was he? Was he just an actor?" The work of art is inseparable from himself. It's *him* 'they' like or fail to like," Guthrie had wisely said. Guinness's first Hamlet, whatever its intellectual qualities, failed to ignite. Guinness might be able to speed up for comedy, but for tragedy he remained slow and searching. For him it was never an intensification of reality, as it was for Olivier, who said, "The only time I ever feel alive is when I'm acting." Edith Evans, when she heard of Guinness marrying, told him – "No-ah!" You're an artist! You shouldn't marry." But Guinness, refusing to be pinned down, has always been much more than an artist. His heresy, in an age which worships the artist-hero, is to insist that art and life are separate departments.

When looking back, Guinness liked to see his own career as if through the wrong end of a special kind of telescope which diminished everything but also through which the tiniest parts came out as much larger than the main roles. This was because the biggest parts gave him the most pain, and this is what he chose to forget, or wanted to forget. Of Shakespeare he once said he could speak with no authority as he himself only acted in two or three Shakespearean roles. It was the Shakespeare roles which gave him the most pain, so they became reduced to two or three.

"I am evasive," Guinness said in 1993. "I do know I'm evasive, because I wish to be. My private life is my private life, and I have very much taken the attitude that I share it with my wife, who is inclined to be rather a shy person. She didn't know when we married that I would make a name for myself."

Guinness may, by his own high standards, have failed as Hamlet but in his work and his life he was to embody more and more of its central message: "The readiness is all." Also Tyrone Guthrie's way was ultimately the liberating way for his talent, while Guthrie's own choice of supporting actors, especially that of Anthony Quayle for Laertes and Andrew Cruickshank for Claudius, brought very definite qualities into influential play over Guinness that were entirely different from those of Gielgud.

Quayle was an excellent but cool, prosaic actor who brought to Laertes a stricken stillness in his grief over his sister's death and a self-harrowing guilt in the duel. Cruickshank, more crucially, was a Claudius who had lost the love of Gertrude and who knew it: "But that I know love is begun by time," yields, in Harley Granville-Baker's suggestion, this interpretation. Cruickshank's performance became a notable exposition of the Stanislavsky theory that an actor playing an evil man should look for the good in him. Looking for the good in his characters was to become, increasingly, the creed of Guinness.

His next move, early in 1939, was to lead a British Council tour of the Continent and Egypt. This tour of mainly right-wing or fascist countries provoked an outcry: "shaking the blood-stained hand of Mussolini", some papers said. Scotland Yard warned of a demonstration outside the theatre, but nothing much happened.

The company travelled with eight productions, including *The Rivals*, *Trelawny of the Wells*, *Hamlet* and *Henry V*. The enterprise, by today's standards, was huge and incredible – a company of forty-two and nearly twelve tons of scenery. They first played Lisbon, where their scenery was lowered into the Tagus by mistake and where the victory of Franco over the Republican-held Barcelona was celebrated with delirium; they played Milan, Florence; they played Rome where Mussolini invited Guinness to take tea with him in his box, then cancelled the arrangement. Pius XI had just died and the audience wore black in Rome and Naples, appropriate for the *Hamlet* which became very popular in Italy and helped promote the lost cause of Anglo-Italian relations. Lewis Casson, who was now playing Polonius, tried to encourage Guinness to show more confidence. Later he would defend Guinness's interpretation as the ordinary man's Hamlet.

They next sailed from Naples to Cairo. Sir Sydney Cockerell, the art historian, was in the audience in Cairo. Cockerell was extraordinary, as his biographer Wilfrid Blunt noted, on account of "the empire he exerted over his innumerable friends". Some questioned if it was toadyism or genuine hero-worship. Guinness became at once a new object of his admiration. "A charming young man of twenty-four, very serious about Shakespeare and about his profession. His wife is on the stage, and is also a lover of literature . . . I hope to see them again," wrote Cockerell in his diary.

After Cairo they played in Alexandria where Guinness saw Katina Paxinou – whom Casson called "the old and fish-wifey" grande dame of the Greek National Theatre – in her most famous role of Electra. In fact she was barely forty and went on acting for another thirty years. Sailing past Rhodes and Naxos they docked in Athens, and then finally on to Malta, where the social activity was intense, but even more evident were the battle preparations of the English fleet in Valetta harbour. One performance of *Henry V*, in which Guinness acted the Chorus, emptied halfway through as men were called back to their ships. The fleet was, as the pacifist Casson put it, "so horribly ready".

This year and the next saw Guinness's involvement with Shakespeare and other classics deepen further. On his return from Malta, in May 1939, he played his first Macbeth with the Sheffield Repertory Company; in June he played Michael Ransom in Auden and Isherwood's *The Ascent of F6* at the Old Vic, to which part, W.A. Darlington wrote in the *Daily Telegraph*, he brought "a sense of the concentration and integrity that belong to genius". In July he played Romeo in Perth, a role he chose to forget, although he always recalled clearly the Apothecary he played when Edith Evans acted the Nurse. When he was off-stage he would hold open doors for her and not "get even a nod, let alone a thank you".*

In August 1939 he began rehearsal for another Michel Saint-Denis production of Chekhov, this time of *The Cherry Orchard*, some of which he had already rehearsed before at the London Theatre Studio. Edith Evans was cast as Madame Ranevsky, Peggy Ashcroft as Anya.

Edith Evans was not much over fifty, much admired by the younger, gentler sort of actors such as Guinness and, in particular, by Michael Redgrave, whose infatuation for her bordered on obsession. She had witnessed the formative shame of Guinness's dismissal from William Wycherley's *The Country Wife*, in the Old Vic 1936–7 season, when he started rehearsing in the role of

---

* Alan Dent wrote of this production in the *Manchester Guardian*, "There was a goodly drawing by Mr Alec Guinness of the Apothecary. But why does the last always have Romeo's poison in his pocket ready to hand? And, incidentally, why does Shakespeare make him fuss so much at being paid? Perhaps in Mantua the chemists were not cash."

Sparkish, and Ruth Gordon, the American star who was playing Mrs Pinchwife, had told Guthrie, "Please! I can't act with this young man", so he had been dismissed. Subsequently Edith Evans consoled him by saying he was not right for the part.

In *The Cherry Orchard* Guinness was cast as the student Trofimov, with the salary of £28 a week. Cyril Cusack, fresh from Ireland, somewhat intimidated at working with the exacting Saint-Denis, sidled over to address the actor with the lofty "Irish patronymic... one that ranks among the Lords of the North" as he put it. The Guinness name, he mused, originally "Mac Aonghusa, son of Aonghus, God of the Birds". He had not been disappointed, or so he reported, for "Mr Guinness admitted diffidently there might have been an ancestral shade or two hovering, however mistily, amidst the hills of Donegal". Guinness was not above using the effect his name produced on others.

But on Saturday 2 September, the day before the outbreak of the Second World War, Binkie Beaumont, the producer, called the cast together on stage at the Globe to tell them they would not be able to open. "Fated never to reach the gods but condemned to limbo at the first off-stage roar of Mars," concluded Cusack loftily.

"Alec, take me for a walk," Edith Evans commanded her protégé on hearing this news. They walked arm-in-arm slowly along Piccadilly to Hyde Park. Edith Evans launched a tirade of self-centred egotism at the slender young actor: "I can't act with bombs falling: what am I going to do?" ... and so on and so on. The future dead, the future dying, the young men lost, the devastation: no concern for any of this, only her own career. Guinness felt chilled.

Next, Guinness formed a little company which they called the Actors' Company with George Penne, Vera Lindsay (later Poliakov, later Lady Russell), Martita Hunt and Marius Goring, to put on "intelligent" work. Guinness had adapted *Great Expectations* and this was their first choice for production. They hired the Rudolf Steiner Hall and planned to follow the Dickens with *King John* and a Molière play: money was raised from Marius Goring (£200), the department store John Lewis (£10), and an unexpectedly generous Edith Evans who insisted on contributing £700, the price of the most recent fur coat she bought. "I can't let actors be out of work when I spend £700 on a fur coat," she told them. *Great Expectations*, which was George Devine's first professional production, was, according to Guinness, very good and also very popular. Guinness, who had earlier worked with George Devine in Michel Saint-Denis productions, played Herbert Pockett, Marius Goring Pip, and Martita Hunt Miss Havisham. They ran for six weeks during the blackout, but were thwarted in their hopes of transfer to the Shaftesbury Theatre, and made a loss. During the run Guinness met Edith Sitwell, who came backstage with her brother Osbert; she had sent him a book, and subsequently invited him to lunches at her Sesame Club where he met literary celebrities including Stephen Spender, Evelyn Waugh and Somerset Maugham.

Guinness was not suited to Romeo, but his next Shakespearean role – after *Cousin Muriel*, an unsuccessful Clemence Dane comedy at the Globe Theatre in which he played the juvenile lead and was paid £30 a week – was as Ferdinand in *The Tempest*. Gielgud's "family" at the Old Vic was gathered for the last time before they were dispersed in battle. Gielgud, of course, was Prospero, Lewis Casson Gonzalo, while Jessica Tandy began as Miranda, to be replaced not long after by Peggy Ashcroft. Jack Hawkins played Caliban, and Marius Goring Ariel, in a production again directed by George Devine.

Sybil Thorndike and Lewis Casson's son, John, had joined the Fleet Air Arm. He was in charge of a dive-bomber squadron on *Ark Royal* when he was shot down over Norway by a Messerschmitt. Sybil went along to tell Lewis before one matinée of *The Tempest* that the Admiralty had telephoned that John was "missing, believed killed". When they played, every line about the drowned Ferdinand appeared to refer to his loss. Casson insisted on going on but when Ferdinand and Miranda are discovered playing chess in the grotto, and father and son are reunited, Casson broke down and wept on stage. In fact John was not dead. Much later he was reported captured by the Germans. While Guinness played Ferdinand, Merula announced to her mother that she was pregnant. Chattie Salaman, mother of six, railed at her, "How dare you bring a child into this filthy world?" Yet for the generation to which Guinness belonged there was always going to be a war.

In this production Guinness worked again with Devine, whose quality he described as "wiry roughness". He followed *The Tempest* with the English provincial tour of *Thunder Rock*, by Robert Ardrey, in which he took over the role of Charleston from Michael Redgrave, who had created it in London.

During this run Guinness was invited with Merula to stay with Edith Sitwell at Weston Hall, Sacheverell Sitwell's home in Northamptonshire; later, during performances of *Thunder Rock* at Leeds, Guinness and Merula visited Osbert and Edith at Renishaw Hall, Osbert's vast and dark house in Derbyshire. They had Matthew, their son, with them in a carry-cot, but Edith firmly instructed them that Osbert must not be informed of the child's presence in his house. Matthew was entrusted to an old maid, called the "baboon" because she "looked like one". Osbert found out about Matthew but assured Guinness he did not mind in the least, "So long as you will excuse me from looking at him".

Matthew was only two or three months old. He had been born in June when Merula and Guinness were living in a bungalow they rented near Ockley for seven shillings a week. By now Guinness had enlisted in the Royal Navy and was waiting for call-up. Twenty-six years of age, he had a wife, a son, and, in the past six years, had played thirty-four parts in twenty-three plays by Shakespeare, Sheridan, Pinero, Chekhov, Shaw and others. To a small loyal public he was something of a star.

After such a concentrated and meteoric rise it is hardly surprising that this young man, whose temperament was so alien to self-advertisement and the other usual trappings of an actor's ego, should enter an intensely spiritual phase. From an early life of dark contrasts, some of it rarefied, genteel yet some of it threatening and ugly, he was set to enter a much larger universe. Here he would need a strong external identity and the will to survive, if survive he did; but he would have to surrender his family of actors, his substitute for the more usual family of parents, brothers, sisters which he had never had.

This was a world of deference where the experienced actors and actresses were always referred to as Mr or Miss: "It was always Miss Evans and Miss [Elizabeth] Bradley, never their Christian names." Yet this formal theatre was about to pass away for good, and gone would be the conventions that required younger members of the company always to wear a tie when they came through the stage door, and never to be seen carrying in parcels in case they might be confused with tradesmen. At that time the actors were respectable and close to their audiences. Guinness remembered that the best nights, when he was a very young actor, were always Thursday because the carriage trade was in and most of the stalls wore a black tie. On Friday they had departed for the country weekend.

There was a feeling of elegance, of going out, that gave the occasion a little extra, even though they were no more intelligent than people sitting in their raincoats in the gods, reading the *Evening Standard*.

12

Shallow draughts and bulk unprizable

Alec Guinness was passed A1, the doctor curious about his ability
to expand his chest – four inches – which Guinness explained as the
result of his voice training as an actor. He was called up towards the
end of 1940 and drafted as an Ordinary Seaman to HMS *Raleigh*,
a shore establishment near Plymouth to do basic training. He was
selected as a potential officer more or less straightaway, but as
with all branches of the Services, everyone had to undergo that
levelling period of being marched and pushed around, in which
spit-and-polish was the order of the day and all privacy was
denied.

Among his intake was another actor, Peter Bull, who had just
been confined to hospital for eight weeks after a bad accident to
his ankle occasioned by carrying a sailor piggy-back in the gym
which had resulted in a blood clot. Bull came from a high-caste
family – his father Sir George Bull was the Conservative MP
for Hammersmith and later Lord Mayor of Chelsea and had
been to school at Winchester. He possessed that inherent class
authority to which Guinness responded, but it was accompanied
by a campness, an eccentricity and an original sense of humour.
According to his godson, Sheridan Morley, "Bully", as he was
known, was "something of an experimentalist who would veer
from stable, live-in relationships, often with younger men, to
occasional ventures into the rough trade". The ambivalence was
attractive to Guinness. Bull also dabbled in the occult; later he
owned a share in an astrological emporium in Kensington High
Street. He possessed a gaiety of heart and made Guinness laugh a
lot; reliable as he was, there was something spontaneously anarchic
about him. He was also enormously fat and greedy; he liked to eat
three lunches.

Now recovered from his set-back Bull had to start training

again in Guinness's intake and became Deputy Class Leader under a "Scottish Laird of great distinction", as Guinness called him, named Algernon Ross-Farrow, aged thirty-eight, a volunteer with a weak heart who subsequently left the service. The trio of older trainees (Bull at twenty-nine, and Guinness at twenty-six the youngest) survived this parade-ground onslaught on their sensibilities. Guinness commented on the irksome conviviality of the ordinary beer-swilling mass of humanity in close proximity to whom he was flung without ceremony, complaining there was hardly a quiet corner to which he could retire and read.

His first feeling was one of intense loneliness, heightened by the painful separation from Merula and six-month-old Matthew. It seemed doubly grievous to be taken from the family he had just started when this was what he most wanted in life. But stripped from the accoutrements of his early, even rarefied stardom, he enjoyed a certain relief at the anonymity of it all. He was absolved from the terror of having to perform and in particular of the first night.

While at first Merula had continued acting – she was with the Young Vic while Guinness was at sea – she now also withdrew from the theatre. "I suppose I was obsessed by acting," she said in a possibly unique interview she gave in 1992. "It was something one could bury oneself in. However, there were awful difficulties in having a small boy and going on tour. I thought to myself that it was no way to be a professional actress and I gave it up." Instead, she took up painting, and in 1947 published a children's story with her own illustrations.

The sense of alienation gave great impetus to Guinness's literary ambitions. He came to find, when he spent some time at sea as an ordinary seaman and then attended Lancing College and HMS *King Alfred* in Hove for officers' training, that he preferred the life of a seaman, although he must have given to his fellow sailors "a queer impression of aloofness or shyness or Puritanism". He found the officers' code of getting drunk dull, expensive and unnecessary. His individuality, he came to feel, was more respected as an ordinary seaman and he commented, "I don't think the officer class (if such a thing exists now) is so tolerant."

He was trying to write a book, an adventure story written from the heart, which, in a letter written towards the end of October 1941, he promised to send to Sydney Cockerell. He was also reading avidly, particularly Dickens, and now *Bleak House*.

Sydney Cockerell, whom Guinness had met in Cairo, had, as the curator of the Fitzwilliam Museum in Cambridge, built up its collection into one of the finest in England. He was also a connoisseur of people. A servant disciple of Ruskin, and one-time friend and companion of William Morris, Cockerell provided direct links to the greatest writers of the age: he knew Shaw intimately, while he had once visited Tolstoy, whom he venerated, in central Russia just to be in his company for half a day.

While waiting for his shot at a commission Guinness served on a variety of ships and felt himself lucky that he was not posted to the Far East for the duration of the war. For a while he was on shore duty at Inverary, on Loch Fyne, where he whiled away several months as a sentry in a box on the sea-shore. He savoured the solitariness and quiet, and on fine moonlight nights the line of the hills and mountains. Here, as he told Cockerell, he was able for the first time in his life to meditate, although adding characteristically that he couldn't think much: "I've a fairly addled brain and am stumped for knowledge whenever any problem presents itself . . . Actors are so hopelessly undisciplined emotionally – this new life is a tonic."

During this period he was able to see Merula and Matthew on weekend leave every two months or so. Passing through London he would look up old theatrical friends. He even found time to record for BBC Radio in February 1942, the fragment of Menander's newly discovered comedy *The Rape of the Locks*, in which Peggy Ashcroft played a part and so did Guinness's old friend Martita Hunt. His mind was also turning to church matters: he was reading widely if unmethodically in St Teresa of Avila, St John of the Cross, the Curé d'Ars and Charles de Foucauld, the Catholic mystic priest whose martyrdom in the desert was to influence T.S. Eliot when he came to write *The Cocktail Party*.

Merula and Matthew lived mostly at Ockley with Michel and Chattie during the war. The London leases of Salaman estates had started running out, while the servants had left to join up. Michel did the housekeeping. He would come down from London with all kinds of exotic food.

Guinness was proud that Cockerell had told him about picnicking with the Tolstoy family in the apple orchard. They were sitting or lying in the long grass under the trees drinking black tea and eating cucumber spread with honey. Tolstoy took them to the "billiard" room where the table was hidden under thousands of unopened letters. Even so, Cockerell somehow managed to come away with a copy of a letter written to Tolstoy by "the late Grand Mufti of Egypt" (as he had told another correspondent more than thirty years before, in 1907) so Tolstoy must have opened some of his letters.

Cockerell was an authority, a mentor, the representative of a higher civilised spirit to which Guinness needed to refer. But Cockerell was also ruthless and a "scrounger of genius," as someone called him, "who had turned a "pigsty into a palace". He was not a formally religious man, but as "a man without any set creed", as he described himself, this "bearded infidel" became an important part of Guinness's search for a spiritual centre to his life. Guinness sought serenity and peace from the basis of someone who had suffered too much inner toil, and material and emotional insecurity. This allied him deeply to the Tolstoy whom Cockerell once defended enthusiastically to Dame Laurentia McLachlan, the distinguished Benedictine nun who was dubious about Tolstoy's religious values:

> Tolstoy is a man who has lived with the principle *Homo sum humanum nihil a me alienum puto** – and he has now after immense struggles and wrestlings arrived at that serenity of mind and indifference to worldly annoyance that comes only to the very wise and the very simple and the very religious, and not always even to these. One has only to meet him to feel that he lives on a different plane from most of his fellows – a plane in which love of family and love of country are entirely merged in love of man and love of God – though what God is . . . he told me he did not know.

In view of what we now know about Tolstoy's treatment of his wife and family, perhaps the nun was more accurate than the humanist.

While Guinness wrote to Cockerell only "occasionally" (he reported that Cockerell in his published collection of letters, *The Best of Friends*,† used "two or three" letters – in truth Cockerell printed nine of his letters), Cockerell replied with brief telegraphic

---

* I am a man. I think nothing of man alien to me.
† Published in January 1956. *The Times Literary Supplement* said of it: "Old-fashioned ideas of privacy have largely crumbled under the bombardment of what is euphemistically called publicity." It is rather ironic, perhaps, that Guinness should have been prominently associated with it, revealing himself as "the possessor of a serious and searching mind".

answers, "like the Lord's Prayer written on a postage stamp".
Again Guinness was using his autobiography as an exercise in
self-diminishment.

There was a certain artifice, however, even a presumption and
self-conscious vanity, in these letters. On the surface they were
eminently civilised and virtuous in their search for values. But they
were not entirely the genuine, humble outpourings of a simple,
unassuming person; they were, sometimes beneath the surface, the
craftily channelled and softened aggression of someone who had
so much rage and unsorted feeling inside him that he needed to
adopt almost the most civilised code and order there was, in order
to fashion self-respect.

In the spring of 1942 Guinness returned to the south coast, to
HMS *King Alfred* in Hove, where he trained for his commission and
"just about" scraped through. Do we have to believe the modesty?
Apparently he passed his selection board because he spoke up with
insincere enthusiasm for an officer whom the Admiral in charge of
the evaluating board had enjoyed seeing in a play. But this was a
game of later years. The officers must have known that before them
stood a young man who had served nearly two years in the Navy,
but before that had played leading roles at the Old Vic and in the
West End and led a famous theatre company on a foreign tour.
Guinness was perfectly sound officer material, as was the "camp"
and extrovert Peter Bull, who claimed that he only passed officer
selection because he produced the Divisional Concert:

> The lowlight of the show was my strip-tease, which I maintain
> got me through my finals. Some years previously I had laughed
> loud and long at Tony Beckwith's performance in a Gate Theatre
> Revue in which he had suddenly had to take the place of a
> burlesque dancer and take all his clothes off. I realised that
> a sailor's uniform was ideal for a similar act and I made my
> first entrance to the strains of "She's My Lovely", dressed in
> full uniform with a gas mask on and webbing equipment. Out
> of the latter I produced cartridges which I threw gracefully at
> the officers in the front rows. I slowly stripped to my pants and
> then coyly retired behind a screen to emerge . . .

Often in his long and effectively light-hearted account in *Blessings in Disguise* of his wartime years, Guinness was performing in
counterpoint with *To Sea in a Sieve*, Bull's classic description of
life in landing craft.

The commissioning of Guinness as a Sub-Lieutenant meant that he was now posted, in early summer 1942, as First Lieutenant to a tank landing craft on Loch Fyne. After three months, further promotion followed. He crossed the Atlantic in late 1942 on the *Queen Mary* to take up command of a brand-new landing craft built to carry two hundred troops, which was nearing completion in a naval dockyard near Boston. The work was delayed for some weeks and when Guinness revived some former theatrical friendships, notably with the actresses Gladys Cooper and Peggy Webster, he found himself being approached by Terence Rattigan who was visiting New York to help mount the American production of *Flare Path*, his play about a bomber pilot which had opened in London earlier that year. Guinness was then asked to play the lead in New York, a part which required outer insensitivity and inner vulnerability (the means by which Flight Lieutenant Graham ultimately, yet unconsciously, salvages his marriage).

In an unusual move by the Admiralty, Guinness was granted eight weeks' leave – he was, he said, the "only available actor with an English accent" – but after three weeks' rehearsal and a week's try-out run *Flare Path* opened on 23 December at the Henry Miller Theatre. "It seems to be another case of an English hit destined to be an English miss," wrote Robert Coleman in the *Daily Mirror*, while George Jean Nathan, the doyen of New York critics commented, somewhat unfairly, "If the play has so much as even one happy, one redeeming feature, it has eluded this critical cunning. The author's purpose and intention is to pay tribute to the valour of the Royal Air Force; what he achieves, so trivial being his equipment, is something that rather puts that admirable body into a ridiculous light." What Eleanor Roosevelt had written up in her column as "a true and moving picture of the RAF" closed after only two weeks. Guinness's own contribution was not remarked upon as special. Had the play been a triumph, and his own performance hailed as outstanding, the history of his war might have taken a distinctly different form.

Guinness reported back for duty two weeks early to join his LCI(L) no. 124 which was ready for him on its Boston slipway. Then began his "wild adventures", as he called them, as Officer in Command of a landing craft, a ship which, for its notorious unmanoeuvrability, always "left its mark" on other ships, lost its anchor or bent lamp-posts from the quays to which it was tied. "Tin Can" and "bloody menace" were epithets generally applied by the crews of other ships.

Peter Bull wrote about how he himself had "five collisions in the first three days" of taking command of a landing craft, so he "got to the stage where I solemnly prayed for the weather to keep us in port". Peter Copley reported meeting Bull in Glasgow at this time where Copley was acting with his wife Pamela Brown. In the classic dilemma these craft presented their commanders, Bull confessed to Copley, "I don't know how to get it under the bridges . . . and I daren't ask."

13

Spirit levels

Hosts of landing craft were converging on the Mediterranean for the monumental invasions of 1942–44. Guinness crossed the Atlantic in sixteen days in a Squadron commanded by an officer with whom he exchanged biblical signals. The trip was full of incident as Guinness's craft met difficulties of one kind or another or developed various faults. He had a Geordie coxswain: "a regular RN, very robust, downright, trustworthy and likeable. He would often advise me on some course of action – and probably very tactfully – but I rarely grasped a word he said. Not wishing to offend him by asking him to repeat everything slowly, I got into the habit of replying, 'very good. Let it be so!'"

Peter Bull undertook a shorter voyage with a flotilla of twelve ships from the north of Scotland:

It was a nerve-racking trip, but during it I became convinced of a special Deity who kept an eye on landing craft throughout the years. The losses were to be miraculously small during the coming campaigns considering the risks, and as the ships had a hard job in even getting recognised as part of the Royal Navy, it was comforting to believe in the existence of such a person. For every craft arrived in Gibraltar, with the exception of one which broke in half during the voyage. Rumour had it that the stern part made a triumphant entry into harbour towing the bows.

Guinness docked at Djidjelli, a port west of Algiers, where they practised for invasion and here, shortly after, he was joined by Bull, who now commanded a bigger Landing Craft anti-aircraft ship with seventy marines on board. They spent much enjoyable spare time together for, as Bull said, "Alec's presence . . . was a life-saver." He wrote in his book: "It was nice sending signals to each other with 'Repeat Nervo and Knox, Donald Wolfit and Phyllis Neilson-Terry' on them with impunity."

They made one trip together worthy of note (both wrote it up) when "Lieutenants Bull and Guinness" were "excused duty" to visit companions of old in an all-star company headed by Leslie Henson, Vivien Leigh and Beatrice Lillie, which was playing at the Garrison Theatre in Bougie, half-way between Djidjelli and Algiers. By the time Bull and Guinness could reach Bougie they were too late to see any of the performance, which was packed out anyway. They were confronted by Binkie Beaumont who told them that he would take them round backstage after the show. They spent twenty minutes backstage, but then became depressed as they wondered how on earth they would get back to their ships.

Vivien Leigh came to the rescue, flattering and cajoling an admiral into sending them back in his staff car. Even so they arrived late and had to join their craft by motor-boat. This hardly qualified as a resounding or a significant event, and if you stripped the personages of their celebrity – and the wheedling, forward sex appeal of Vivien Leigh in her Scarlett O'Hara persona – it would hardly be worth recounting at all. Yet it filled two pages, or roughly one per cent, of Guinness's autobiography. Even in this account Guinness was notably absent from the event, while Bull demonstrated a keener and fuller recall of the way Vivien behaved, and of the niceties of rank.

Guinness was keeping his distance. "I, Alec Guinness, do not matter," he was reiterating, "and I cannot possibly be of interest to anyone." Yet at the same time he was conspiring and colluding with the reader/spectator in being somewhere interested in Alec Guinness, as if he would like to report on himself without being seen as being there, as if he would somehow like the reader/spectator to be enthralled. After all no one would want to show himself as keeping a secret unless he wanted in the first place to attract the attention of the person from whom the secret was being withheld. This was an important part of attracting an audience. This form of secrecy was not a true desire for secrecy, for it would easily have been possible for Alec Guinness not to act, to become genuinely a nobody, had he really wished rather than had a *partial* wish for it which he was, instinctively, converting into a powerful professional ploy and, later, a major and genuine part of his attraction. The deliberate form of this secrecy, as created by Guinness, was really just as inordinate a demand for attention as the most aggressive or extrovert of showmen could have displayed. But it was reversed. In the kingdom of the blind the one-eyed man is king. In the hothouse of the theatrical world the elaborately modest and self-effacing star appeared, and indeed could be, infinitely more tantalising and virtuous a proposition than the self-puffed celebrity. But was it more than a subtle and sophisticated means of achieving fame?

In time Guinness's secrecy was to become highly aggressive, the flip side of an intense desire to show off, compounded of shame and guilt over that desire. As Ronald Harwood observed, "This trait may seem to some an affectation. To the outsider, it may be incomprehensible that anyone, especially an actor, so famous and acclaimed, should for a moment doubt his own importance or, professionally, so lack in confidence." Yet to the actor himself this diffidence was real. Here was the conundrum.

Guinness's account of his war service carried this eerie sense of absence to an extreme. While Peter Bull was at the centre of *To Sea in a Sieve*, Guinness, who would appear most willing to write about himself – he submitted accounts of his wartime experience to *Penguin New Writing* and offered a long description of grounding his craft on Sicily on 9 July 1943 to the *Daily Telegraph* – remained unsure of expressing himself directly. It was still primarily an exercise in angling and directing the spotlight away from the central figure in the narrative, while making the reader always aware he was present. He tantalised himself, but without becoming self-conscious about any trickery involved.

Some may see this as akin to the deep self-duplicity of the spy whose desire to remain hidden and clandestine in his activity really concealed a powerful and even vain wish to be more clever and more important, and ultimately more famous, than anyone else. But specifically and unselfconsciously – and probably unconsciously – Guinness had by now adopted this means of becoming a famous actor. That he then became remarkably in tune with and expressive of his own age – and in tune with the medium of film as opposed to stage acting – is in no way his fault but the reward of his own inner consistency.

The real Guinness of the letters to Sydney Cockerell wrote of his reading the lovely "filigree" work of Hooker's *Laws of Ecclesiastical Polity* (in ten volumes, a little unlikely), and the remarkable *The Screwtape Letters* of C.S. Lewis. As he sat curled up in front of an electric stove listening to a furious wind, he thought of John Gielgud whose performance as Macbeth in a mask-like make-up he had seen in January 1942:

I see the press has attacked Gielgud's Macbeth for lack of soldierly qualities – they've quoted "Bellona's bridegroom," etc. They seem to have some notion that fine fighting-men look like prize-fighters, and that Macbeth must above all suggest a great eater of beef. Actually Gielgud manages to suggest great physical activity and alertness. My limited observation of first-class soldiers and sailors makes me think they are more inclined to be like that than the heavy type.

Gielgud continued to be important to him. Guinness still recognized so much of Gielgud in himself and still had ambitions to play those great parts, such as Macbeth and, once again, Hamlet, in which English actors dreamt of making their names. Close to his heart was also a vague and grand literary ambition. He spent his spare time writing his novel. This gave way for a while to adapting Dostoievsky's *The Brothers Karamazov* for the stage. All this was part of his continuing search and need to find himself and to find God. Cockerell expressed the idea to him in terms comparable to those he used to Dame Laurentia McLachlan:

Tolstoy and Dostoievsky were both men seeking God and their novels are a record of their search. Dostoievsky went further and in *The Brothers Karamazov* he presents us with a world which has found its centre in Christ. Tolstoy never found peace and died in a last frantic effort to escape from a world in which he could no longer believe. But this makes the search for God all the more moving . . .

14

Knocked about and exposed
to every climate

At the Allied landings in Sicily on 9 July 1943 Guinness was ordered
to embark two hundred soldiers from a troopship on a very small
island west of a lighthouse on the south-eastern tip, and, in the
confusion and disorder of the wind and the high seas, failed to
receive a signal to delay his landing on the sea coast by one
hour.* Charging ahead, but still unaccountably accompanied by
other landing craft who presumably had also not been informed
of the change of plan, his craft ran ashore on a narrow sandy
beach from which his soldiers disembarked without opposition.
The whole non-event of this landing provided Guinness with perfect
material for an anti-heroic, little-man-caught-in-the-middle-of-big-
events-beyond-his-control, account, ideal for his form of deadpan,
throwaway humour. It was even capped by his turning the tables on
an angry Commander RN who asked him why he had arrived early
on the beachhead, whereupon Guinness reproved him in his best
West-End manner by pointing out that, when a curtain is advertised
to go up at 8pm, it goes up at eight and not an hour later. This
was indeed a fitting instance of how not only Guinness but also
Peter Bull, when delivering his engagingly humorous account of
these years, managed to reverse any kind of expectation or reality
that one or other of them was actually in command of one of His
Majesty's fighting ships. For such humour to work there had to
be an authority or higher command actually in command and

---

* He knew exactly where to go because he and Bull, some two or three weeks before
the invasion, saw on a slide at a top-secret tent briefing in North Africa a scratched
number indicating the height of the lighthouse near the invasion beam ("183 or
something") taken from submarines. Later, on board his own vessel, Bull worked
out from the *Mediterranean Pilot* the landing place as Cap Passero, Sicily. "A woeful
lack of security," Guinness called it. "It was a terrible burden to carry."

respected as such. The figure of authority who failed to command fear could no longer be a source of humour.

Yet there was another side to Guinness who, when writing up his landing, reflected, like Hamlet failing to be stirred by Fortinbras, on its dullness. "Many other ships," he remarked in an article in the *Daily Telegraph* in August 1943, "had as uneventful a time as I did, but there were yet others – and maybe they did not. But on the whole, it was as if the Italians wanted us to come, and only made a little resistance to avoid being clouted over the heads by their German brothers.

"How dull, how dull all this is. And yet, presumably, it's a good-sized page in the history books already."

But also like Candide Guinness "cultivated his garden". For the previous two years he had prided himself on his "floating library" of forty or fifty volumes, glowing against the pale grey paintwork of the bulkhead: "Shakespeare, Dostoievksy, Tolstoy, Jane Austen, Friedrich von Hügel [the Catholic theologian and philosopher], Eliot, Saki, Disraeli, Plato, Max Beerbohm, Graves and company, and even an unread paperback thriller . . . My little library used to cause joy to a few visitors, but more often pained or languid surprise. "Nothing sexy? Anything funny? Got a good 'tec'?" One day when his ship was confined to Naples harbour with a wire round the screw or a dirty filter, a friend lent him a copy of Joyce Cary's *The Horse's Mouth*.

"I accepted his gift with alacrity . . . I imagined to myself a few happy hours of relaxation while the crew welded, hammered, painted, scraped and generally clattered about the resounding iron decks of my forlorn L.C.I. (L)." But this was not to be. After a dozen or so pages he wearily snapped it shut.

> The flicks of colour that Cary jangled before my eye (a man is sick of colour after two years in the Mediterranean and longs for the glaucous line of Sussex Downs), together with the short, knotted sentences and the facetiousness, made me restless, if not downright ill-tempered.

But a few months after this Guinness experienced a deep shock which struck his being to its very centre: a violent Adriatic storm on the first day of 1944 brought him near to death and his vessel close to complete extinction. They were sailing in idyllic conditions to evacuate women and children under cover of darkness from an island off Yugoslavia when he fell asleep and awoke with the ominous sensation that some terrible end was about to overtake them. A hurricane from Egypt and Libya whipped the sea into an ungovernable fury and they were blown about all night and for most of the following morning almost completely out of control, expecting wreck at any moment.

For Guinness the scene was as vivid as the moment in *Hamlet* when the Ghost prompts Hamlet into calling up "angels and ministers of grace" to defend him. A particularly eerie visitation for Guinness was the visible emission of light flowing around the ship's rails and hawsers like a bluish brandy dance on a Christmas pudding, until the sight of the ship became dizzying. This was a phenomenon caused by the storm but a Glaswegian crew member was heard to bawl, "Is it spirits?"

Here, for Guinness, was the unreal, unearthly event, the moment of terror from which he genuinely did not know if he would emerge alive. He emphasised the passivity, as if he was still at heart that small boy being dangled over the banister by his stepfather, the "captain". For Bull a similar moment came in Valetta harbour when his ship was bombed and strafed by German aircraft. For actors of powerful imagination these were formative events which remained with them for ever. Bull wrote much later, "I have a habit of comforting myself on first nights by trying to think of appalling experiences during the war, when terror struck from all sides, but the windiness felt on the Italian beachheads and elsewhere was nothing to compare with one's panic on that evening of 3 August 1955" (he was referring to the first night of Samuel Beckett's *Waiting for Godot*).

The thoughts that exercised Guinness when faced with extinction were, first, what would become of his wife and son, and how would they survive? Second, how would Merula cope with the burden of caring for his mother? He answered to himself that she would not have sufficient funds to do so, for her pension as a naval widow would be small. Here, possibly, was some insight into what was still a deep preoccupation. The responsibility for his mother was here powerfully revealed, with all the shame and embarrassment it might and could cause.

It was further symptomatic of Guinness's desire that life should be unified and whole, that while most people would have dismissed the storm as an event of an imperfect, nay even randomly malignant natural event, Guinness should apply Hamlet's "There's providence in the fall of a sparrow" to this storm and feel quite relieved when there was no inquiry called into its cause or his own handling of his ship. The notion that he could not be blamed for his ship being written off subsequently – as it was when he managed in the end to limp into Temoli harbour on the eastern Italian coast – seemed hardly to have crossed his mind. The guilt and shame deeply residual in his being was ready to be triggered off on all occasions. As he asked himself, on the deck of the ship when the storm was at its height, "Why on earth was I wearing a collar and tie?"

The next six weeks or so were spent in a state of unpleasant recovery – two weeks' leave in Malta followed by an office job until a new command was found for him. The shock of the storm took time to wear off and he felt ill mentally rather than physically. He walked in the sun and wind as a tonic to recovery. His crew was dispersed, and so ended a pleasant association.

During 1944, in a new landing craft, Guinness was running supplies to the partisans in Yugoslavia. But the tension of war activity slackened and he seems to have had more spare time to work on his Dostoievsky adaptation, and also on his plans for the post-war period. In August 1944 he confided to Cockerell that he had received an invitation for after his demobilisation to play with the Old Vic Company at the New Theatre. Boredom, frustration, the dreariness of separation from those he liked now tormented him more and more. In the heat, all he and his new ship's crew could do was sit about in shorts and dark glasses and listen to the sea slipping by – while sipping iced water to pass the time.

In such conditions he finished his adaptation of *The Brothers Karamazov*:

> I say finished – that is, the play *exists* and *could* go into rehearsal tomorrow, but actually there is still quite a lot of work to be done on it. A playwright friend, Benn Levy, has pointed out weaknesses in the first act, and there is much polishing to be done. However, I'm disgustingly proud of myself for having completed the play – I so rarely finish what I start.

He and his fellow sailors were also busy making toys for Greek children at their ports of call on the way to Yugoslavia. As Cockerell wrote to *The Times*, copying directly from a letter Guinness wrote to him, the following were the words of a well-known actor in the RNVR "who has changed the part of Hamlet for that of the commander of an unnamed vessel, perhaps HMS *Pinafore*":

> I've even made a large woollen ball myself, which caused a

great deal of amusement among my more masculine friends. We happen to know a wretchedly poor Greek convent, where eighty small children, all orphans, are cared for. The very best that can be done for them is done, but it amounts to practically nothing – they are more than half-starved. Many of the babies are red-raw because they have to be washed in sea-water, fresh water being so precious that it can only be spared for drinking. None of them has ever known a sweet or seen any sort of toy. The proud possession of the children was a small ring of steel which could be rolled along the floor – not even a tin to beat with a stick, for every tin is required as a cooking utensil, and all sticks are fuel.

A naval officer I know happened to have a wooden yellow duck on wheels on board; it was an intended Christmas present for a niece in England. He presented it to the convent. It caused stupefaction! It was received with wide-eyed silence and gaping mouths – and then solemnly led by a daring four-year old out into the street. In absolute silence all the children followed it, and soon a regular procession was started, with old men and women, soldiers, priests, everyone, and they all followed the yellow duck through the main street of the town. Someone found a Union Jack and hoisted it on a pole. A tattered dirty drummer appeared from somewhere, and a fiddler with a squeaky fiddle. They played, almost unrecognizably, "God save the King". The yellow duck, a hideosity, was led like the Trojan horse back into the convent. And so we make toys for them now . . .

This letter was given a prominent position in *The Times*, yet it was also highly personal, which explains its charm and its power, for Guinness was clearly identifying with those Greek children, at the same time expressing a deprivation from his own child.

So the year of 1944 drew to an end. The Allies were well-established on the continent and in the rear of the forward thrusts the theatre companies began to assemble among the "*poys* and the luggage", as Shakespeare calls them in *Henry V*, the rearguard of the invading armies.

Guinness lingered on in his war, riding out the Mediterranean swells, sometimes with a five-days leave as escape. On one such he visited Rome, in which he paid homage to the spirit of Keats by a visit to his grave in the British Cemetery and found the terrible inscription on the tombstone emotionally shattering:

This Grave

contains all that was Mortal

of a

YOUNG ENGLISH POET

who,

on his Death Bed,

in the Bitterness of his Heart,

at the malicious Power of his Enemies

Desired

these Words to be engraved on his Tomb Stone

Here Lies One

Whose Name was Writ in Water

Feb 24th 1821

He also met Pope Pius XII, whom he found gentle and decisive and blessed by a ravishing smile. He spoke of God at the same time raising his eyes and arms, which made Guinness realise how simple and beautiful such a movement could be. For the first time in his life he believed that he had seen a saint. Yet he was not, or so he said at the time, especially taken with the Roman Catholic Church.

But Hamlet, too, continued in his thoughts, although, as he conveyed in a letter to Cockerell in February, he had sworn never to read anything about that enigmatic prince again. Freya Stark, the explorer to whom Cockerell became literary counsellor,* had written about Hamlet; what she had to say about John Dover Wilson's psychological theories about the prince intrigued Guinness although he felt Dover Wilson lacked being in theatrical touch with the play in the way that Granville-Baker was. He would, he said, if anyone gave him the chance to play Hamlet again, "avoid all scholars like the plague". In 1938, he felt, he had been very influenced by Dover Wilson and by Dr Ernest Jones,

---

* "Strip off the veneer of distinguished men and women from whose friendship or acquaintance I have gained an unfair lustre, and what remains?" he had written in 1930 to Viola Meynell. But the truth was that a great deal did remain.

the biographer of Freud who had expounded Freud's theory of the Oedipus Complex in relation to the play. But now, "my own desire is to be influenced by Shakespeare and what I have seen of life in the past six years. I am tentatively feeling after a theory that Hamlet's failure was due to a too abundant sense of humour."

Pictures of Guinness in uniform, later during the war, revealed a lean and even gaunt-faced Royal Navy Sub-Lieutenant with a toughened air. The Senior Service had been a wearing, weathering experience. The sea was no beautifier.

"You know," Guinness told John Mortimer, the playwright, "the most difficult part I ever had to play was to be an officer and a gentleman for three years in the Navy." The experience the Navy had given him was to make him real, namely to give him a direct formation in the qualities of heroism and resourcefulness on which he was able to draw continually for stage and film roles in later life. Faced with death, there were few disguises.

If Guinness's theatrical background in the 1930s now stood him in good stead so that he would always be able to play complex character parts brilliantly, both on stage and on screen, it was his serving years in the Navy which equipped him in a broader way to play world leaders and heroes such as Disraeli, The Cardinal, Colonel Nicholson, Lawrence of Arabia and even Freud and Hitler in such a way that they became real people. He had doubly guarded and developed his own sense of loneliness and destiny, and had experienced at first hand heroism and the need for resourcefulness.

Guinness's wartime years were very different from those of theatrical stars ten years older. Gielgud had spent the years feverishly and wholeheartedly working for ENSA under Basil Dean, acting in such plays as *Blithe Spirit* and *Hamlet* in order to keep up civilian and service morale; he continued to bathe in adulation; he accepted homage as his due.

Olivier and Richardson joined the RNVR and became seaplane fliers but both kept their star status and were frequently released to make films or for other appearances. Neither was allowed in the thick of danger or serious action, for their death or incapacity would have been considered a propaganda victory for the Germans. Both tried to do more than fly around the obsolescent navy planes entrusted to their shaky care, but their attempts to expose themselves to the full rigours of war were refused by a wise and, in a broad sense, patronising higher command. Olivier enjoyed the feeling of patriotism and service: "The best part I ever played", he said. But the pair remained first and foremost actors; and they were released early so that they could join the Old Vic Company at the New Theatre where the repertory opened in the autumn of 1944 and scored its first triumphs with *Richard III* and *Peer Gynt*, starring Olivier and Richardson respectively.

On 5 June 1945 Guinness was back in Southampton, waiting for his release from the Navy, and, having applied for four months' leave to play Bob Acres in *The Rivals* with Edith Evans, full of high expectation for the future. But he was loath to lose the comfort, the security and the command of being a naval officer to launch himself once again on the ontologically unstable life of acting. Actors are well known to take on the colouring of their surroundings. Some assume them in imagination and appearance, remaining themselves. Some absorb their environmental identity at a very deep level. By now, after long years of service, the role of naval officer and Alec Guinness were one and the same person.

One of the few photographs of himself that Guinness allowed to be printed in his autobiography showed him in uniform. He had been proud of being captain of a ship with a small group to command. When he arrived back in Liverpool, he met Judy and Tyrone Guthrie at the Adelphi Hotel. They, as his alter ego figures, castigated him for his grand and British manner, and ascribed it to his uniform. They didn't, he commented, realise he had grown up a little.

Shortly afterwards, a colleague recalled, Guinness arrived at the New Theatre to see Olivier. He was still in uniform. Not the well-worn uniform of a long-serving officer. He was immaculately turned out "like a tailor's dummy". He wore white gloves and he carried a cane, a black walking stick. "It all looked so new," the colleague commented, "as if he had dressed up to play a naval officer. Perhaps it went back to the time everyone was telling him, 'Don't be an actor, you have no appearance, nothing . . .'"

Playing the part of a naval officer had been a difficult, a very difficult assignment. As captain he had been almost always alone: but there was a close connection between the many violent transformations to which the sea was subject, and the individualism of the man who managed his ship. In such a very English role he had succeeded.

PART THREE

Mystery and Mischief

I have been surprised at the observations made by some of my characters. It seems as if an occult Power was moving the pen. The personage does or says something, and I ask, how the dickens did he come to think of that?

Thackeray

Essentially I'm a small part actor who's been lucky enough to play leading roles for most of his life.

Alec Guinness

15

Winter kept us warm

Although Guinness never went into it deeply, the war, one felt, had had on him a profound, disturbing and transforming effect, and it became for him the background of his conversion to Catholicism some ten years later. Over the next few years he was, however much he might behave to the contrary, making his peace with God over his past, over his difficult and contrary nature, and to some extent preparing to sacrifice his own will to what he considered the will of God.

Unlike most people at this time he was not seeking new relationships or sudden illuminating insights but looking for an integration, as well as a wholesomeness in himself which he now understood to come from change of inner attitude. Out of the evil of his early life, out of its torment, confusion and out of the dark contrary moods of his own nature, he sought to realise that sense of well-being and readiness to embrace all of life. He was still following Hamlet, but this was now a Hamlet who had left the cosy pre-war family atmosphere of the theatre and grown up, a Hamlet who could, as Roberto Rossellini did in his post-war films, especially in *Germania – Anno Zero*, draw a universal conclusion about the evil he had just experienced. Rossellini's epigraph for *Germany – Year Zero* summed it up:

> When an ideologue strays
> from the eternal laws of morality and of Christian charity
> which forms the basis of men's lives,
> it must end as a criminal madness.
> It contaminates even the natural prudence
> of a child, who is swept along from one
> horrendous crime to another, equally grave,
> in which, with the ingenuousness of innocence,
> he thinks to find release from guilt.

Guinness was never an ideologue. He sought unity of spirit, not self-gratification or fulfilment of some over-riding ambition. He grew in receptivity. He was as remote from the post-war ethos of "grab what you can" as it was possible to be. Yet, like Menenius in *Coriolanus*, his stance was patrician, aloof. With his first two post-war productions his self-expressive powers were still limited and confused, they limped behind his experience as a man, hardened though in some ways he had become.

For most people the immediate post-war period may have been a long celebration, but Guinness's way of marking the return to normality was to immerse himself in two of the darkest and most gloomy masterpieces of European literature. For these he teamed up with the twenty-year-old Peter Brook who had just left Magdalen College, Oxford. Brook had tried to enter the secret service in 1943 but the Medical Board would not grade him, so instead he had read languages and become president of the Oxford University Film Society for which he had directed a film of Laurence Sterne's *A Sentimental Journey*, an enterprise frowned on by the college authorities, and for which he was fined five pounds for neglecting his work and almost sent down.

But directing was his first and only love: "I want," he said at the time, "to be a vampire of the outside world and at intervals to give back the blood I have drawn out, in some creative form. I want to change and develop, and dread the thought of standing still." Even so young as he was his influence over others was powerful. To Kenneth Tynan, three years his junior – who had, unlike Brook, positively manufactured his low medical grading in order to escape conscription – Brook was a hero fit for the wildest fantasies of an aesthete: he looked edible, and Tynan had the notion that "if one bit into him he would taste like fondant cream or preserved ginger". Tynan felt he had never travelled anywhere on foot or on buses, but was "wrapped up in silk and carried".

Brook and Guinness were a severe contrast. Guinness was now a hardened and quite bald ex-naval-commander of thirty-two. The works they elected to do were Dostoievsky's *The Brothers Karamazov*, and, a month later, Jean-Paul Sartre's *Huis Clos*, his powerful study of the proposition that "Hell is other people". Imbued with the feelings of a Frenchman who has lived through the German occupation of France and maintained his spirit of liberty, it became a flag bearer for a new, popular philosophy of self-fulfilment, or selfishness, known as existentialism.

They rehearsed in May and June 1946. Brook was wasting little time after taking his finals in launching himself into a triumphant West End career. They used Guinness's own adaptation of *The Brothers Karamazov*, even though it was somewhat loose and unwieldy. Surprisingly Guinness elected to play Mitya, the parricide in whom the Karamazov family sensuality had become a devouring fever. It was hardly type-casting, but it seems that Guinness's interest in the work and his desire to play Mitya came from his preoccupation with his own illegitimacy. It could be seen as an exorcism of anyone's repressed feelings of anger or bewilderment over an unknown father, and, to a great extent the novel absolves Mitya, or at least finds in him redemptive or saving graces. It was this, especially, that attracted Guinness.

Mitya's defending counsel underlines how old Karamazov was a misfortune as a father which it was impossible for the impetuous Mitya to survive:

> He is wild and violent, and we are now trying him for that, but who is responsible for the circumstances of his life? Who is responsible for his having received such an absurd upbringing in spite of his excellent propensities and his grateful and sensitive heart? Did anyone teach him to be sensible? Did he get any proper education? Did anyone love him ever so little in his childhood? My client grew up by the grace of God, that is to say, like a wild animal. He may have been eager to seek his father after so long a separation. Remembering his childhood as though in a dream, a thousand times perhaps, he may have driven away the horrible phantoms that haunted his childhood dreams and longed with all his heart to justify and to embrace his father! And what happened? He was met by cynical sneers, suspiciousness and attempts to cheat him out of the money that he claimed belonged to him . . . at last [he] saw his father trying to entice away his mistress from him, his son, and with his own money . . .
>
> The love for a father who does not deserve such love is an absurdity, an impossibility. One cannot create love out of nothing, only God can create something out of nothing. "Fathers, provoke not your children to anger," the apostle writes from a heart burning with love.

Guinness must have felt very close to the feeling in these lines: his father had created shame in him. They had had no relationship:

he had felt himself rejected even as he needed to express that love which a son has for his father.

Mitya offered no relief or solution. The careful anecdotal way Guinness distanced himself when he wrote later of the production only reinforce our impression of this alienation from his feelings. He was striving outwardly for effect, and in spite of his adaptation being ferociously directed by Brook, he could not reveal anything deeply about the soul and character of Mitya. In fact he was still using his acting – still, for the present that is – as a form of self-defence and, although he would choose parts which touched upon his deeper preoccupations, he would embrace them intellectually rather than commit himself to them. Those who recall this production have expressed deep surprise that he ever came to play the part, yet found him excellent at times, although inconsistent. To one view he gave the impression that he was suffering from a prolonged attack of anxiety. Kenneth Tynan wrote to a girlfriend that he had seen "Peterkyn's" production of the "Bros Tara [sic]" in Hammersmith. It was visually brilliant, he said, with Valk [Frederick Valk played old Karamazov] "huge and hirsute, bellowing and pricking at folk with a big avalanche of beard and voice, swallowing up Mr Guinness' heady nail-biting at each bounding syllable". But Tynan found the tedium bottomless.

James Agate was respectful but lukewarm, deleting from his article the quip "Alec Guinness is good for you! . . ." He also deleted a reference to the effect that Ernest Milton's Father Zossima was twin brother to Hermione Gingold's King Lear. It was just as well he did for Guinness, who had persuaded Milton to play the part, was terrified that Milton would receive bad notices and actually commit suicide. He saw much of himself in Milton. What possibly endeared Milton to him was that the older actor's feelings were as confused as his own. Guinness would probably have been far better in *Karamazov* realising, in a complete way, the character of the Saintly Alyosha, yet it is a propensity of the incomplete personality that he or she invariably chooses to grow by attempting something he or she cannot achieve.

As Garcin in *Huis Clos (Vicious Circle)* Guinness, with a shaven head and playing opposite Beatrix Lehmann and Betty-Anne Davis, was superb, but because the portrayal of lesbianism meant that the play failed to pass the Lord Chamberlain's censorship, it could only be staged before a club membership.

Huis Clos is Sartre's best play, written before his plays became schemes to illustrate his ideas: as it had only three characters and one set, Sartre may be said to have innovated the small "chamber" play which quickly became a common phenomenon, for reasons of economy if nothing else. The geographical location impressed Guinness: it was set in "hell" and its three characters were condemned to live there for eternity. The statement "Hell is other people" ("L'enfer, c'est les autres") admirably summarises the atmosphere generated although it has been (or so Sartre claimed in a postscript) misunderstood (it is "other people that are important in ourselves and in our understanding of ourselves"). Garcin is a self-portrait of Sartre, a man alienated from others, a man who is a prisoner of himself rather than of others: Guinness was intellectually subtle enough to make the crucial distinction. The concentration of emotion in *Huis Clos* worked extremely well: it was Sartre's most actable play, and he wrote it, on his own admission, for three friends none of whom he wanted to feel had the biggest part; thus he deliberately constructed the piece so that no-one could leave the set. This was ideal for Guinness, for he did not have to suffer the burden of "carrying" the play on his own shoulders. Above all, it gave him the opportunity to play a character who was in essence like himself, someone who nursed a secret shame which distanced him from others.

Although the Sartre play ran only briefly the production and its performances received wide acclaim and provided Guinness in particular with many tempting offers to appear in films.

16

Intimate Aside

In 1946 the Redgraves, that is to say Michael Redgrave and Rachel Kempson, his actress wife, with their small children, Vanessa, Corin and Lynn moved to a fine house, No. 1, Chiswick Mall which they bought for £12,000. Guinness, Merula, and his son Matthew now lived around the corner at No. 7, St Peter's Square, a square of narrow tall houses built for the victorious generals of Wellington's army in the early nineteenth century. Corin and Matthew became close friends because, after a short attempt by both sets of parents to integrate them into the state system of schooling, they joined a small group that was privately taught, and then, with this group no longer functioning, they were tutored, just the two of them, by a Miss Holly at the top of the St Peter's Square house.

Matthew was slightly younger than Corin, who recalls the house being particularly suitable for the Guinness temperament. "He had a colossal dignity about him, quite awesome, he would sit in a high-backed leather chair and address you in this even-toned and measured voice."

Corin Redgrave never thought of Guinness as a deeply spiritual person, but uncommonly decent and kind. He genuinely showed his care, and, as his son's best friend, Corin remarked on how he went a long way to find out what you liked, or he would be there to meet you at the station from a train, all the while demonstrating an extraordinary courtesy. Matthew, for Corin Redgrave, was extraordinary too: innocent, of an open nature, he seemed like one side of the actor in essence. His father, Corin believed, may have been rather too much of a disciplinarian, and had too high an expectation of his only son, picking him up on small details in front of a friend, which used to make him feel slightly embarrassed.

Corin Redgrave remembered how his own father was fascinated by Guinness as an actor, as indeed he was himself; he heard stories about how his inventiveness on the set, for instance in *The Three Sisters* in which Michael Redgrave also appeared, used to land him in trouble. He sometimes had a certain difficulty in reconciling this fastidious father – who had always banked at Coutts before it became fashionable to have a merchant banker – with the shiny bald head, the moon-faced smile.

Corin Redgrave on the whole identified closely with Guinness and with his son, because his own father was deeply reclusive and shy, a remote figure; but Guinness was very different for he had "the qualities of a great mime, and his face could assume any shape". Later Corin Redgrave felt Guinness became much too associated with "quasi-spiritual" parts and never got properly used.

Matthew, after the conversion of his father to Catholicism, was sent off to Beaumont College, the Catholic boarding school, a move which Corin regretted because he lost touch with him. He had heard Guinness talk wisely and lovingly of Shakespeare, but he had never once talked about religion or spiritual matters, so the conversion came as a surprise. Most of all Guinness left on him an impression of almost incredible decency, as shown perfectly in the D'Ascoyne husband, in *Kind Hearts and Coronets*, the one who is so kind, so nice, and so deeply in love with his wife – and who gets blown up in the woodshed.

In the early 1980s Corin Redgrave, a committed Trotskyist, wrote to Guinness and asked him to open a training shop in Brighton for unemployed youngsters, and Guinness agreed. "Well, I'm not political," Guinness had said. "One assumes he is a conservative," said Corin. Then the press, hearing of this, got on to Guinness with a vengeance – the great actor-knight mixing with Trotskyists – and Guinness spent all day reeling with shock. But, having given his word, Guinness did not withdraw and he opened the shop. "He was absolutely admirable," said Corin, "and he gave the training shop quite a large sum in cash."

17

Not likely to promote himself

The main reason why Guinness did not launch straight into films in this post-war period is that he had been selected by the powers-that-be, namely the Old Vic board, for future leadership of the English theatre. Although still on the board Tyrone Guthrie was no longer directing the Old Vic. His successors, Laurence Olivier and Ralph Richardson, were leading the newly constituted Old Vic company playing at the New Theatre in St Martin's Lane. Their first two seasons, with a main course of Shakespeare (*Richard III* and *Henry IV, Parts 1 and 2*), and with *Peer Gynt* and *Uncle Vanya*, had gone down superbly well. By the end of 1945–46 season Olivier and Richardson had become such magnetic figures that, on their last night, St Martin's Lane was blocked by 2500 fans shouting for their heroes. They now left for a New York tour. But Richardson, who with his Falstaff was at the peak of his career, and Olivier, who wanted – a want never to be fully satisfied – more time with Vivien Leigh, needed to find suitable and powerful leading actors to follow in their footsteps.

Guinness was chosen. Guthrie was an ardent supporter of Guinness, his idea of the ordinary, down-to-earth, non-actorish leading player. Society stood on the threshold of the era of the common man. Guinness, ten years junior to Olivier and Richardson, was to be groomed, ultimately, to take their place. The Old Vic management was convinced that, ultimately, it would lose Richardson and Olivier to Hollywood.

Guthrie had fallen out with Olivier, who had chosen to play Mr Puff in *The Critic* and Oedipus both on the same night, as a double-bill. Guthrie considered this a gross piece of self-aggrandisement. George Jean Nathan, the outstanding American critic of his generation, supported his view that the Old Vic Company was built mainly around a star actor and that actor is Olivier. In the five plays it has shown, Olivier has been the star, in the Broadway sense, in all but one. Though Richardson is the star in that one, the second part of *Henry IV*, he plays second fiddle to Hotspur in the first part, second fiddle to Astrov in *Uncle Vanya*, since the doctor's role is theatrically much showier than the name part, third fiddle as Tiresias in *Oedipus* to Oedipus, and tenth fiddle as Lord Burleigh in *The Critic* to Mr Puff.

Guthrie began actively plotting to have Olivier and Richardson removed from the directorship of the Old Vic in 1947-48. Richardson was at any rate booked to do a film in Hollywood, while Olivier had tentatively agreed to lead an Old Vic Company to tour Australia and New Zealand. Guthrie proposed to John Burrell, who was co-director with Olivier and Richardson, that they should form a second company for 1947-8 with Alec Guinness at its head.

In the meantime Guthrie was to direct Richardson as Cyrano de Bergerac in Rostand's romantic masterpiece, Burrell to direct Olivier as Lear, and – a most eccentric decision – Ralph Richardson to direct Guinness as Richard II. As Guinness himself understood it, he was "to be given a total variety of parts for these two seasons, because I have no idea where my talent lies, or if it exists any more." And, of course, they had little idea of his exaggerated humility.

Olivier's Lear was by all accounts poor: Sybil Thorndike even, his most ardent admirer, said he lacked the stature. He never attempted to play the part again on stage for it demanded of him an understanding and a spiritual self-awareness that he did not have (he played it later in life on the television, portraying well the pathos of the old man cracking up, but little more). Guinness played the Fool, which many critics considered the best they had ever seen. He acted it with a clown's white face and wistful eyes. He would show a baleful dejection anticipating the tiredness of his witty thrusts. Philip Hope-Wallace, the *Manchester Guardian* critic, remarked upon his "sad, bilious loyalty". Guinness restored the Fool, wrote J.C. Trewin, to his proper place, "wry, quiet, true, with a dog's devotion; when at last he slipped from the play we felt for a moment that the candle was out". The actor Harcourt Williams wrote in his Old Vic memoir, "It was an epitome of all the wisdom in the world falling in stray shreds from a clown's chalked face. It had the beady eyes, the questioning eyebrows, the comedy and pathetic inability to cope with life that was once Grock's. It had that strangeness too, which, Bacon tells us, is to be found in all excellent beauty."

"I made a critical success, I believe," Guinness later told Alan Strachan. "That's because, I believe, the Fool in *Lear* has sixty lines and Larry Olivier wisely cut them down to thirty, so that you couldn't get bored with the doggerel that goes on, and also I was always in his light wherever he went on stage." In sum he stole the show from Olivier – and Olivier never forgave him for it.

Guinness told the present writer he had difficulty in finding the right image for the Fool: "One has to be careful of one's own psyche with certain elements in Shakespeare." He then described how one night he had a visit from the Fool. It was shortly after he was demobbed. He went to a party, then came home. He fell asleep but woke up in the middle of the night. He had a waking dream. "The fool was sitting at the end of my bed. He had a dead white face and he spoke in a certain voice." He could tell the others at rehearsal that he had seen him. Perhaps because of this visitation Guinness's Fool lived longer in the memory than Olivier's Lear.

But it was a miniaturist's part: so what should this Nicholas Hilliard among players attempt next but the foolish young Bisley, a nondescript role in Priestley's *An Inspector Calls*? The author himself marvelled at it: "He had only to walk upstage, his back to us, to give us a further display of the character of this thoughtless youth." Guinness would have been ideal casting for the role of the Inspector, but Richardson, also perfect as a ghostly caller, was there first to play the enigmatic policeman. One evening Richardson commented that Guinness's patent leather shoes squeaked horribly: "Try water." Guinness did nothing but next performance when he rushed in to change into these shoes he found them in a bucket of water where Richardson had stood them. "I squelched noisily through the last act and then missed two performances through near pneumonia." "Oh, have you been off, I didn't notice," said Richardson later, never alluding to the shoes. A familiar Guinness story.

Guinness next played De Guiche in Guthrie's production of *Cyrano de Bergerac*, during the rehearsals of which confrontation between Guthrie and Richardson was continually expected but never quite happened. Once Richardson – who was forever harassed by Guthrie, "For God's sake, Ralph, play the scene! Play the play!" – stopped the rehearsal and came to the downstage edge of the stage, "peering gimlet-eyed from both sides of the great Bergerac nose up to where Guthrie stood". "I was brought up to find my lights," he said, "And I'm finding them and for the first time in your production. So . . . don't call me a bloody fool, old cock . . ."

Guinness's own performance was a remarkable small study of a bitter and self-regretful aristocrat: he looked like a portrait by Van Dyck, but once again he emphasized the icy interior of a man displeased with himself.

He acted next what he has often described as his favourite role – he repeated this somewhat odd assertion as late as 1992. This was the part of Abel Drugger in Burrell's acclaimed production of *The Alchemist* which opened just before the beginning of the big freeze-up on 19 January 1947. Not only were there big cuts in the fuel-ration – electricity was cut off for five hours a day – but coal and wood supplies were scarce.

Surprisingly Ben Jonson's comedy was a hit, with George Relph's Alchemist perfectly matched by Richardson's Face (the well-known photograph of Richardson bears astonishing similarities to Guinness, as if Richardson stole something of Guinness for his make-up). Although the company was shaky on its words just before it opened, there was no doubt that *The Alchemist* showed it at its peak.

In contrast to his Fool in *Lear* Guinness wore little make-up as Drugger, the innocent gull of a tobacconist who is unenviably deceived by Face. The essence of a comic victim, Drugger has few lines but they give the actor an opportunity to create on stage a whole being. Here once again was a chance for Guinness to show perfection, but on a small scale. Guinness felt that this was the one time in his life when he was putting himself in danger by acting: "He's such an extraordinarily innocent character. I felt as though I could go on acting him all my life and never escape from him." Possibly he was again scaling himself down to the size in which as a child, neglected by his father, he felt himself comfortable and secure.

Kenneth Tynan, who was now beginning to review plays informally in letters to his friends, quickly grasped the essential quality of Guinness who was far from playing Drugger as David Garrick had, by inflating the role into much more than Jonson intended.

Guinness made the most of the limited opportunities available, and expanded them from within:

> Mr Guinness manages to get to the heart of all good, hopeful young men who can enjoy without envy the company of wits . . . His face creases ruddily into modest delight, and he stamps his thin feet in glee. In a later scene, he demonstrates a very rare gift, that of suggesting the change that comes over a man when he is alone. Drugger is commissioned by Face to bring him a Spanish costume as disguise. He trots away and returns, shyly clad in its showy cloak and hat. Waiting for Face to answer the door, he begins to execute timid dance-steps under the porch. He treads a rapt, self-absorbed measure with himself, consumed with joy. Then Face appears: the pretence is over, he recognises his intellectual master, and, not regretfully or pathetically, but smartly and prosaically, he sheds his costume and hands it over.

Was this the secret of Guinness's magnetism, as Tynan claimed? "He can seem unobserved; he can make every member of the audience an eavesdropper on a private ceremony. His art is the art of public solitude." Tynan eloquently and instinctively understood the suspiciousness of the lonely illegitimate child who wanted to be observed and loved in his privacy – and therefore no longer alone – because he, too, was illegitimate. This brilliant empathy was entirely unconscious. Neither man knew of the bond of illegitimacy they had in common.

Guinness in time came to show the much stronger integrity: he trusted the hierarchical "family of actors" world; he distrusted the celebrity world which Tynan embraced as a substitute mother and father love. He sought something more deep and more lasting. The unresolved question remained; would he, as Tynan believed all men and women could, find salvation through art and fame, or would it be something else?

The hard weather continued without a thaw almost until April 1947. Conditions backstage at the New Theatre grew appalling. Guinness had to make up wearing his overcoat. The washbasins were frozen. And the rehearsals for *Richard II* had to be scrapped. Guinness recalled that he was bidden to meet Clement Attlee, the Prime Minister, at a bun-fight at 10 Downing Street which was otherwise attended by sixty elderly ladies in velours hats and coupon clothing. Balancing a tea cup and saucer in his hand he leaned against an open door which felt as if there was someone crunched up behind it. He eased the door a bit and a rather squashed Prime Minister emerged from behind it. Guinness thought he must be hiding from the "more serious ladies who had calculating eyes on him". He mumbled an apology and fled.

Perhaps the postponement was fated. Richardson and Guinness had similarities of background but these served to set them apart rather than to bring them together. The closeness of background appeared in numerous ways. Each had been abandoned or neglected by his father and suffered a strained or constrained upbringing and a single child relationship with his mother. Both had money and privilege somewhere in their backgrounds: neither had any serious professional training. Neither had a degree or higher qualification. Both had to start earning their living at a very early age. Each possibly saw mirrored in the other elements of insecurity and fear in himself which neither wished or wanted to confront. Both were fiercely anti-psychological.

Both, above all, were imaginative actors, who brought the vulnerability and pain of their upbringing to bear in their work. Richardson had primarily a poetic quality, Guinness almost the opposite, a kind of quintessential nakedness of thought, but both in their best work drew on the marrow of themselves. Both were reticent yet not modest, egotistical yet sure that they were not in the showy, first division of actors (which for them only meant being in the same class as Olivier and Gielgud). Both were, in one sense, the more exciting actors: they were guardians of the secrecy of life. They believed that, as a quality, mystery was far above explicitness, suggestion far above displaying everything.

But in *Richard II* Richardson was in charge. He was enjoying everything, at the peak of his fame. During the run of *Cyrano* he had been knighted, even before Olivier, that is, who flew into a rage of jealous pique, saying, "I should have been the fucking knight." Backstage they would now call Ralph "Sir-rano".

So, one feels, he never quite became engaged in the anti-heroic aspirations of his junior. When Guinness asked his director what kind of a Richard he had in mind he got the answer, "I'll tell you, old fellow," and snatching a beautiful Venus pencil from the table Richardson waved it in front of Guinness's face: "Like that. Sharp and slim, that's what we want." "I don't know how to play a Venus pencil," Guinness remarked later. "I've been asked to play Piccadilly Circus by Michel Saint-Denis and that was easier."

As reported by Michael Warre, the actor and designer, Richardson's ideas about the setting were just as vague: "I have a strong feeling that the set should all be wood . . . You should be able to go in and out of it."

"Permanent?" inquired Warre.

"Perhaps we could change it from time to time . . ."

"We must have an upstairs for Flint Castle and probably for the lists too . . . this is leading us towards a formal structure . . . which is Elizabethan," pointed out Warre.

"Why not?" said Richardson.

"Costumes?"

"Why not Elizabethan structure . . .?"

"With fourteenth-century costumes?"

The most important thing for Richardson was that it should be made of beautiful wood and the actors should handle it lovingly. Through this set Guinness had to track the insecure ego of his protagonist:

> Thus play I in one person many people,
> And none contented.

It was as much part of Guinness's identity crisis as it was King Richard's, but Guinness probably did not see it like that at the time. Instinctively, though, Guinness understood how Shakespeare was dramatising his own self-consciousness, a necessary stage in his evolution towards the writing of *Hamlet*. He had shadowed forth Richard, his Player King, who was bewildered and lacked understanding of himself. The tragedy of Richard was not quite a tragedy because the King enjoyed, with aesthetic pride, his own decline. Likewise Shakespeare was always watching himself and taking note. Guinness explored this whole perception of Richard with considerable skill and intelligence.

But Guinness was still too much under the influence of Gielgud when he rehearsed with Richardson. Later he called his performance a "partly plagiarised, third-rate imitation". In fact many people at the time thought it bad because he played it against himself, wanting to play it like Gielgud. But he was growing aware of the problem of his identity as an actor (very bound up as it was with that of the person).

A subtle actor, Richardson the director was none the less fairly untouched by all this subtlety. The production secretary who was taking notes from Richardson found that he kept on saying unrepeatable, dreadful things for her to write down — using the grand, formal method of dictation. These consisted mostly of blistering comments like "bloody awful" or "ghastly", which she had to repeat to Richardson when he asked airily, "What did I say about Alec?", all impression of the performance having vanished entirely from his mind. A photograph of the newly knighted Sir Ralph, in double-breasted suit and holding a hat, staring madly in the opposite direction from a timid, be-costumed Guinness and Renee Asherson as the Queen, summed up perfectly the style of his direction.

The critics failed to grasp what Guinness was trying to do with his Richard. Some said he had no voice, others that he had no tragic emotion, or instability of mood, that he projected surface melancholy rather than the flame and agony of tragedy. Yet it was hard, others noticed, to dismiss it as a failure. The intelligence behind was unmistakable.

For Guinness *had* captured the quickness of brain, the need for secrecy, all those inner qualities of genius that he himself refused to believe he possessed in common with Shakespeare (and Shakespeare possessed in common with Richard II and Hamlet). As Lionel Birch wrote in *Picture Post*:

> Guinness's conception of Richard of Bordeaux was of a man always capable of standing . . . a little apart from himself and looking at himself. The man outside observing the man within — but both men resident in different worlds. Private worlds indicated by private jokes which started at the corners of Guinness's mouth . . . some people might find this interpretation too cynical and insufficiently "poetical" for their pre-conceptions. To me it seemed the true apocalyptic link between this cat-and-mouse king's tweaks of sadism at the beginning of the play and his twists of masochism at the end of it.

Birch might have been writing years later of Guinness as George Smiley.

Harcourt Williams noted Guinness's rare facility for altering the quality of his appearance without the aid of make-up. This he attributed to the muscles in his face: "One dreads to take one's eyes off him even when he is not speaking for fear of missing some flitting shade of thought". But this was not a big stage, histrionic quality, but the attribute of a film actor.

Kenneth Tynan pointed to the set imperfections: "Possibly the most impractical that man ever devised. One cannot but stare when Northumberland, swarming with difficulty through a maze of pillars and posts, complains of these wild hills and rough uneven ways: and it is even odder when Bolingbroke . . . refers to the set as the grassy carpet on this plain. It was about as carpet-like as a porcupine."

As for the director, he stole the show. Richardson's collarless costume as John of Gaunt made him appear to Guinness like a large, bearded Peter Pan; Guinness was fiercely instructed, "Never come within six feet of me on stage, old cock," with the result that he would huddle up with Bushy, Bagot and Green. Richard's failure to blaze meant, one critic said, "The other characters seemed to take on a corresponding importance, and a beautiful study of the dying John of Gaunt proved the dramatic highlight for the connoisseur of acting." Richardson was wicked.

After this production was over they would meet again socially, but they never again acted together on the stage and were hardly involved together even in the same film. Richardson also never acted on a stage together with Olivier after these New Theatre seasons, but he did act again with Gielgud. Olivier never acted with Gielgud although Gielgud did lead a company at the National Theatre when Olivier was in charge. Guinness simply never acted again with any of these three great actors with whom he had begun his career.

Guinness next played in the John Burrell productions of Shaw's *Saint Joan* and Gogol's *The Government Inspector*. In the first he was the Dauphin, a nobody whom he played with hands hanging in a slightly abnormal position and a lack-lustre eye reflecting a numbed mind; in the second, he was Hlestakov, the Inspector, a nobody mistaken for a somebody, who then tries to live up to it. At least he was moving on from the Olivier–Richardson season which had become a "hot-bed of false noses". He ended this round of Old Vic involvement with Menenius Agrippa in *Coriolanus*, in which John Clements played the title role. Here, as the veteran peacemaker, Guinness transformed himself into a stately old man to capture the best notices, but he failed to satisfy the Old Vic's *éminence grise*, Harcourt Williams, who commented that Guinness deservedly won rich praise, but that he wondered if he was not carrying an intellectual approach to his work further than was wise. In reaction, said Williams, "from over-emphasis and false sentiment he exhibits a cold reserve which seems to prevent a scene from catching fire".

Guinness finished playing at the Old Vic in May 1948, by which time he was already filming with David Lean in *Oliver Twist*.

18

The beginning of Lean times

Guinness had been much involved with Dickens and *Great Expectations* just after the war began. He left the Navy with an adaptation of *The Brothers Karamazov* in his pocket, and with a greater love of Dickens from his reading. Like a delayed gift, one could say a resurrection, from those two experiences, there had come along in 1946 the film of *Great Expectations* to launch him into his film career.

In reinvoking the horrors of his own early life, the deprivation of taxing manual work, the constrictive atmosphere of small rooms, the taunting claustrophobia of being dubbed "common", Dickens had dared to express some of the grotesqueries the past had caused in his imagination. The novel of *Great Expectations* is dense with ghosts, with secrecy, with darkness, yet it is that very weight which gives it its quality of exhilaration and comedy. Guinness's revenge on his own past – or if not revenge, purging – was to be more subtle, sophisticated, more gradual and perhaps in the end more complete. So he did not play Pip, but John Mills did: as at the Rudolf Steiner Hall he played Herbert Pocket. It was characteristic that he should be closely related to *Great Expectations* as adaptor, and even more closely related in human terms to what the work embodied, yet *not* play Pip, the main character who, like himself, was a self-made "gentleman" and whose values were formed in the darkness of his early life.

David Lean, the director of *Great Expectations*, had not been strongly drawn to Dickens, knowing only *A Christmas Carol* before being taken by Kay Walsh, his actress wife, to see the Guinness adaptation at the Rudolf Steiner Hall in 1940. During the war Lean had directed Noël Coward in *In Which We Serve*, the moving propaganda story of a ship at sea; its tense, epigrammatic style made it seem like the epitome of all war films, and it caught perfectly the conflict between personal feelings and a sense of duty to one's country. After the war Ronald Neame, who had also seen the pre-war *Great Expectations*, wrote the script of it for Lean to film. Lean became friendly with Guinness and this friendship blossomed in an exchange of vivid and courteous letters between the pair. Yet at no time did he show himself to be carried away by the thought of Alec Guinness in his film. At the time he was making *Great Expectations* his great craze was for Ralph Richardson, whom he was to direct later in *The Sound Barrier*.

Lean and Dickens were well-matched. Lean found himself responding to the extravagance of imagination and he fell in love with the subject, as he had to do in order to make a good film. But he was a difficult man; brought up a Quaker he was unlikely, temperamentally, to see eye to eye with Guinness in the long run, although there was no clash between them during *Great Expectations*. Guinness's Herbert Pocket was, as it should be, entirely charming, completely credible. As the pale young gentleman, his ears were pointed, his eyes shone with eagerness, his mouth curled up at the corners. Exhilaration was the keynote of this performance.

But he was frightened at first of overacting in his first film role, although he knew he was terribly lucky to be doing something he had first done in the theatre. "I was very nervous and self-conscious," he later remarked. "I hated my wig. I didn't want to say it wasn't as good as the wig I had in the theatre as it hadn't got the sharpness to it . . . and it was all a bit softened." At one point when he had to laugh uproariously he felt he was in extreme danger of becoming exaggerated. Lean took a break in the film, led Guinness aside and said to him, "Let's rehearse without the cameras rolling." He then told him some stories and Guinness started laughing. But Lean cheated and the cameras had been filming all along.

Guinness would in time develop a unique way of measuring a performance during the making of a film: his stand-in would come over to him after he had rehearsed a scene and say, "I loved the way you did that, Alec." What a sweet and generous sentiment, Guinness would respond. But then some instinct would tell him, "Oh, no, that was noticed, it must come out." He would come to rely a great deal on the stand-in for praising something which he knew must be stripped away immediately.

Ronald Neame, the scriptwriter of *Great Expectations*, was a big fair man with a boyish character who was originally a cameraman. His compact, judicious script and Lean's natural sympathy for Dickens's instinctive montage made the film extremely successful in somewhat the same way as *Les Enfants du Paradis* became popular in post-war France. Both films expressed a return to traditional national values, especially those of humour. Both films expressed joy in dark times.

Lean next made *Oliver Twist*. Guinness wanted so much to play in more Dickens that he asked Lean out to dinner to try to convince him that he should act Fagin. It was the only time in his life, he said later, that he "wined and dined" a director with a specific part in view. But Guinness's memory was slightly faulty: it was only lunch – at the Savoy. "You think in terms of types," Guinness told Lean. "You won't find what is inside other people." Lean, unconvinced, ("He's going to be covered in crêpe hair and it'll look awful"), made him audition and do a screen test. In fact Guinness demanded the test, which was described as only "quite good" by one party – or did Lean fall about with enthusiasm? – while Robert Donat who tested for the role of Bill Sikes was "terrible". "I got mine by the skin of my teeth and Robert didn't," said Guinness. "Of course I was bowled over by it and Alec got the part without another word," said Lean. Not much diversity of opinion here!

During the shooting Guinness would arrive at 5 a.m. or 5.30 a.m. to be made up as Fagin. The evolution of that make-up, based on George Cruikshank's drawings of the old Jew, was itself remarkable for Stuart Freeborn, the make-up artist, had experimented with new plastics, enlisting the help of ICI to achieve flesh-like materials which were not only supple but semi-transparent, so that you could see the blood vessels. So passionate was Lean in achieving the right appearance for Fagin that he had Freeborn try out numerous variations on Guinness: at one time, said Freeborn, "he looked just like Jesus Christ". Lean sent the filmed tests off to the States for approval. It was only because Freeborn could manage to make the PVC (Polyvinyl Chloride) into a very soft, foam-like exterior that he finally achieved the right effect with the nose. But America said "no" to the nose. "To hell with them," Lean responded.

Even though Freeborn made a wax mould of the nose he modelled for Fagin, and then made a cast – and then evolved a technique for enabling the melted plastic to dry at different densities – it still took three and a half hours each morning at

Pinewood to make up Guinness. Fifty-two multiplied by three and a half hours is a lot of time to spend sitting still: "I won't speak; I shall be very quiet; you need all your concentration", Guinness told Freeborn, who pushed tiny rolls of cotton wool into the nose to absorb the perspiration. So well did the crews and set-up come to know the Fagin face that one day, when Guinness was not required for filming and he wandered on to the set as himself, he was somewhat perturbed to find no-one recognised him and said "good morning".

As he became more famous this kind of story multiplied. The best example was that of Guinness and Gielgud lunching together one day in York. A waitress asked them to sign the table cloth. "I'm sure she doesn't know me from Adam," said Guinness. "She'll be very disappointed if I sign my own name. I shall sign Jack Buchanan." He did and the waitress was thrilled.

The impersonation which finally emerged in *Oliver Twist* was masterly. Guinness brought to Fagin's harsh, rasping utterances a pantomime gentleness of movement, while the apocalyptic mood of Lean's direction was powerfully underlined by the music of Arnold Bax. But the exaggerated traits of character were still enough to provoke accusations that his portrayal was anti-Semitic. "That was, I believe," said Guinness later, "about the only time since the war when the Russians and Americans united in protest.* They all walked out, I'm told, when the film was first shown in Vienna. It was *so* ridiculous, because we fell over backwards to ensure even that the word 'Jew' shouldn't be mentioned. I really don't think the film did any harm. I must say that after it came out here, Jewish taxi-drivers used to greet me *most* affectionately and refuse to let me pay my fares." But in New York, where soon after the film was shown he was playing in *The Cocktail Party*, a hostess at a party said to him, "I wonder you dare to come. I'd rather give my children prussic acid than let them see your picture."

Then, as much later, Guinness never minded thoroughly evil people, whom he found more interesting to act than good ones. But they had to be evil, not weak. "I don't like playing weak characters because I suppose I'm frightened of my own weaknesses."

---

* In March 1950 *Oliver Twist* was banned by the American Film Industry's Production Code; seven minutes — consisting almost wholly of close-ups of Fagin — were cut before it was allowed to be shown in the US.

Lean taught him to perform the same action identically from take to take. Being neat and liking precision he found that Lean reinforced his taste for understatement and simplicity. Lean steered him through the new world of the cinema and turned him from grimacing his way through a role to relying on thinking.*

* This is what he told Richard Findlater (*Observer*, 9 December 1984).

19

I have that within which passes show

At the New Theatre Alec Guinness received much appreciation for his direction of *Twelfth Night* in 1948, but the Old Vic was now in crisis. Olivier and Richardson had just been sacked as directors, while John Burrell, their co-director, had fallen ill. Guinness, having been coached to supplant them, had, as an actor, proved to have neither the power nor the stature. To fill the gap in policy and continuity, he was now given a popular comedy to direct.

Unfortunately the production was not wholly under his control. He had taken it over because John Burrell was absent and it was Burrell's cast as well as the sets that Burrell had approved which he had to work with, neither of which he wholly liked, nor would have chosen himself. He put his stamp on it, however, by subtly grafting on to Robert Eddison, who played Feste, much of his own vision of the melancholy fool. He saw Feste as the centre of the play and in love with Viola, as someone commented, "like a consumptive prince in exile". Cedric Hardwicke, whom Richardson had dispatched from Hollywood as his replacement while he made the film of *The Heiress*, played the most gentlemanly of Belches – a "whisky-and-soda man". According to Donald Sinden, who was cast as Sebastian to play the twin to a Viola whom he closely resembled physically – only to find her pull out and be replaced by Jane Baxter who was four inches shorter and not even remotely similar – Guinness's production was "very distinguished and saved the Old Vic's reputation".

Popular and commercially successful though it proved, it did little to help Guinness's disenchantment with himself in the role of classic stage actor belonging to one of the great English theatre companies. He had asked the Old Vic for four varied and contrasting parts to show in what direction his talent lay, but the strong answer had come back: in four different directions. Or, perhaps, in any direction he was given or chose to take. He would never act again in a permanent or semi-permanent company which performed a classical repertoire. With *Twelfth Night* he parted for good from the acting peers of his generation. This was nearly his twentieth encounter with the plays of Shakespeare, whose spirit at so many points resembled and touched upon his own, yet none of these had resulted in much more than a costly expense of spirit.

But now, after the production of T.S. Eliot's *The Cocktail Party* at the first Edinburgh Festival in August 1949, he was something of a celebrity.* As he was about to depart to New York to open the Eliot at the Henry Miller Theater he could afford to unbutton himself just a little, as he did in a talk given in Oxford to the Dramatic Society. The report in *Isis* on 20 October 1949 remarked that off-stage Guinness was most unlike an actor:

> . . . almost shy in his self-effacement, and one could well believe that he was so upset when bullied once by Mr Gielgud that he lost his voice. To recover it he visited an elocution specialist, an old lady, who we feel must have looked like Margaret Rutherford in a character part. Muttering about doggie-woggies, she hurriedly pushed young Guinness on to his knees and made him scramble about on the floor barking "Bow wow". The treatment was unsuccessful. Next he saw an actress, who seized hold of his upper lip and said in a toneless South Kensington voice, "My dear, it's quite flat – no good to you at all. You might as well get rid of it." Mr Guinness still has the lip, and seems to find it useful.

Guinness went on to talk about acting, again striking out in a direction very different from that of Olivier, Gielgud and Richardson. "An actor needs a slightly mystical approach to the stage, for after all you can't force a character on yourself; you must absorb it into every pore."

He next told his student audience that actors were born and could never be made, and that four months was long enough to be in "Rep" for "inevitably this week's character study suffers from that of next week's". But, he added, twenty years' experience was necessary before one became an actor. The *Isis* reporter added – tartly or tactfully one is not quite sure which – "The exception

---

* Earlier in 1949 he appeared as Dr James Simpson, the pioneer of chloroform, in *The Human Touch* at the Savoy, described in the *Telegraph* as "an exhibition of shadow boxing".

proves the rule, for Mr Guinness himself has been acting for fifteen years."

Guinness had first read T.S. Eliot's early poems when he was seventeen. He became an instant admirer and subsequently bought each new work as it appeared: "Sweeney Among the Nightingales" from the 1920 *Poems*, with its obliquely exotic South American background (Geddes was always said to have been a South American banker), was his favourite. Sweeney himself was the "coarse average man", while the poem's ending, Guinness believed, had some of the best lines in the whole of our literature:

> And let their liquid siftings fall
> To stain the stiff dishonoured shroud.

As he pointed out, "liquid siftings" meant bird droppings.

In early 1939, when he arrived back in London after the Old Vic tour of the continent, Guinness heard that *The Family Reunion* had been published that very day. He managed by the afternoon to buy it: "All I can say is that I sat up that entire night reading it twice through with intense excitement."

His first personal contact with Eliot came when, as an ordinary seaman in naval barracks, he heard him talk on the radio. Eliot mentioned a book but Guinness failed to catch the title. Riveted by what Eliot had been saying, he subsequently wrote to him at Faber and Faber, and received a reply in which Eliot recalled seeing Guinness play Hamlet before the war. Again Guinness was showing this ambitious trait of seeking contact with his heroes to confirm and develop some aspiration in himself, a trait Tynan also possessed, although in the latter's case with exaggerated effrontery. Guinness later perceptively pointed out how that talk of Eliot's contained "words and phrases which cropped up in *Little Gidding*, which he hadn't at that time written".

When, in the spring of 1949, Henry Sherek, who had been spreading the word among his friends that Guinness was "the best actor in the world", asked him to appear in *The Cocktail Party* at the first Edinburgh Festival, Guinness waited anxiously for the half-dozen or so sheets of the text to appear, "hot from T.S. Eliot's typewriter", sent round daily from Sherek's office. He was thrilled to be one of the first half-dozen people to read a new work by Eliot, and he "used to have the pages spread out on the floor at home anxiously and [was] cliff-hanging for the next batch to come the next day. Oh I loved, loved it as a play!"

During rehearsals his admiration for the poet, his senior by twenty-six years, deepened further, while later he accidentally found himself in Eliot's company on one of the liner Queens crossing the Atlantic:

> I found him a man of immense good humour with a richly warm laugh and he loved his dry martini and had no, not a shred of arrogance.

As an example of this Guinness cited his behaviour at rehearsal one day when Guinness, in the course of delivering his lines, suddenly said to him, "Oh Mr Eliot, haven't I said this speech before, rather?"

> Eliot looked at the script and said, "Oh yes, you're quite right", and he put a pencil through sixteen lines without a qualm and a little later in the day I said I cannot get from here to there across the stage . . . and there'd have to be a pause. And he again took the script and wrote four superb lines, they just flowed from him which enabled me to do the thing I wanted to do . . . The only other person I've come across who can do that is Graham Greene who again has the same masterful hand at seeing his own possible mistake and helping the poor wretched actor.

The Cocktail Party expressed something of Eliot's fear, which he shared with Shakespeare and in particular with Hamlet, that to enjoy love was to destroy it. Guinness was often playing against the bent of his genius: like him, but as a dramatist, T.S. Eliot was not an explicit artist, rather one who modelled much of his dramatic craftsmanship on the indirect, thwarted action of *Hamlet*, the supreme play of inner life. It was therefore perhaps to be foreseen that Guinness would triumph as Harcourt-Reilly, the Harley Street psychiatrist who becomes Eliot's arbitrator of love and wrecked marriage, and the authoritative voice in *The Cocktail Party*. The temperature of the piece never soars very high, but in this production, there was a powerful current of feeling beneath the surface, similar to Hamlet's "I have that within which passes show".

Coincidentally, Celia Coplestone's missionary zeal was based on the life of the religious visionary, Charles de Foucauld, who had fired Guinness's enthusiasm some years before while he was serving at sea, by his mysterious power of holiness. Born to wealth and social position, Foucauld practised as a priest in the Sahara, living in a stone hermitage and giving medical aid to tribesmen, until he was suddenly killed, in 1919, by marauding Arabs. While *The Cocktail Party* was somewhat rigged with rather forced and theoretical ideas about the love of God versus the love of man, Irene Worth as Celia brought an inner sensuality to help clothe Eliot's words in flesh, while Guinness himself tapped the hidden depth of feeling with a kind of sinister potency. Irene Worth described the impact Guinness had on the play and on her own performance:

> When I, as Celia, had the good fortune to play the "break-up of the affair" scene with Robert Flemyng . . . Robert's performance had been so profound that he had prepared the ground for the great "consulting room scene" to follow. Alec Guinness then said "Yes", and brought the house down . . . When the couple left, Alec lay down on his own consulting room couch and put a handkerchief over his face. The telephone rang, he answered it and said, "yes". I don't know what alchemy he used. I often watched him from the wings before my entrance. There was nothing to see – only Alec at the telephone and the audience laughing with delight. His brilliance defies explanation.
>
> After the laughter, Alec prepared a stillness for my entrance which made it possible for us to play the ensuing scene sitting, without a move, until it ended perhaps twenty-five minutes later. His stillness allowed Celia to pour out her heart. His stillness was like the stabiliser of a great ship. Alec's love and knowledge of the sea are not wasted. His stillness was like the sea.

Later Guinness did not speak highly of this production or of the one he did at Chichester in 1968, which transferred to London. E. Martin Browne, the director on the first occasion, was very much on Eliot's wavelength but he had no great theatrical sense. He directed it, so Guinness said, as a smart drawing-room comedy of the 1930s although Guinness was probably "more Sinister Street than Harley Street", as someone at the time teased. It probably did more than justice to the play: it became the touchstone for the short post-war revival of poetic drama. It also had a powerful influence on Guinness's subsequent conversion to Catholicism. Guinness's performance had fascinated Harold Hobson, who, on the death of James Agate, had become the critic of *The Sunday Times*:

> On the surface Guinness was light-hearted and playful, but fundamentally he was immensely serious in his treatment of the psychological problems presented to him by the Chamberlaynes'

guests, and by the Chamberlaynes themselves. It is to one of these guests, Celia Coplestone, that Harcourt-Reilly, like Hamlet showing his mother the two pictures of his father and his uncle, compares the life of domestic utility with that of dedication. On the one hand:

> If that is what you wish,
> I can reconcile you to the human condition,
> The condition to which some who have gone as far as you
> Have succeeded in returning. They may remember
> The vision they have had, but they cease to regret it,
> Maintain themselves by the common routine,
> Learn to avoid excessive expectation,
> Become tolerant of themselves and others,
> Giving and taking, in the usual actions . . .

which is to be compared with the life of sanctity and martyrdom:

> There *is* another way, if you have the courage . . .
> The second is unknown, and so requires faith.
> The kind of faith that issues from despair.
> The destination cannot be described;
> You will know very little until you get there;
> You will journey blind. But the way leads towards
>   possession
> Of what you have sought for in the wrong place.

Hobson described how all this was beautifully spoken by Guinness. Of course it was not the ordinary humdrum domesticity that attracts Celia but the way of martyrdom (bizarrely devoured by ants in some savage country, which was an idea Eliot copied from Michael Innes's *Appleby on Ararat*). However it did not, "for all the beguiling fascination of Guinness's voice . . . for a moment make me believe that Eliot believed in the glory of martyrdom". Hobson admired, but did not feel himself conquered.

But Guinness, by virtue of his next choice of role, Hamlet, may have been on his way to becoming the martyr himself. That he was aware, perhaps only at an unconscious level, of the importance of this choice, was registered in him by his purchase, with his first week's salary, of the gold vest-pocket watch which he had once imagined he might inherit from his father. This signified at last he had earned some money that counted. He carried the watch during all the performances of *The Cocktail Party*. And what did he have engraved, on the inside – and not on the back, so it would be essentially a private gesture to himself – but Hamlet's "The readiness is all".

This was in recognition by him, and to himself, that he had arrived.

Guinness won great critical acclaim as Harcourt-Reilly both at the Edinburgh Festival (Lyceum Theatre)* and on Broadway, which established Guinness's reputation in America although he played only half of the play's 49 performances,† leaving to make *The Mudlark* and *Last Holiday*, his next two films.

When I met Guinness in 1989 he told me that he had nothing "imaginative or even sensible to say about Shakespeare," and that he could not possibly be described as a Shakespearean actor, having appeared in only "three" of his plays over the previous thirty-seven years (this takes one back to 1942). In fact Guinness appeared in six Shakespeare plays after the end of the Second World War. The most disastrous of these was his second attempt to play Hamlet, which opened in May 1951 at the New Theatre. The failure of this production was critical to all that subsequently happened to him and seminal to all he did. The modern version he played with Guthrie in 1938 when aged twenty-four had in his view been ridiculous, "water off a duck's back". This time he was thirty-seven.

He was now to show great self-confidence, backed by Henry Sherek, in masterminding a new production of that play which was as large and mysterious and elusive as himself; which he cast himself; and in which he was to dare to play the title role.

In the *Spectator* of 6 July 1951 Guinness wrote that he had seen nine previous Hamlets, crediting that of Ernest Milton as the greatest: "When I came to play Hamlet for the first time, in 1938, in Guthrie's modern-dress production at the Old Vic, I was merely a pale shadow of Gielgud with some fustian Freudian trimmings, encouraged – he will forgive me, I know – by Guthrie. I list these things, as I believe they are important in the way of tradition and as showing how an actor

---

* The success of *The Cocktail Party* took everyone by surprise and there was no London Theatre available for it, although it played at the Theatre Royal, Brighton. It did not open in London until May 1950, where it ran for 350 performances.
† It was a sell-out: Brooks Atkinson in the *New York Times* called the play "verbose and elusive drama that has to be respected"; another critic said American playwrights should go home and break up their typewriters.

can react against the traditional and yet be steeped in it and love it."

Guinness had recently read the essay *On Hamlet* (1948) by Salvador de Madariaga, which convinced him of the necessity of having a Spanish designer to show him how much Elizabethan England was influenced by Spain. He engaged Mariano Andreu. Clearly when it came to the set design he still had the nightmare Richardson production of *Richard II* on his mind. It was partly the result of reaction against permanent, semi-permanent and realist sets in Shakespeare, and above all, of a stubborn dislike of raised acting areas:

> Rostrums, apart from cluttering the stage, tend to produce a one-foot-up, one-foot-down sort of acting which I find peculiarly dispiriting. I have very few conversations on the stairs in my own house, and see no good reason for making God's gift to an actor – a flat square stage – into something like the entrance to the Athenaeum.

The casting of *Hamlet* indicated perhaps that it was just as well that Guinness had had no hand in casting *Twelfth Night*: his perception of the ability of others to deliver finished performances was naïve, for he gave the heavy roles mostly to actors who had little experience in Shakespeare (e.g. Walter Fitzgerald as Claudius; Robert Urquhart as Horatio; Ingrid Burke as Ophelia; Lydia Sherwood as Gertrude). This last was perhaps the oddest casting of all because she was thin and nervous, not at all voluptuous, sexy or motherly. Yet he clearly had intuitions about the casting on which he relied, probably based on whether he felt those he chose could become real in the parts, while he did not do badly in picking Alan Webb for Polonius.

For Rosencrantz Guinness selected a twenty-three-year-old newcomer, Robert Shaw, who was playing a page in *Much Ado About Nothing* at Stratford-upon-Avon. He went round to his dressing-room after one performance, humbly introducing himself "I'm Alec Guinness" to the unknown actor who never removed his feet from the dressing-room table or stopped provocatively rocking back and forth in his chair. Shaw agreed to play the part for £20 a week, an almost unheard-of sum then for such a small role. His Rosencrantz had a sinister appearance with a black patch over one eye. He and Guinness became friends and Guinness invited him several times back to his house, and later helped him to a small part in *The Lavender Hill Mob.*

Perhaps the most eccentric piece of casting of all – almost as if Guinness was willing self-destruction – was that of Kenneth Tynan as the Player King. He had seen, in January 1949 at the Rudolf Steiner Theatre, Tynan's notorious Oxford production of *Hamlet* (in which Tynan had acted the Third Player Queen). John Schlesinger and Robert Hardy had also been in this production. In what seems like a fit of wildly extravagant behaviour, Guinness wooed the young critic to appear for the first time on the professional stage.

Yet was it so extravagant? Perhaps the two men were drawn to one another because of the – as yet undeclared – secret each sensed in the other. Both were illegitimate. Both shared a preoccupation with the play *Hamlet*, at whose centre was a hidden impostume or boil. Tynan, besotted with theatrical illusion of all kinds, was obsessed with the play and its leading role, which he had acted at his Birmingham grammar school. Both, by an even odder coincidence, had the same birthday, 2 April, although Guinness was the senior by thirteen years.

The two men met in the White Tower, Guinness's favourite restaurant. Invited there by Guinness, Tynan wore, as Guinness said, "bright green from top to toe". Guinness found him very amusing, slightly "startling" was the word he used. Something about Tynan may have struck Guinness to make him so especially attractive: something, perhaps, of himself. Guinness noticed that, when animated, Tynan did not seem to stammer, so he was not much bothered by this. He was used, anyway, to stammerers, for he said, at Ealing Studios, "pretty well everyone stammered. I think there was a great fashion at that time – it was considered rather elegant."

Guinness wanted Tynan as the Player King to be rich and ornate: as Tynan said later, "I, an attenuated twenty-four-year-old, was alarmed at the prospect of playing a robust and bearded tragedian."

But, alarmed as he was, he leapt at what he thought was the offer Guinness made him at lunch, so that on 15 December 1950 Guinness wrote in reply to him saying he had not made him an offer but had only asked him if he would be interested in playing the part. Guinness said firmly that he was not in a position to offer parts as he was not the management, though he sincerely hoped

Tynan would play the part. He suggested Tynan badger Sherek for further information.

Guinness also engaged Frank Hauser, a young BBC producer with whom he had recorded Jean Anouilh's *Antigone* for the radio, in which Guinness acted the Chorus, Peter Ustinov Creon, Denholm Elliott Hymen, and Mary Morris Antigone. Hauser had written and asked Guinness if he wanted an assistant. Guinness said yes. Later they lunched at the Caprice where Guinness told Hauser that, "You may want to resign when I tell you that I have cast Kenneth Tynan as the Player King." In fact Hauser, who had been at Oxford with Tynan, knew his acting and had high respect for his ability to play old men – Tynan had played the Old Judge in *Winterset* and Holofernes in *Love's Labour's Lost*. Anyway Hauser himself had never directed a stage play before, so he probably felt in good company.

The idea was that Guinness should "block" the play and then hand over to Hauser. But, did not Guinness believe, in accordance with the ideas of Guthrie, that actors should not write down pre-determined moves, as Gielgud would have wanted him to do? Guinness also arranged for a great plastic ear to be made for the Player King to be poisoned through, to be worn over Tynan's own ear. So rehearsals began for the opening at the New Theatre (in fact it opened six months after Guinness lunched with Tynan, so time for preparation was never a problem).

At the first few rehearsals Guinness propounded some wonderful ideas. For instance, as he later wrote himself, "I followed Granville-Barker's advice and did not drop the curtain, as is usual, at the end of the 'Rogue and peasant slave' soliloquy. Now this seems to me to be the only daring, original and exciting thing we did in the whole production, and it escaped the critics' notice." In place of the customary thudding curtain, he pointed out, the audience got: "'To be or not to be' within a minute and a half, followed by the 'nunnery' scene, followed by the social ease of 'Speak the speech' – in fact, they get the greater part of Hamlet's character stripped bare before them . . . And all in the space of about fifteen minutes." After this he took a back seat and invention seemed to wane. Gradually the inability of Guinness to commit himself to sole direction began to work not only the downfall of the production, but of Guinness's own performance. There was criticism that Andreu, who lived in Biarritz, had little time to adapt his gouache designs to the needs of the actors.

In the last week of rehearsal everyone in the cast became extremely insecure. Tynan was a demoralising factor. Every morning he would arrive at rehearsals dead tired: he would try to get into psychiatric analysis of the characters. Guinness was worried about him: he was a bit light, "a bit bored", he commented politely. One night Guinness blew his top at one of the others in the cast and they had a screaming row: "I remember Ken was very near me. Suddenly he was nodding vigorously. I felt he would have much preferred the whole thing to be played in high emotion."

Tynan kept silent. Guinness had his way. It was his production and his Hamlet, and carried in every way the stamp of his own emotions and preoccupations of the moment. It restrained and repressed feelings. Towards the first night it tapered away and diminished.

After their first run-through, when Hauser gave the cast their notes, Guinness said to him, "You said nothing to me". "I thought you understood," replied Hauser, "you were magnificent." "He thinks I am so bad I am being left out," said Guinness as if to someone else. Hauser then realised that, in the theatre, silence invariably conveyed disapproval.

Tynan was later told by Guinness about the events leading up to the moment the curtain rose:

> He [Guinness] arrived at the New Theatre far too early, and killed time by strolling round the corner to the Garrick Club. After glancing at the newspapers, he was about to leave when his eye fell on the new bust of Forbes-Robertson, standing on its pedestal in the entrance hall. Ever a hostage to superstition, he looked about him and, seeing no one, reached up on tip-toe and touched Sir Johnston for luck. Duly consoled, he made for the door; and then noticed the bust of Irving. Warily, compulsively, he touched that too. These things going in threes, he thought he had better do the same for Shakespeare. The pedestal proved too high for him. Undeterred, he dragged up a heavy club chair, climbed on to the seat, and, wobbling, achieved his object. Having appeased the fates, he sauntered back to the theatre, where the fates quickly showed him what faithless harpies they are.

The first night was something of a fiasco. As many have observed, on first nights Guinness's confidence was at its lowest ebb; he was never the kind of actor who rose to the chemistry of first-night hysteria and glamour. Normally he developed a crippling pain in his knees and back. But this Hamlet far exceeded in torture everything he usually suffered. The new electronic or computerised lighting board in the New Theatre went mad, and the lighting for the Elsinore battlements became that of the Court scene, and vice versa. *The Times* kindly said in its review that the lighting had first night nerves; someone remarked backstage that Guinness was calm, but the reply was, "It's the calmness of despair". There were boos after the curtain came down. "It was my fault. Don't blame yourselves," Guinness told everyone after the final curtain. "I gave up in the first act."

Guinness did not receive many good reviews for his performance and was deeply hurt and shaken by the whole experience. Tynan later wrote that it became "Hamlet with the pilot dropped," and was a self-inflicted wound.

"I made a balls-up of Hamlet," Guinness told me. "I did it out of revenge . . . (This was for Rex Harrison playing *The Cocktail Party* in London, which had been promised to Guinness). "I was sick every night. I retched every night. I was overcome with nausea."

Tynan benefited most from the bad reviews; Beverly Baxter wrote, under the banner "Worst Hamlet I have ever seen" that Tynan "would not get a chance in a village hall unless he were related to the vicar. His performance was quite dreadful." But Tynan *was*, in an obscure and mysterious way, "related to the vicar". Tynan was much criticised for making so much critical capital out of the fiasco, for shortly afterwards he joined the *Standard* and a year later ousted Baxter from his post: he also wrote anonymously a damning review of *Hamlet* in *Harper's Bazaar*, described by Hauser as a "virtuoso piece of treachery". Even Guinness complained in a gentlemanly way when Tynan wrote a "hysterically frank letter . . . I felt he should have come to the management". This was presumably Tynan's reply to Baxter's review in the *Evening Standard* when Tynan said, "I am quite a good enough critic to know my performance in *Hamlet* is not 'quite dreadful'; it is, in fact, only slightly less than mediocre. I do not actually exit through the scenery or wave at friends in the audience."

To this day Hauser has admired much of Guinness's performance: it was, he said, "very very exposed, very brave. He played the closet and nunnery scenes ruthlessly, savagely." Hauser deplored the fact that, owing to the mockery of the critics, Guinness shaved off the beard he had grown. He thought the whole performance had been extremely well thought out: it was a "remarkable, magnificent performance which never got properly credited but needed a John Dexter to come along and take the whole thing in hand".

Tynan's picaresque Player King ear provided undoubtedly the mesmerising last image of this great theatrical disaster:

> phosphorescent paint had been applied to the crown, the vial of poison and a great plastic left ear which I wore over my own: these glowed in the darkness, and the tableau as the poison was poured took on the aspect of an advertisement for a proprietary brand of rum . . . I remember handing the ear over to the stage manager and feeling, for a moment, remarkably like Van Gogh.

Harold Hobson wrote in *The Sunday Times* that Guinness apart, you would never hear of the actors again: the arrogance of this so enraged Guinness that it was the only time he felt like taking revenge against a critic. Except, he said, for the Ophelia ("Who did go mad"), and several of the others, "every single member of that cast became a star of some sort. No one could afford it now." The cast included not only Alan Webb and Robert Shaw, but also Stanley Holloway and Peter Wyngarde.

Guinness could have added that, while he might not have been able to pick the right actor for the right role, he knew how to select other geniuses. "We knew he was a magnificent actor," wrote J.C. Trewin, "but it was not his night." The *Daily Express* was more blunt in its headline: "Guinness's Hamlet booed". Matthew told Guinness he got chivvied at Beaumont College because of this poor notice, and this upset Guinness: "You begin to think, 'Hey, hey, hey?'" The production closed on 31 July 1951 and lost between £12,000 and £15,000.

One night during the run, Guinness recalled twenty-five years later, he had slapped Robert Shaw's face when he put a Rosencrantz line too rudely to him, a "quick temper" reaction on his part:

> It had an impolite edge and Shakespeare hasn't written the comeuppance line and there was nothing to do but crack him across the jaw . . . I was very distressed, I'm not given to that sort of thing.

There was perhaps more to it than that. On 9 August, Robert Shaw's twenty-fourth birthday, Guinness threw a large party for him at the White Tower restaurant, inviting Shaw's friends such as

Barbara Jefford and Robert Hardy, as well as former student companions. Speculation for the reason behind such lavish generosity to the young Shaw was rife, reported John French in his life of Robert Shaw published in 1993: "Didn't you know?" one friend volunteered, "Alec's fallen in love with him." Also after *Hamlet* had closed Guinness asked Shaw and Russell Enoch, another actor in the company, to stay the weekend in Brighton with him. Shaw himself recalled, French wrote, that there was a frisson in the Old Ship Hotel when Guinness touched his hand for a second or two, "but the 'love' remained only a friendship".

His second Hamlet marked a turning point in Guinness's life, finally causing him to abandon the specifically English challenge of becoming a great stage actor in Shakespeare. The tantalising or binding power of the event over our imagination comes from the likelihood that Guinness, had he known how to marshal and integrate both his force and his intelligence, would have been one of the great Hamlets of all time. And he should ultimately have played the role on film. But it was a film that was never made.

It is the comic spirit that tends towards the enjoyment of disintegration and chaos, and even recently, when Guinness has talked of Hamlet, it was the comic discontinuity of the role he saw, pointing out how Hamlet displayed a "different personality" in each act. The many-sidedness of Hamlet possibly dismayed him because he had to confront in it his own unresolved many-sidedness which perhaps spilled over into real-life relationships. In real life he was much too like Hamlet to be able to act Hamlet well: he related to him more as a literary man might, a Coleridge or a Goethe, than as a jobbing actor.

As an actor he was still intellect-bound, as the critics rightly observed. He refused to "let go", blaze or show himself. He could only satisfy himself by the somewhat academic criterion of "small is beautiful", hence his emotional security in making small roles perfect. He would have to find a way to grow which would not be so much the clichéd, late twentieth-century way of opening up, confronting himself and losing all inhibitions – baring his soul or his body – but still keeping life and acting separate, a true way of growth in accordance with the laws and individuality of his own being.

Lady luminaries: Guinness with Edith Evans in *Cousin Muriel*; with Margaret Leighton in *An Inspector Calls*; with Beatrix Lehmann and Betty Ann Davies in *Vicious Circle*.

His favourite dupe: a study of Abel Drugger in Ben Jonson's *The Alchemist* by John Vickers.

The Fool directing the storm with Olivier's prostrate Lear, and Nicholas Hannen as Mad Tom; as Celia Johnson's Dauphin in *Saint Joan*; Guinness as De Guiche, Richardson with the great Cyrano de Bergerac nose; "in one person many people" – Richard II with Bolingbroke (Harry Andrews).

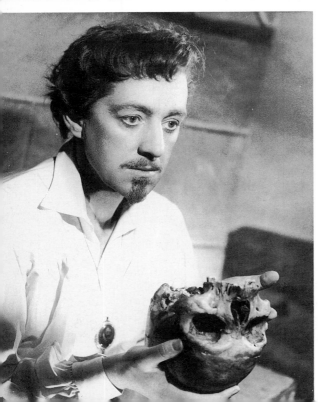

The house that Alec built;
bearded Hamlet with
father's picture and
memorabilia.

20

The dark side of the moon

How do we connect the shame of illegitimacy with the terror of exposure on the stage? To some extent Guinness must have assumed the paternal, authoritative role of the father he never had, just as faithfulness and loyalty to his wife and family were articles of faith, for they were something he had not directly experienced from his own mother and father. Yet at the same time he had to deal with the opposite sides of all these qualities – in his case a sometimes uncontainable feminine side crucial to his acting – while these antithetical statements and feelings were also part of his nature.

There were the occasions – such as the one reported by John French in his life of Robert Shaw, or others attested by colleagues who considered that in any account of him these should be acknowledged as important to the understanding of him as an actor – when the attraction of someone of the same sex, an image of himself perhaps, might lead him into behaviour outside the norm. Yet it is remarkable to find that, with all the insecurity in his background, he never thought of himself as a condemned man, shrinking from the responsibility of permanent relationships. He repudiated the romantic, Tennessee Williams approach which later became so fashionable, as summed up by "We're all of us sentenced to solitary confinement inside our own skins." Aspiring continually to do better, and again like Hamlet the character, he was to come to terms with himself in a distinctive and original way. It is perhaps not too extreme a claim to view his modesty as an act of defiance in the face of a self-gratifying society, while this modesty remained always based on a sense of his own faults and shortcomings.

The defiance of Guinness, if such it was, remained always vulnerable. He was at heart and always remained, in the way that it is something you never get over, an unwanted child. As someone who suffered the stigma of illegitimacy herself, Guinness's friend Angela Fox – the wife of Robin Fox, the theatrical agent, and the mother of the actors Edward and James and the impresario Robert – knew only too well that sense of not belonging anywhere. She was herself the illegitimate daughter of Frederick Lonsdale, the playwright, who had also another, legitimate, family on the go. She also came to terms with this deprivation in a courageous way. "You think they had you by mistake," she said. "You feel rejection, by life, by people, and by God. My mother never looked at me as if I was an ordinary child. You were a problem. And don't forget they tried so hard to get rid of us." Desperate feelings sought desperate remedies. "You do something stupid for relief or get blind, bloody drunk," said Angela Fox.

But desperation could also be the explanation for Guinness's comic gift too, a desperation shared with many excellent comedians: Tony Hancock, for instance, who, unhappy for reasons other than illegitimacy, ultimately committed suicide; or Peter Sellers, an anxious and desperate man without any sense of his own identity, who died prematurely from a heart attack; a sense of annihilation, too, which Guinness had not managed to express fully through Hamlet. "The mother," said Angela Fox, "loathes the illegitimate child for he or she makes *her* feel a mess." Guinness knew his own mother was selfish: once, before the war, as he was beginning to make a reputation for himself, she had raided his bed-sitting room and carted off any realisable assets such as spare cash or pawn tickets. It sounds as if she was sometimes trying to get her own back on him.

But, for Angela Fox, Guinness paradoxically and in spite of his mother's treatment of him, loved women in a very special way: few men had such a wide range of liking women, especially older, eccentric or great women, as Guinness showed. He never saw women primarily as sexual objects and therefore never rejected the majority who were no such thing. In fact, if there is one proof of the universality of the genius of Guinness, it was this ability to perceive and celebrate women of all kinds. He deeply appreciated Sybil Thorndike, surely the best, the most saintly woman he ever met,*

---

* Guinness once summed her up to Herbert Wilcox: "If everyone loved someone as much as Sybil loves everyone – what a wonderful world it would be."

as well as Mrs Thatcher, who was briefly his hostess at Downing Street

> I had never seen her in the flesh before and I was astonished, indeed captivated by her splendid appearance ... Mrs T was most elegantly dressed from top to toe in some glittering, form-friendly gown which appeared to be made of minute metallic tiles: black, dark, green and midnight-night blue. Perhaps it was bullet-proof. But it is the eyes that have it; they are amazing and totally mesmeric. I couldn't help feeling that she might single me out and whisper, "There is a tree in the midst of the garden of No 10, with a magnificent apple on it. Come with me and you shall have a bite."

There is little evidence that Guinness was a good mixer. His intimates were of the kind of Peter Glenville, the director (who was the handsome son of the Irish comedian Shaun Glenville, and who had been educated at a Jesuit school), or the breed of essential chaste men as represented by Catholic priest or monks. And, much later, Alan Bennett. He was a loner. He tended to withhold himself from aggressive men, especially if they worked for the media, so that they viewed him as a friend, yes, but not as a close one. Yet even friends of a lifetime found him "very difficult to get to know," as Margaret Harris said. He remained continually guarded, as why should he not be, for he had had no relationship with a father which built in him any trust towards members of the same sex, especially in the responsible use of his capacity for fatherhood. Who knows how many legitimate half-brothers, or sisters, his own father might have fathered, or if indeed he did not have a whole family tucked away somewhere, all of them in excess of thirty years senior to him. Someone might at any moment emerge from the shadows. But what was true was that Guinness did always have an extraordinary gift of friendship with women, with whom he became involved in a completely non-sexual way. And he knew the force of Dr Johnson's dictum: "Sir! A man should keep his friendships in constant repair."

"Is not this, perhaps," wrote C. Kerenyl, "the secret of every true and great mystery, that it is *simple*? Does it not love secrecy for that very reason. Proclaimed, it were but a word; kept silent, it is being." Above all Guinness knew the essence of mystery; to be silent about the feminine side of his being, or about wife and son or other personal matters, was not, in his case, a concealing weakness. It became the essence of his being, it acquired a truth in the way that frankness and openness never could. The mystery was acknowledged and not repressed. He made continually the point that it was there. And it was, of course, in *being* that the power and quality of Guinness as an actor lay. In *being* rather than doing. If not in doing nothing, then in trying to do less and less to establish the life of a character, and giving the appearance of life.

As an illustration of that high-spirited sense of fun, that lightness of being, that Kierkegaard once showed could only come from a corresponding dynamic darkness or depth which lifted it like a lever, Angela Fox recalled going backstage one night in 1967 with her husband Robin, after a performance of Simon Gray's dark comedy *Wise Child*. In this Guinness played in drag as the outrageous Mrs Artminster. In his dressing-room they found him just emerged stark naked from the shower, and Angela Fox described with glee this strange, pale, forked creature joking and clowning without inhibition. Then the stage-door keeper knocked on his door and announced the name of a theatrical agent who insisted on calling: "Vere Barker" – "Oh no, I've seen enough of agents: on no account let him come round," commanded Guinness. "But, but we're too late," expostulated the stage-doorman. Guinness seized a towel with which to cover himself and in walked an extremely "gorgeous" black gentleman who was the Kabaka of Buganda.

Guinness was also extraordinarily generous in an unassuming, secretive way. A well-known acting couple who were suffering severe financial hardship were discussing their debts one evening with Angela and Robin Fox. Guinness was also there. "Let's write down all you owe," Robin Fox suggested. They did so and it came to £500. Guinness yawned, said he was feeling tired, and that he must go home. He disappeared. An hour or so later the couple were still discussing with Angela and Robin what they should do about their plight when they all heard a plop on the door mat. A large fat envelope had arrived. And there inside, with no message, was £500 in cash.

Although some of the time disappointed and bitter, and often under deep strain, Guinness was always what Angela Fox called "a huge personality . . . Alec was as near to complete understanding and as near to God as anyone could be".

21

Steep

Guinness had always been a south-coast man; as a child he had attended schools exclusively in seaside resorts, as if his mother insisted on his inalienable right to be surrounded with the wholesome air that had attended her brief encounter with his father in the summer of 1913.

> Seaside breezes
> Lift up the chemises
> Oh Jeses, oh Jeses.

Later he married the daughter of a Surrey squire, immersed himself in the world of village greens and picturesque brick and tile-hung houses. In the war he joined the Navy, so therefore yet again home was identified as a south-coast haven. It came as little surprise, then, that he and Merula should buy, in 1951, a fourteen-acre field near Petersfield, on the Hampshire side of the border with Sussex, and build for themselves an £11,000 house on it, first as a week-end retreat, later to become their permanent home.

The landscape around Steep Marsh, a hamlet on the edge of Steep, itself a quite small village close to Petersfield, was very gentle. Petersfield, with its fine equestrian statue of William III, had become important as a watering place on the London–Portsmouth Road, well inland of course, notable from the twelfth century onwards for its wool market. A mile or so to the north-east rose the ground that contained the Parish of Steep, still, at the time they bought the meadow, quite remote with no regular village centre, a strung-out affair of scattered large and small dwellings along the roads or tucked down bridle paths, dells, or in hidden-away copses. There was something about its inaccessible winding ways and yet its general mildness which appealed strongly to Guinness. The beechwoods that clothed the slopes that surrounded the meadow where he built his house; the slopes themselves, Butser Hill, Harting Down, and the Hangers – the names might well have been part titles for the *Four Quartets*. East Coker (near Yeovil and more deeply in Hardy's Wessex than Steep) was perhaps its twin, with its enfolding landscape of deep lanes shuttered with branches, dark in the sultry afternoon light of summer hazes, and, above all, its houses rising and falling. Home is where one starts from. Here he could find stillness and quiet: at the still point of the turning world.

But, apart from spiritual satisfactions – "listening to the precious silence, broken only by an intermittent sleepy bird" – Kettlebrook Meadows answered a more basic need. Guinness was a very English type: like Wemmick's in *Great Expectations*, his home became his suburban castle with the drawbridge up. Guinness sometimes felt ashamed not to be living "out of a clothes basket, with no home", but the truth was that "not having a home as a child I spent a great deal of time wanting it . . . I *need* my house – the thing itself with its walls and foundations . . . I love the sense that my possessions have been there for years, and that what has been planted has come up in *my* soil."

Bedales, the co-educational school, was just down the road; Edward Gibbon once had his family home in a nearby village; Trollope had lived several years in another; the cottage of Edward Thomas, the poet who died in 1917, was not far away either: what could have been more safe, secure, and a better place to hide away from the glare of the spotlight, as well as a better place for the long hoped-for calm, and later the autumnal serenity and the wisdom of age?

Much had to be done. The verandaed, largely timber-built house was constructed at the end of a long tarmacked drive. A five-barred gate, rarely to be closed, was at the main entrance. Here the actor made for himself a territory all of his own: "His seclusion," wrote one reporter, "has created a useful myth, that no such person as Alec Guinness exists behind the many masks." Certainly his profile as a local resident never became high. J.B. Priestley had a friend who lived near Guinness who told him that "Alec could wander around or attend local functions and yet never be recognised." The local library could find no cuttings on him in the file: he was never "written up". When something happened to him, like a fire which severely damaged the whole lower floor of his house in 1987 there was the shortest of reports:

"They sat in one of our police cars while firemen dealt with the fire." No fuss.*

For three or four years, after their house was built, Guinness still lived much of the time in St Peter's Square, but by 1954 he was writing to friends, saying how the house was "gorgeous" and that they must come down to stay. Merula, having given up acting and taken up painting, had always loved horses and they now kept two ponies, two dogs, a car, a parrot and a horse with one brown eye and one blue eye.

Irene Worth, who played with him in Feydeau and Eliot, was one visitor some years later:

> Alec won't live in the bustle of a city. He and his wonderful wife Merula, their son Matthew not too far away, live in the country and their love and knowledge of nature is strong. There one finds them in their element, without pretension, with their animals, books, paintings, answering the telephone, reading, writing. There are no photographs or paintings of Alec standing about.

Coral Browne was another, who described her host as the "soul of discretion ... and "a truly formidable, invisible man". She and Vincent Price, her husband, went to Kettlebrook Meadows on one of "those rare, halcyon English summer days that erase all the grey drizzle from the memory ... The entire house and its grounds bespeak everything about this generous, adorable and self-confessed odd couple ... The idyllic garden ... owes much of its charm to the interests, rural hobbies and loving care of Merula. 'This England' in a nutshell."

Of Guinness himself, Coral Browne observed: "I am not aware of any troubles that ruffle his serenity ... However, I have never known him to laugh volubly, rather a silent amusement, his merriment contained to a mischievous smile." When she left the parting was all too perfect, too:

> Alec waved a farewell to me and I looked back at him framed in the doorway. His attire – cardigan and well-worn trousers – had been exactly right for this day in the country. But, I knew for sure that should our next encounter be anywhere in the city

---

* The fire was caused by their French-style Aga, which overheated. Peter Glenville was staying with them at the time. There was also a smaller fire in March 1955 which Guinness attacked with his jacket.

he would be head-to-toe immaculate. Mr Impeccable poses a constant problem for the likes of Jean Marsh, Eileen Atkins and yours truly . . .

Was Coral Browne saying that she was being put on her mettle by Guinness almost as one would be by another woman?

"Pain is at the centre of all his characters," wrote an astute commentator in *Time* in 1958, quoting Guinness's own admission of "a certain uncomfortable void" at the centre of his life, and of a friend who said of him: "I would call it Alec's personal abyss. There is this great sense of absence in the middle of him. This lack of identity. One seldom sees a man who lives so intimately with nothingness."

With his conversion to Roman Catholicism, subsequent to the building of his rural retreat, would he now become like the quiet-voiced elders of East Coker, deceiving themselves, and bequeathing to others merely the receipt for deceit?

> The serenity only a deliberate hebetude,
> The wisdom only the knowledge of dead secrets
> Useless in the darkness into which they peered
> Or from which they turned their eyes.

Who could know? As Eliot remarked, there is only a limited value in the knowledge derived from experience.

22

Commanding absences

Guinness cemented his reputation as a leading English film actor in the next few films he made. He became known as the man who could disguise himself as often and as variously as he wanted, yet even here there was much dispute about whether he disguised himself in these roles, or actually "became" them.

At this time in the film world the "studio with the team spirit" was coming into eminence: six acres of dull tarmacked drive and studio in Ealing, West London, it had opened in 1931 and churned out historical romance after historical romance, largely under the direction of Basil Dean who resigned in 1938 and, throughout the war, ran ENSA. Since then these studios had been run by a Birmingham-born, South African Jew, Michael Balcon, who had already created the reputation of Alfred Hitchcock with *The Thirty-Nine Steps* and *The Man Who Knew Too Much*, and of Robert Flaherty with *Man of Aran*.

During the war Balcon had nurtured a group of young film-makers who had mostly begun as editors, many of them with Oxbridge backgrounds. The directors included Charles Frend, Robert Hamer, Charles Crichton and – from Brazil via France – Alberto Cavalcanti. Balcon produced several powerful war films which for their uncompromising documentary exactness had roused Churchill's wrath, but were praised by high-ranking service personnel enough to escape banning. T.E.B. (or Tibby) Clarke, the war reserve policeman turned scriptwriter whom Balcon discovered, wrote *Hue and Cry*, the first film of a distinctive Ealing style: this tale, set mostly in London, of street urchins who eccentrically capture a criminal, established what Balcon called "the new story-documentary technique . . . which I believe is going to be the most important trend in the cinema from now onwards."

Yet documentary trends apart and in the words of the popular adage, "Everyone at Ealing is a character." Here was the productive paradox at the heart of the studio's achievement. Above all, as its head, was this autocrat or benevolent dictator whom some called rigid and puritanical in the traditional manner of a Jewish patriarch, yet who formed a group of technician-based film-makers who stayed together for fifteen years so that, quite unusually for the cinema anywhere in the world, they formed a unity of style. Balcon was admired because he had already taken a lot of chances, and after the war came Ealing's big chance. As Charles Crichton, director of *The Lavender Hill Mob*, said, "The war made a lot of difference: for a while American films were invisible. It was a period of emotional stress and this stress came out more in the comedies than in the war pictures. The comedies were more sincere – more human, more warm."

The first film that Guinness made for Ealing was *Kind Hearts and Coronets*, directed by Robert Hamer. In it Guinness played the whole of the Ascoyne-D'Ascoyne family. It was a black comedy of murder and intrigue of a typical English gentry vintage with monsters of arrogance and cruelty being bumped off by a rather effete murderer Louis, played by Dennis Price, who dealt a good hand in ruthless epigrams such as "Revenge is a dish which people of taste prefer to eat cold."

Robert Hamer had a first in mathematics from Cambridge; fair in complexion he worked with a "buttoned up" manner; his small face has been described as "like a clenched fist". He first offered Guinness three of the family roles which he, together with John Dighton, had scripted. Guinness then suggested, "If you want seven or eight people to look like me, why don't I play them all myself?" Hamer agreed; if three why not eight; he persuaded Balcon to let Guinness play the whole family.

Hamer and Guinness got on extremely well together. "We talked the same language. We laughed at the same things," said Guinness. *Kind Hearts and Coronets* was shot mostly on location at Leeds Castle, Kent, whose lack of size and grandeur at first upset Guinness, recalls Michael Relph the art director, in spite of its perfect air of hereditary privilege and its position in the middle of a lake. Douglas Slocombe, the cameraman of many notable Ealing pictures, remembered how meticulous Guinness was in his preparation, how he would arrive every morning at six to start being made up, and how his memory was perfect.

Optical processes were quite primitive and the famous split-screen trick shot when Guinness appeared as six D'Ascoynes in contiguous church pews at the same time had to be shot in an old-fashioned way. The lens was laboriously shuttered and finely adjusted to open in part for each new impersonation. It took three days at Ealing to shoot the requisite number of fifteen-second shots, while at any moment the whole composite picture could have been ruined if Guinness had not complied exactly with the technical complexities of the placings.

On set one day Guinness recounted to Douglas Slocombe how Matthew, now aged seven, had suddenly snatched up a crucifix which his father had brought home, stared at it in a very puzzled way, then suddenly grasped it by the shaft, held it between thumb and fingers, parallel to the floor and made arabesques in the air with it, to the accompaniment of a "zooing" sound.

When they were staying on location in Kent, Guinness, with his co-stars Joan Greenwood, Valerie Hobson and Price, would play 'The Game', an entertaining pastime of association and memory first made popular by Noël Coward. Each player had to repeat everything previously said by another player and this could run to sixty or more inconsequential words or ideas which had to be recalled exactly in the order they were said. Robert Hamer had a phenomenal memory: he could read a column upside down in the *Daily Telegraph* and repeat it verbatim. But Guinness could surpass even Hamer.

Guinness later identified models for one or two of the family whom Louis bumps off. An ancient admiral had once reprimanded him for wearing a scarf over his impeccable uniform on a freezing icy day on a Scottish loch and ordered him to put on a collar and tie (which he was already wearing). Guinness said he watched the admiral depart through his "quizzes until he was as small as a mosquito," rehearsing to himself Hamlet's lines to Polonius about the actors, "Let them be well used for they are the abstract and brief chronicles of the time. After your death, you were better to have a bad epitaph than their ill respect while you lived." And now he was playing this senior officer going down the bridge of his ship his mind jumped back "to that cold morning near Inverary. I am ashamed to say it now, but I had my little revenge and it tasted sweet."

Kind Hearts and Coronets, when it was released in mid-1949, became one of the most successful films ever made at Ealing, and in time a comedy classic. It also brought Guinness hitherto undreamt of acclaim, but a new complication: fragmentation of character into multiple impersonation. Or, as he put it, "False noses are too easy." Essentially, in those eight speaking parts, one non-speaking part and a portrait in oils he was showing different aspects of the same physical and mental constitution. The key to his complete immersion in each role was that he could disguise himself not only physically but mentally. But here were only eight Abel Druggers in the same film. True psychological complexity remained with the murderer. Although *Kind Hearts and Coronets* established Guinness as the most gifted character actor in England, he dismissed all these roles as thin stuff – "Pretty cardboard". What happened in the darkness after each D'Ascoyne snuffed it – the mysterious limbo in which Guinness would transform himself into something quite new – became much more intriguing to himself. Who really was he?

In failing to rise to portray that psychological complexity, Dennis Price failed to mature as an actor and while Louis murdered the D'Ascoyne family, the screen success of Guinness as the family of his victims became the instrument of Price's own destruction. For while Price could have expected a lot of praise for playing Louis, Guinness stole the show. Price, a highly sensitive being, apparently felt rejected and suffered all his life from being overshadowed; he ended his life by committing suicide. T.S. Eliot, whom Guinness had met on several occasions through playing in *The Cocktail Party* and who had, as Guinness remarked, "a surprisingly coarse laugh", disapproved strongly of *Kind Hearts and Coronets*. Eliot thought it immoral to make a funny film about murder. Could it be that Eliot was right? Although one hardly dare support such heresy, was there more connection between crime and its light-hearted depiction on screen than one would care to believe possible?

Last Holiday, Guinness's next Ealing film, was a much more typical Ealing film than *Kind Hearts and Coronets*; while not altogether a success, it was also more prophetic of Guinness's future development, both on and off the screen, as well as more revealing about the human condition of being Alec Guinness. In *Last Holiday* Guinness played the first of his "little men" and demonstrated his extraordinary capacity for ordinariness.

J.B. Priestley's characteristic, but wayward, script tried to draw a social message out of a man dying of an incurable disease but this unfortunately stopped *Last Holiday* from being the more interesting film it might have become had the story been developed more subtly. Priestley himself felt the London critics missed the various depths of irony as "they shrugged it away". As George Bird, Guinness, in double-breasted pin-stripe suit and under sentence of death from "Lempington's Disease", attempts to enjoy his last weeks in a "high-class" seaside hotel. It seemed that only Guinness could ever convey that special melancholy of holidaying in a run-down, quality hotel. Unaffected in every way by the illness, Bird withholds his secret from the women and other characters to whom he becomes attached, and gains the power, love, and social distinction he previously could never enjoy. Then Bird finds out the diagnosis is mistaken, but dies anyway – in a car crash on the day of his reprieve. Self-doomed to anonymity, Guinness gained magnetic power in solitude. As Priestley commented, "The scenes were not shot in chronological order, which meant that Alec had to be ready every morning to present his young man at some different stage of his development, jumping forward or backward in time. And this he did beautifully." Also, for the first time, he showed the ability to convert the screen into an intimate, private means of communication, as if revealing something special to each member of the audience. But he still watched and withheld.

Last Holiday was the prelude to five films made in quick succession, interrupted only by Hamlet at the New Theatre. The first of these was The Mudlark, occasioned by his Edinburgh and Broadway success in The Cocktail Party, and in it Guinness impersonated his first historical genius role, that of Disraeli. This was also his first Hollywood picture, directed by Jean Negulesco, although much of it was shot on location in England. Prestigious and successful as it was at the time – Guinness won the Picturegoer Gold Medal for most popular actor and the film was chosen for the Royal Command performance – it sank in mid-Atlantic condescension. The Times called it a "hybrid". The photograph images of Guinness's Disraeli make-up remained potent.*

The Lavender Hill Mob, however, became part of folklore. Guinness played the devious bowler-hatted Mr Holland who seduces a manufacturer of cheap souvenirs, played by Stanley

---

* The high point of the film was a moving speech Disraeli made in Parliament, punctuated by a long, dramatic silence, which, commented Darryl Zanuck, was one of the most effective moments of silence in film history. Since the script had not called for it Zanuck asked Guinness later on how he came to think of it. "I didn't," Guinness told him. "In the middle of my speech I forgot my lines – dried up."

Holloway, into turning bank robber with him. For this picture Guinness was paid £6,000 (to Edith Evans's utter amazement when he told her of it). "It had to be written and rewritten," said Clarke, "eleven times before it satisfied all concerned – and a really good climax eluded me through three or four versions." Guinness spent several days with the script, weighing up each line and making illuminating suggestions that would never have occurred to Crichton, the director, or Clarke. "I see Holland as a man given to handwashing gestures," he pronounced. "Anyone who usually does that is on the plump side so I think I ought to be slightly padded . . . we should somehow point the incongruity of a person like Holland seeing himself as the boss of a gang. It might be a good way to get the right effect if he were to have difficulties in pronouncing his R's."

Guinness could in some ways become over-meticulous, recalled Crichton. He would hate having any pre-ordained moves; he would never allow a double to walk in the distance for him, although once in *Oliver Twist*, when Guinness was off for some reason, Lean had made up as Fagin and, doubling for Guinness, had himself filmed walking down a street. One day they were filming the scene at the kiosk at the top of the Eiffel Tower. Guinness had not been called until later. A double was standing in. There was only one position for him to stand, and an assistant had put down some marks: "For Christ's sake," said Crichton, "take those marks away. If he sees those it'll be disaster."

Guinness's performance, if not revealing of his deeper self in any way, had complete relaxation, together with an element of the commanding absence he sometimes managed to place at the centre of his best film performances. Here was the elevation of Ealing's "little man", the quiet rebellious type who was to find his apotheosis in Guinness's next film and its best directional exponent in the work of Alexander Mackendrick.

23

The guise of conformity

"An Ealing comedy – we know ... Sir Michael Balcon's jolly gagmen have established a style," wrote Kenneth Tynan, who was deputising for Milton Shulman on the *Evening Standard*, about Guinness's next, much more significant film:

> We know that there probably will not be a hero – or that, if there is, he will be slightly comic if not downright weird: that we shall not spend much time in the boudoir or the countryside: that we shall see a good deal of the Civil Service, the police force and the small shopkeeper: and that the theme will be the bizarre British, faced with yet another perfectly extraordinary situation.
>
> The writing will be crisp and astute (Ealing all but invented scripting as a full-time profession in England) and nobody will rupture a blood vessel to make us laugh. Ealing offers an exceptional middle-class man's view of the middle-class. The novelty is to find a film studio with any point of view at all.

For his new director, as Guinness wrote, "The enemy was always lurking behind the portals and façades of the hierarchy. In short he is an artist, and like all artists wants his own way. Rightly."

Up to this point Alexander Mackendrick had led a wayward, even erratic career. Born in 1912 in Boston, Massachusetts, he was repatriated when he was seven to Glasgow, where he lived with his Calvinist grandfather. His mother was an alcoholic who walked out on him and became a Catholic convert: "Frankly, I preferred her when she was a tippler," said Mackendrick later, who felt injured by her desertion and kept up a lifelong aversion to religion.

Lonely and unhappy as he was, Mackendrick nursed, in spite of his mother and albeit grudgingly, some moral feeling and when, after a brief spell at Glasgow School of Art (which he left without a degree), and outstanding work at J. Walter Thomson's on "Horlicks continuity ads", Mackendrick landed the job of directing *Whisky Galore*, he brought to the Ealing comedy a special preoccupation which work with Guinness deepened. For, set on the whisky-starved Hebridean island of Todday, on whose rocks a cargo boat carrying 50,000 cases of the spirit vital above all to Ealing – the directors and crews were notorious drinkers and would invariably "repair" after shooting to the Red Lion opposite the studio gates – *Whisky Galore* seethed with moral ambiguity. The way people saw things, their modes of perception, came to the forefront as the hopes for intoxication in the subversive part of the community overthrew the structure of authority. The innocent rejected what they could not see; the experienced blinded themselves.

All this thematic depth was important to *The Man in the White Suit*, Mackendrick's next film which was based on a play by Roger MacDougall, his cousin, and further developed by John Dighton of *Kind Hearts and Coronets*, and by Mackendrick himself. Guinness was surprised to find, on the first day of shooting, pinned on a board in the studio a sort of strip-cartoon Mackendrick had sketched of all his intended shots for a scene. Although they were, as he thought, "admirably and vigorously drawn", he was immediately on the defensive for they signalled rigidity of approach, something of which he had a horror.

The Man in the White Suit gave Guinness the opportunity to portray his first eccentric man of genius, the inventor Sidney Stratton. Stratton invents an artificial fibre of such impossibly perfect qualities that it threatens the livelihood of millions of textile workers. In that threat there is a disintegrating factor at work – as in *Whisky Galore* – what the playwright Samuel Beckett identified as "the principle of disintegration in even the most complacent solidities". As Charles Barr, a chronicler of Ealing wrote, "Outside Mackendrick's work, how many British films have intelligence as a central concern, valued in the characters as it is expressed in the organisation of the film?"

When Mackendrick adapted MacDougall's play he "took Roger's hero and gave him a minor role, and pivoted the whole story around a secondary character, the one played in the film by Alec Guinness, to make a new story entirely". This was a remarkable discovery of Mackendrick – "that there is a character you need in a play, but don't need in a film because the camera takes over from him. It's Enobarbus in *Antony and Cleopatra*, it's Horatio in *Hamlet*. The camera becomes that character who holds it all together – the viewpoint character."

The imaginative breadth of *The Man in the White Suit* was Faustian, beginning with the Dickens "Coke Town" landscape of smoky chimney and grimy back-to-backs: scientific discovery was destructive, the work of the devil, and Mackendrick imbued the whole atmosphere with a kind of uncertainty bordering on catastrophe, a mind-at-the-end-of-its-tether or stop-the-world-I-want-to-get-off atmosphere. The documentary style was where it began. The nightmare was where it would end.

For Guinness it was an exemplary picture. He and Mackendrick shared a concern, even an obsession, for detail. Both were painstaking, even over-meticulous in establishing the comedy in precise detail. The solid carpentry of imparting information and laying fuses was what both enjoyed most. The film was completed in fifty-nine days. Both also relished the private joke, the comically enriching closeness between the textile town Stratton throws into confusion and the world of Ealing itself, which had a strong enough identity to be satirised. The mill-owner's paternalism, for instance, owed much to Michael Balcon's benign presence being manipulated by subversive noise-makers. Philip Kemp noted in his biography of Mackendrick that "Guinness borrowed traits from a young studio technician whose innocently self-absorbed air he had noticed." The noise of Stratton's invention created particular delight. Obscene bubbling sounds which the sound supervisor described as "like breaking wind in the bath". Tynan, in his review (which failed to pin down the unique quality of the film), called it "chortling and burbling . . . like a sort of plumber's zither".

When the invention causes strikes and Stratton is pursued in his gleaming suit of the imperishable textile through claustrophobic alleys, the film deteriorates somewhat into hysteria. But Guinness's innocent and blinkered quality made Stratton glow from within and generated a rich comic sympathy. In fact there were many obnoxious qualities about the inventor but the story was built so that the audience was pre-disposed to side with him. Guinness concealed the scientist's obsession by spending much of the time trying either to hide himself or his clandestine research from the rest of the characters. Privacy and a quality of mind were at the core of his attraction, yet the overall effect turned more and more into the Buster Keaton vein.

Guinness did not like some aspects of working at Ealing, especially how the studio was, as he thought, more geared towards serving the needs of technicians than of actors:

> They rather thought actors got in the way of things and they were always trying to get me killed. I remember on *The Man in the White Suit*, I had to climb down a wire rope. I thought it looked dangerous. "Nothing to it," said the technicians. "It can withstand a tension of ten tons – so it will certainly hold you." I said I had some experience of wires and ropes in the Navy during the recent hostilities and I wasn't so sure. I climbed down just the same. The rope snapped. I fell. All they said was, looking a bit surprised, "It shouldn't have happened." But they didn't say sorry. That was the way it was.

That the director was all-important to the success of a film was demonstrated by the one outright failure Guinness suffered in this early batch of Ealing comedies. Just after *Kind Hearts and Coronets* he had played the part of a journalist in Charles Frend's *A Run for your Money*. Frend was an integral member of the Ealing team. But the two films he made with Guinness, *A Run for Your Money* (1949) and *Barnacle Bill* (1957), failed to ignite although Guinness enjoyed Frend's easy raconteur wit and his compendious knowledge of pubs and beer. Not that this interested Guinness much, but like many Ealing figures Frend was known as a "character". The contrast between his working self and his social self was remarkable; a colleague has described how, when on the studio floor, Frend would become eaten up with nervousness and self-doubt, and as a result fierce towards actors and crew alike. He was his "own worst enemy" and gravitated towards subjects of tragic dimension, if not tragedies: *The Cruel Sea* was one; *Scott of the Antarctic* another.

In *The Card*, the film version written by Eric Ambler of Arnold Bennett's novel, Guinness played another comic upstart, Edward Denry Machin, who rose from humble obscurity to become Lord Mayor in a provincial town, while his path was strewn with the maxims of the self-made man: "The road to success is fraught with hardship; it's the woman's duty to adapt herself to the man." Some have attributed this choice of role to a desire in Guinness to win audiences outside London – he had never done the customary stint in an out-of-town touring or repertory company. Others have claimed that Machin, a man who set out to conquer the world, presented the challenge of a new kind of hero. Certainly the parvenu capitalist was a most unlikely role: Guinness invested him with tantalising ambiguity so it was never clear if Machin's actions were above board or if he was going to be caught as he charmed his way into wealth and prominence.

But once again an Ealing film caught the moral ambivalence of English society in that muddled post-war period. "What great cause has he ever been identified with?" sneers a political opponent on the eve of Machin's adoption as Mayor. "I think I can tell you," retaliates the Countess of Choll. "He's identified with the good cause of cheering us all up." Beyond Machin, Guinness conveyed the philosophy of Mr Sleary in *Hard Times*, who defends the pleasure of the circus to Gradgrind: "People mutht be amuthed. They can't be alwayth a learning, nor yet they can't be alwayth awarking, they an't made for it." Peter Copley, another actor in *The Card*, commented on the continuous alertness Guinness showed to props during the filming. At one point, warned by his co-stars Valerie Hobson and Petula Clark, he stopped a heavy studio lamp toppling on the heads of the crowd. He was always on the lookout too for comic opportunities: in the tailor's shop, for instance, when Machin gets promoted, he was longing to pick up and do something with the tailor's shears.

24

Mephistopheles, the tall tempter

In April 1952, with courageous promptness after the failure of *Hamlet* – like a thrown rider immediately re-mounting his horse – Guinness returned to the West End, this time to the Aldwych Theatre, to play the Ant Scientist in Sam and Bella Spewack's *Under the Sycamore Tree*, a revenge play along the lines of *The Insect Play* – the satire on the human race by the Czech brothers Capek. In this, as a multipede, Guinness not only had to progress to the age of ninety, but adopt multiple professional roles. The play was not brilliant – somewhat more bite in the dialogue was required – but its favourable notices revived in Guinness deeper theatrical aspirations. He was in this frame of mind when Tom Patterson, a Canadian who was organising the 1953 Stratford Ontario Festival under Tyrone Guthrie's direction, visited him in his dressing-room between a matinée and evening performance.

Guthrie, in order to attract Guinness to work with him again – but also because he was genuinely supportive of his old friend and protégé's ambition to conquer one of the highest peaks – had told Patterson to offer Guinness Hamlet again.

Wisely, at their first meeting, Patterson suggested to Guinness the tentative fee of $3,500 dollars, omitting to make any mention of Hamlet. The fee was tempting for six weeks of rehearsal and four weeks of playing. Guinness was interested, but next day, when he and Patterson met for lunch, he received the suggestion of Hamlet very coldly and grew suspicious that Guthrie was out to show him up: he remarked tartly, "that a certain gentleman was very good at encouraging actors and quite good too at slapping them down when they became stars". He agreed finally to appear; the plays chosen were *Richard III* and *All's Well that Ends Well* (in which he was to play the King of France).

Guthrie's account of this new venture with Guinness was very different from Patterson's. Guinness and Guthrie read all of Shakespeare's plays. *Richard III* was agreed upon. "Guinness wanted to play it. We both felt that the complicated genealogy, the rather obscure historical background, were probably drawbacks for Canadian audiences but might be offset by the strong threat of melodrama." Guinness was delighted in the new transformation he could effect upon himself. "Do wish you were able to come to see me and my wig as Richard III," he told Tynan in March 1953.

The whole venture nearly collapsed because they had, after all, to erect the Festival Theatre, even if it was only a huge semi-permanent tent, as well as rehearse and act in it. Funds grew low and they were unable to meet their bills. But the contractor who was preparing the site had, according to Guthrie, "decided that the honour of the community was at stake and that, whether he was paid or no, his part in the whole plan would go forward". The big top of the Festival Theatre was finally up (and blessed in a service of Dedication by five ministers of different denominations) as they assembled in Ontario for the remaining rehearsals. To the last rehearsal Guinness and Guthrie fought over the amount of ooze on the outside of the sack which held the severed head of Hastings. Guthrie had also neglected to calculate one unexpected effect, for multitudes would lurk in the spring twilight outside the skirts of the great tent. On the whole their behaviour was impeccable but, occasionally,

a juvenile head would appear under the canvas, momentarily, slyly, six inches from the ground. Then an enormously magnified whisper from outside would say, "Well?" The head would withdraw. Then the huge whisper would reverberate, "You're sure it was Alec Guinness?" The head would reappear. The actors, led by Guinness, would make desperate efforts to get on with the job. Pay no attention. Go ahead. Over the dialogue would float the enormous pervasive whisper: "Well, what's he like?"

The acoustical peculiarity was solved two days before the first night by covering the whole floor with coconut matting. Then throughout the day of the first night the cars rolled up: in one of them was the Governor-General, Vincent Massey. As Guthrie's biographer wrote

The young volunteer ushers . . . moved like naval cadets putting the ship to sea; got people aboard and seated with courtesy. Trumpets blew. The red geraniums were in place round the tent.

A yellow pennant – present from Stratford-upon-Avon, England – floated from the top of the tent. A gun fired. The play was on. Guinness took the stage, as Richard III.

"Now is the winter of our discontent/Made glorious summer . . ."

Both plays resulted in a personal triumph for Guinness, while in *All's Well* his triumph was subordinate to Irene Worth's stunning portrayal of Helen, a part which Guthrie regarded as Shakespeare's finest female creation.

> I remember [said Irene Worth] the loneliness of his Richard III as he sat, horribly alone, silent, his Coronation train covering the stage, his eyes filled with fear and guilt, his voice, in a rasp, saying, "I am not in the giving mood today." I remember his dying, exquisite King in *Alls's Well*, whom I wheeled about in a wicker bath chair. I hear his gentle voice: ". . . since I nor wax nor honey can bring home,/I quickly were dissolved from the hive".

The festival was a big success and was extended for two weeks. According to the designer, Tanya Moiseiwitsch, many people came who had never before seen a stage play. The presence of Guinness in Ontario was germane to this new festival which grew to become of world status, and as such created a whole new community.

For the rest of his stay Guinness was to be seen riding about on a bicycle, "trilby on head and decently clad, moving smoothly and sedately along the tree-lined streets, like a character right out of one of his Ealing comedies". Not Professor Marcus, one of his future characters, one hopes. In August he sat for a portrait by John S. Coppin, a Canadian artist. With the enthusiastic notices and his personal satisfaction at an all-time high, he could withdraw from the Shakespeare stakes with honour. He was only, ever, to appear again twice in Shakespeare in the theatre.

In November his film, *The Captain's Paradise*, in which he played an adulterous sea captain, was banned in Maryland for mocking the sanctity of marriage, but when the ban was lifted it went on to make a great deal of money in the United States. At Christmas, 1953, he was back in England, "sponging off" Binkie Beaumont who had inadvertently sat down on a chocolate trifle at Peter Brook's yuletide party.

25

Missing the mainstream

When Guinness made *Father Brown*, his next film with Robert Hamer, the director of *Kind Hearts and Coronets*, it seemed like a firm return to the circumference of character acting. But, "In Father Brown," wrote G.K. Chesterton, "it was the chief feature to be featureless. The point of him was to appear pointless; and one might say that his conspicuous quality was not being conspicuous." It sounded ideal casting but Guinness did not achieve invisibility so well as he did with later roles such as George Smiley.

The attractive feature for him about Chesterton's character was his concern with the spirit.* Father Brown roots out the criminal in any situation because he has identified in himself the criminal instinct which we all possess, and which used to be called by most people "original sin". "No man's really any good till he knows how bad he is, or might be . . . till he's squeezed out of his soul the last drop of the oil of the Pharisees; till his only hope is somehow or other to have captured one criminal and kept him safe and sane under his own hat." It was the same observation of Sir Thomas More, who, watching a murderer being taken off to execution, observed, "There, but for the grace of God, go I."

In the film Father Brown voices his mission: "I want to help man . . . to cure him of the sickness of his soul", but this became secondary to the detective work. Self-identification led him to the murderer – in other words it was a creative process similar to that of a writer or indeed an actor. As the script of the film indicated "I try to get so far inside a man. I move with his arms and legs." There were, in short, many strong and distinct similarities between Chesterton and Guinness.

* Father Brown was modelled on Monsignor John O'Connor, a venerable Irish priest, who received Chesterton into the Catholic Church.

But he confessed himself dissatisfied with this film and one can see why. Although Father Brown is horrified by the secret and shameful knowledge that every one of us is capable of crime, Guinness's portrayal remained a matter of harmless externals, and he was always owlishly visible. He failed to penetrate the man more than superficially. Guinness was not yet ready to take up full residence in the spiritual centre of a role. But he was wrong to blame himself for not achieving the full stature of Chesterton's conception: this was probably the fault of the director and other elements in the film, such as the semi-farcical script with its Chaplinesque chases. He remained peripheral: as the reviewer in *The Times* commented, this film gave Guinness only "half a chance and Mr Guinness takes that half even though he cannot turn it into a whole".

It was a long time now since Guinness had been anticlerical and "shuddered" if he passed a priest or a nun. He had always been receptive to quasi-mystical or spiritual experiences but one night during the filming of *Father Brown*, which was shot in a village near Mâcon in Burgundy, an incident firmly turned him in the direction of conversion to Rome.

He had finished filming. It was dark, and he was still robed as a priest as he began the walk of a mile or so back to where he was staying. As he told a reporter over twenty years later:

> It was absolutely dark. I heard little footsteps running after me. Suddenly I felt my hand taken by about a seven-year-old boy, who walked with me all the way back to the village swinging my hand and chattering. I only caught little bits of what he was saying. I didn't dare utter a word in case I frightened him with a foreign accent or my clumsy French. I remained absolutely silent, and eventually he squeezed my hand and disappeared, and I thought it was simply marvellous that a child in the kind of dark, in a dark lane, will run up to a man, because he's dressed as a priest. And it totally changed my attitude . . . I don't base my religion on that but it's the attitude. No, I think it's marvellous that a small boy has confidence . . . I've always looked back on it as a magic moment.

It was still to be some three years before Guinness embarked on the enormous step of becoming a Catholic. He was thirty-nine years old when he played Father Brown; as he told a friend later, "The years between thirty and forty are the worst of all. You have got so far, and you are struggling to reach the very top, finally to arrive."

From playing Father Brown and after two further films, *Malta Story* and *The Captain's Paradise*, both entertaining but of no great value or significance, Guinness next went into a London West-End play which seemed to focus all his career and his spiritual search into one complex yet strong and united beam.

The Prisoner, by Bridget Boland, drew from him a performance which for some surpassed *Look Back in Anger*, *The Sport of My Mad Mother*, *The Birthday Party*, *Waiting for Godot* and the other, more garish beacons of the age soon to be conflagrated. Although this play, written by an eccentric spinster – who had worked for British Intelligence during the war, was destined to vanish into obscurity, its actual theme – as opposed to its often second-rate means of expression – of the spiritual superiority of Roman Catholicism to Communism, or of God to materialism, was overlooked in favour of Beckett's pauses, or Osborne's unchecked but fashionable English malice.

The Prisoner ends up far from glorifying God or even establishing the heroism of the unidentified Prisoner. Like the many statues of the "Unknown Political Prisoner" current as sculptures in the early 1950s this prince of the Church had a somewhat grey if universal identity. The progress of Boland's play was towards the man's disintegration – a peeling away of his defences before his shame.

The Interrogator, the antagonist, played on stage by Noël Willman, was attempting to convert the Cardinal from his faith into becoming a supporter of the communist, totalitarian system. What he uncovered as the Cardinal's weakness was his lack of love for his mother and for humanity in general – "I do not love my mother, I never have" – as well as excessive humility and inverted pride. In fact, the Cardinal hated himself with self-gratifying masochism. As a celebrated leader of the Church he was an egotist indulging in secret treachery, an ambitious man who tried to hide away the fact that his mother was a whore; he was intent, above all, on justifying himself to himself – "to me, not to God".

The interrogation achieved his spiritual cleansing, his purification, as if the Interrogator, in some clever ironic way, became himself the agent of God, and by trying to destroy what was the greatest threat to the socialist, materialist way of life, in fact ended by losing faith in that system. "To do my job," the Interrogator finally says, "I had to get so close to you that we were like two sides of the same man talking to each other. And I came to love and pity the other side and hate what I made it do."

Boland was a near, country neighbour of the Guinnesses': a very questioning and forthright woman, she was a brilliant, even pugnacious conversationalist who always had an unusual point to make. Born in Ireland, she read PPE at Somerville College, Oxford, later becoming a major in the ATS engaged on Intelligence duties. At the end of the war she visited Belsen four days after it was opened up; a lifelong Catholic, she was one-time Secretary of the Catholic Truth Society. She would, for instance, burst out laughing at the statue of Oliver Cromwell in front of Parliament, observing something to the effect that "only the English could manage to put that up there — 'without which he managed to rule for eleven years etc . . .'". Her first play, *The Cockpit*, had centred on the problem of Serb and Croat refugees. Awkward and tall, she could suddenly blow up into a temper over the world's injustices.

There were many biographical touches buried in *The Prisoner* which suggest that Boland knew her Alec Guinness well and was painting in some of the emotional background of his own stinging experience of family life and deprivation. The details may or may not be true. But Guinness was portraying deep emotions from the inside. Boland was a powerful and intuitional writer who could depict men as few women writers for the stage have ever done. Whatever the profound cause may be, there was no doubt that this play resulted in Guinness's greatest performance to date, for his acting achieved an authority and a sensitivity which had never until now quite become integrated into a whole. The Cardinal's shame, his darkness, his sense of guilt and sin, his aspiration towards the good, above all his faith, all were absolutely convincing.

The Prisoner ran at the Globe Theatre and was then made into a film which Peter Glenville, who directed the stage production, again directed faultlessly. The London audiences, although they flocked to see it, viewed it ambivalently. Communism was the bogey, for sure, but persecuted Catholicism behind the Iron Curtain was a remote and unknown quantity, while there was still a large proportion of English society which viewed papism with as great misgiving as they viewed communism. The spirit of the English theatre was largely left-wing and pro-Brechtian, and priests were often treated as objects of obscene derision, or as props of a decaying order.

But the film of *The Prisoner*, in which Jack Hawkins took the part of the Interrogator, was paradoxically an unqualified and lasting triumph. Ralph Richardson once said, after a taxing role, "It's a funny thing about acting, I have nothing to say about it at all which is a bit odd because one does take such immense trouble to try and find the character, to create the character, that it is rather as if the memory vanishes. Perhaps it's rather a painful experience, really, and one forgets pain very easily, thank heavens." Perhaps this was Guinness's feeling. If that intensely moving sense of isolation that Guinness created on stage, and that astonishingly still presence in prayer and remorse, were absent in the film, the close-ups of Guinness's face on screen more than made up for them. His expressions, and the underlying passions they represented, registered perfectly the effect Jack Hawkins had on him as he peeled away the priest's layers of defence not so much by tormenting his flesh as by undermining his sensitivity and revealing the impure motives for his vocation. Some triggers of the guilt were not entirely convincing, but the film quickly reached a tragic dimension it never lost.

In *The Prisoner* Guinness placed before us for all time the naked soul of a prince of the Church driven increasingly to desperation: "I wanted to justify myself to myself . . . To me, not to God . . . I succeeded. I can serve . . . But I can't care." Playing without hairpiece or other form of disguise Guinness sacrificed neither ordinariness nor humbleness, but in addition suggested depth and greatness. "Try not to judge the priesthood by the priest," the Cardinal tells the young prison guard after his humiliation, echoing St Peter's denial of his Master before the cock crows three times.

Guinness also eschewed sentimentality and embraced simplicity. The acting was quite inimitable, for nothing spare, nothing excessive, gave away the actor. "I wouldn't," as we have once quoted him saying, "go to a psychoanalyst in case he revealed something and said, 'And that is the springboard for such talent as you have.' I would feel it was just that, was it, instead of having something almost magical . . . like an empathy with animals, something you can't explain, something tucked away inside."

Here for once in his life, and definitively, was the undisguised, naked Guinness. But although he did describe staying in Bridget Boland's flat in Rome,* he never mentioned *The Prisoner* in his autobiography.

---

* Italy, in fact, banned *The Prisoner* as being anti-Catholic; but the Archbishop of Westminster, Cardinal Griffin, said, "This is a film which every devout Roman Catholic should see." It had a great reception in the US where it was voted the best foreign film of 1955.

Unlike Richardson, who turned down the part of Vladimir in *Waiting for Godot*, Guinness never expressed regret over not playing Estragon, the other tramp, which he was also offered at this time. I have found no reference to his views on Beckett, although I suspect they may have accorded slightly with those of his old friend "Bully", who played Pozzo in the first English production, and who relished with disgust the appalling effect acting in Beckett had on him. "I noticed," Peter Bull wrote, "that my friends were clearly mortified at having to hear my lines and Bob [Robert] Morley had thrown the script from one end of his garden to the other."

Bull opened in *Godot* on 3 August 1955. He described the horrors of performing in a play whose ambiguity has lent itself to the efforts of academics to explain it. His account deserves to become a classic. He found the people who liked Godot alarming – "they either sat spellbound in respectful silence or laughed their heads off in such a sinister way that the actors thought they must have forgotten to adjust their costumes . . . and it didn't help me in my portrayal to learn that Pozzo represented Fascism, Communism, Lord Beaverbrook, Randolph Hearst, Mussolini, James Joyce, or rather surprisingly, Humpty Dumpty."

Bull published his trial by *Godot* in *I Know the Face, but* . . . Bull concluded that *Godot* was

> the oddest theatrical experience of my life and had a nightmarish quality that is difficult to recapture in words. Both physically and mentally it was a disturbing play with which to be associated. The bleakness and sordidity of the set and the clothes, the spitting and drooling that formed part of the pattern, had a most depressing effect on me and I came to dread going to the theatre. I also found, as time went on, that I started to disbelieve in the merits of the play and to become more and more intolerant of the praise and importance that were bestowed on it in certain quarters. I got wildly bored by the endless banging-on at parties, in the street and particularly in my dressing-room. But of course it was all this *brouhaha* that helped to pay my rent for so long.

26

Dull as ditchwater

What was it like to be the subject of Kenneth Tynan's first biography of an actor, published in 1953? Here, perhaps, the mirror-image aspects of the pair are too strong to be ignored. This was the first and only complete – as far as it went – biography that Tynan wrote, while it was the first book which anybody wrote about Guinness. This was surely more than a coincidence. Although it was short, a monograph more than exhaustive study, Tynan's book was concentrated and full of detail. The ambition to write a full biography was to elude Tynan all his life, and sadly *Alec Guinness* and *Bull Fever*, the book immediately following (which Guinness loved) were the only books he managed to complete that were not collections of reviews, magazine articles or newspaper pieces.

Tynan researched and wrote the whole of his study of Guinness in 1953, just before he became drama critic of the *Observer*. Surprisingly, Guinness cooperated with Tynan fully. It was the first and last time he ever did such a thing. As he was still climbing the ladder, he could not, or so it might seem, afford to be secretive and off-putting in the way he became later. He allowed Tynan to borrow all his assiduously collected and assembled press cuttings. The documentation of Tynan's book was impeccable, and it was peppered with long quotations from the many hundreds of reviews of his early performances Guinness had collected.

They had last seen each other during the disastrous *Hamlet*. But now their friendship flourished, so that Elaine Dundy, whom Tynan had married two years earlier, recalled his "bubble of calm serenity" when she and Tynan visited him at St Peter's Square, "with his beaming boy face. You live well – good for you!" she remembered thinking in the "spacious and stagnant" Regency

Square, with Merula and Matthew, two dogs, a Siamese cat and grey parrot.* Here, as Tynan wrote,

> I have seen him make many outlandish faces; describing perhaps, a rehearsal mishap, maliciously observed and not for publication. "And so," he will cry, acting it out, "one came capering on, one pranced across the stage, with all *this* going on" – a wild waving of the arms – "and all of a sudden one felt terribly silly, because . . ." He pauses to cover his mouth and chuckle. The use of the impersonal third person is characteristic. It brings us back to where we started: to the persistent, ubiquitous anonymity of Alec Guinness.

Elaine Dundy recalled that he was quite without the usual actor's mannerisms, "No stories about how we should have or didn't, or might have played that part." Although much later Guinness disclaimed reading any more notices about his work, he seemed at this time to have been quite careful, or attentive to self-shaping, and he must have felt there was something to be gained from an association with Tynan. The latter had just taken a television directors' course and they discussed the possibility that Guinness should appear in a television adaptation of Orwell's *1984* which Guinness had just been "horrified" to read. He found it "quite in the first class of nightmares". But he also, as he told Tynan, felt it was "fearfully formless and consequently often monotonous and repetitive". He was fascinated to see what Tynan would make of it as a script, as he was anxious to do a really good television play – while, as he also said, "I've never appeared in bright blue in the Oxford Street stores."

Guinness was prepared to spend, even allowing for the rigours of his film work, several Sunday afternoons with Tynan "discussing whatever horrors about me you want to know". Whether he revealed his illegitimacy to Tynan we do not know, for Tynan remained quiet on this subject, while otherwise and surprisingly for him (or untypical of his later manner but not of his earlier quality), respectful towards whatever Guinness may have told him in confidence. Probably he did not, however, for in view of how Guinness did reveal it later, it still remained a secret: as Chesterton wrote of Dickens, "He never talked of his nightmare but kept it deadly silent . . . the unbearable but impersonal shame."

Later, when he was nearly seventy, Guinness grumbled at certain

* The move to Steep was not complete until 1955.

aspects of the book, at a mistake in it about his 1938 Hamlet: "I wish he'd just checked up." It's hard to detect this mistake now, although he seemed not to have liked Tynan quoting Agate, and wished he had quoted Ivor Brown's better review instead. The book was – because it was about Guinness – "in a sense as dull at ditchwater", although "highly readable". At the time, however, he felt enormously pleased with it, for he thanked Tynan (on 29 October 1953) for writing such a worthwhile and, as far as he could see, honest book about him. He suggested another side of his personality which he was soon to eradicate more or less entirely, for he described the book as being like a long and flattering session with a fortune teller in which his ego could bask delightedly. He affectionately hoped they would meet soon, pull the world to bits and put it together again in happier colours.

Towards the end of 1955, Peter Bull transferred in *Godot* to the Criterion Theatre, Piccadilly Circus. Guinness was now rehearsing the role of Boniface in Feydeau's *Hotel Paradiso*, again with Peter Glenville as the director. As Glenville explained, the characters in the play were "straightforward types, without over-subtlety or complexity". It must have been a relief for Guinness after the soul-baring of *The Prisoner* to find himself in the intricate, ordered world of farce.

But the rehearsals were "hard and gruelling", as Glenville outlined the conditions for making *Hotel Paradiso* a success. "There usually comes a moment when the actors cannot believe that such scientific hard work will ever induce laughter at all. There can be no rewarding conversations between director and cast about the mood, the inner motivation, or the subconscious. This necessity for precision work is like the making of a Swiss clock."

Two years before, Anthony Armstrong Jones, a twenty-four-year-old freelance photographer, had photographed Guinness in his Pimlico studio. "Uncle Oliver recommended me" – he meant Oliver Messel, the designer – and Armstrong-Jones, later Lord Snowdon, was surprised to find Guinness was as nervous as he was, a nervosity which showed in the slightly wooden, self-conscious portraits. Armstrong-Jones arrived at the photocall at the Winter Garden Theatre and took the remarkable picture of Guinness as Boniface with the mad, staring eyes. This was his first commission for *Vogue* and over the next forty years he was to photograph Guinness more than any other actor: he complained on that occasion that he had to work from the stalls with a long lens and because it was a weak shot had to do a rescue job on it:

> I wanted a close-up of Guinness's head to avoid showing he wasn't in costume. So I blew up a section of the negative, using an 8mm ciné camera lens in the enlarger – if I had blown up the whole negative it would have been twenty-foot square. It came out grainy and flat. I then put potassium ferrocyanide on the whites of the eyes to bleach them, which made it almost into a caricature.

Hotel Paradiso opened at the Winter Garden Theatre just prior to *Look Back in Anger* at the Royal Court Theatre. Guinness made his entrance sharpening a pencil, slicing away at it with his pen-knife until he had nearly walked over the footlight into the laps of the audience. Only then did he become aware that anyone was watching him. The critics in their ecstatic reviews of this production, which toured over England, talked of Guinness "letting his hair down" as Boniface, but that was not at all his way when he played the character Glenville called "the timid husband with a roving eye". As Glenville explained it, "Any attempt on the part of the actor at comic elaboration or subtle undertones will disrupt the pattern and rhythm of the play." Tynan, his mind still full of Guinness, wrote of his "exquisite stealth" as Boniface; "the chubby, crafty little fellow obsessed by an urge to break out and show the world his mettle". "When Alec had hidden from my husband inside the chimney," wrote Irene Worth, who played Marcelle, "and returned, quite black with soot, he said, 'It's me, Marcelle,' with such concern and reassurance to me that the audience began to laugh louder then ever. I shouted to him, over the roar, 'Shall I wait or go on?' He shouted back, 'Go on!' We did."

After one performance Alan Brien, the critic, visited him backstage, observing him emerge from the character:

> As we talked he held in his hand a cloth-faced wig-rest upon which someone had lightly pencilled some vague human features. Between sentences he removed his toupee, his eyebrows, and his moustache and transferred them to the dummy. Then he picked up a towel and wiped off the rest of his make-up. I forgot what he was talking about. But I stared in amazement at the man with the face as blank as a balloon who was holding in his hand an exact effigy of Alec Guinness as a Frenchman. (*Daily Mail*, 7 March 1958)

Guinness had now become something of an eminence: more than a star, less than a celebrity. Although only forty-two years old he was already the "father" of his company, and he had formed the regular habit of taking the cast out to dinner. Kenneth Williams and Billie Whitelaw played juveniles in *Hotel Paradiso*. Williams said they both were overawed by the Maison Restaurant in Glasgow: "Billie Whitelaw suddenly launched into an hysterically enthusiastic account of *Picture Post*: 'They have a fascinating article this week on this Dutch community in Staines . . . They've managed to preserve their own cultural traditions, even clothes! All the women wear Dutch caps' – hardly observing the full stop before adding hastily 'on their heads I mean'. Alec smiled unperturbed and mercifully ordered for us . . ." At another time Williams related how Guinness manoeuvred him upstage behind potted plants because he did not want the audience to notice he had left his flies undone. Guinness was the soul of generosity towards his understudy, at first omitting to thank him for taking his place for two performances, then sending a gracious note and a crate of whisky; then, on being informed whisky was not the understudy's drink, he changed the bottles to gin.

So, remarkably, Guinness was now a leader of his profession, an authority, a role model in the way few actors or actresses can or have ever become.

27

The dead of night

In the Spring Honours List of 1955 Guinness was made a Commander of the British Empire. In the summer he descended into the lowest circle of criminality in the film *The Ladykillers* at Ealing with Mackendrick again directing. This became Mackendrick's best film to date, and some say his best film ever, although he went on to Hollywood to make *Sweet Smell of Success* with Burt Lancaster as the venomous columnist J.J. Hunsecker, and Tony Curtis as the sleazy show-biz press agent Falco. *The Ladykillers* was Mackendrick's last film for Ealing and he directed it when Ealing had passed its prime, and was soon to be sold off to MGM, although still run by Balcon. His script-writer was William Rose, an American expatriate who told Mackendrick of a dream he had had one lunchtime when they were drinking in the Red Lion. Rose, from Missouri, had dreamt a whole film: "complete" and "original".

It was, as he told Mackendrick, about five criminals "who lived in a house with a little old lady and she found them out. They decided they had to kill her, but they couldn't and so they all killed each other". When Rose outlined the idea to Michael Balcon, Rose recalled Balcon watching him with those strange hooded eyes all during the telling, "never taking his eyes off me – just once in a while glanced at Sandy [Mackendrick] as if to say, 'Is it just he who has lost his mind, or have you both lost your minds?'"

Rose's "dream", as developed, at least partly borrowed from *The Amazing Dr Clitterhouse*, an earlier comedy-thriller play (in which Ralph Richardson had successfully starred in the West End for a record-breaking run), had the gangsters posing as a string quartet.*

---

* In the US film of *Clitterhouse* they were led by Humphrey Bogart and called the "Hudson River String Quartet" – the film also had a character called "The Professor", played by Edward G. Robinson.

Kemp, in his biography of Mackendrick, described how the crucial casting of *The Ladykillers* came about, the part of Professor Marcus being originally intended for Alastair Sim. But Balcon stepped in: "We're making money with the Guinness films, we're on a run of strength there. It's got to be Guinness."

Guinness read the script and told Mackendrick, "But dear boy, it's Alastair Sim you want, isn't it?" They assured him it wasn't. With Guinness they also cast Cecil Parker, Herbert Lom, Peter Sellers (who played the Teddy Boy plus the voices of Mrs Wilberforce's parrots), and Danny Green, an ex-boxer. As the old lady, again with much opposition, Mackendrick cast the seventy-seven-year-old Katie Johnson, who had played countless tiny roles of old ladies but never a big part in her whole life.

Mrs Wilberforce's innocence is absolute. The evil of the criminal gang wavers in squeamishness: as Rose explained to Mackendrick, "In the worst of men, there is that little touch of weakness which will destroy them." In fact, however, in Guinness's academic of dislocated mental genius, there was plenty to redeem the deformity. Mackendrick observed how Guinness worked on the character: "He has a strange habit of working from the outside in. In the early stages he's very much a putty-nosed character, working off gimmicks, funny voices and so on. But then he gets it down and discards the inessentials and finds the core of the character – even when he's dealing with a comic grotesque." The model for Professor Marcus had also a strange personal reflection, especially as that model had just written a book about Guinness.

Apparently the first idea Guinness had was to play Marcus as a cripple – with a dislocated hip which was, as Mackendrick says "quite gruesome but horrendously funny". This was discarded because the "boss" (Balcon) would never stand for it. Guinness sulked – "and went and looked out of the window. And while I was talking about the script he was snipping away with a pair of scissors, and he made some paper teeth which he stuck in, then turned around and grinned at me."

The portrait which now developed – "snaggling teeth, lank hair, trailing scarf, the cigarette between second and third fingers" – was, so Mackendrick said, "an absolute personal portrait of Kenneth Tynan", although Guinness naturally disclaimed any such intention. "I think I had in mind the wolf in Red Riding Hood. When I first saw myself in make-up I remember saying to Sandy, I look remarkably like an aged Ken Tynan; perhaps I'd better smoke cigarettes the way he does. But that was it. Nothing really deliberate."

Or, one might add, conscious. But, unconsciously, this was Tynan to the core. Exaggerated though it was, the role grew into a "gestalt" cartoon of the naked psyche of Tynan, perhaps in a kind of (completely unintentional) revenge on him for writing a book about him. In some way, albeit at a comic, slightly ridiculous or even ironic level, it had to be a reassertion of control, of power, over the critic. Here, anyway, was Guinness's own private biography of Tynan, and, curiously enough, it revealed something accurate about the brilliant although often misguided mind of the young critic, described by one of Tynan's friends:

> The eyes, the whites above the pupils, dart right into the farthest
> recesses of your psyche, the hollow cheeks crease into the shape
> of a stylised gargoyle, and more fangs than one had believed
> possible fight like maenads to jockey themselves to the front.

Buck-toothed and macabre as he is, Professor Marcus lives and makes us laugh because the portrait Guinness gave the audiences was rooted in reality and observation. The criminal mastermind was endowed with eccentricities both disconcerting and reassuring – kindness, intellectual scrupulousness, which are as much part of the comedy, as the terrifyingly enlarged teeth. To Elaine Dundy, Tynan's wife, there was absolutely no doubt that he was playing Ken. "They admired one another tremendously."

It was an affectionate, ironic and many-layered portrait of someone who was by now himself becoming something of a caricature – an immature, nightmarish person who was then at his peak but who was, as he always had been, operating at one remove from reality. This showed especially, for instance, when he would write a review of his old hero Orson Welles as Othello, calling him "Citizen Coon" and an amateur, the next inviting him to a party and expecting him not in any way to react in an unfriendly way to his review. Guinness was alert to the treachery of the brilliant mind and immortalised it in his depiction of Professor Marcus in a completely comic and harmless way. It was a portrait in which the spirit of G.K. Chesterton breathed beneath the surface: a diabolical visitation by a man who believed increasingly in the existence of the devil. He might even have quoted Chesterton: "St John the Evangelist saw many strange monsters in his vision, he saw no creature so wild as one of his own commentators."

The Ladykillers was filmed in North London in the vicinity of King's Cross Station: with its image of a decaying England, its genteel horror, its Dickensian scale of character – and indeed of good and evil – it mingled mirthfulness and icy macabre in such a way that it drew a wide following and became a commercial success. The American critics failed to register its subtleties – it was compared unfavourably to *The Court Jester* with Danny Kaye – yet it did well at the box-office.

Mackendrick subsequently left Ealing, the studios were sold off to the BBC and Balcon took his Ealing entourage with him to Boreham Wood under the wing of MGM. Balcon was now joined by Kenneth Tynan, who became Script Editor in spring 1956, to a studio which he described as a kind of "outsize Anderson shelter" in a corner of the Metro lot. Later he advised on two not very distinguished Guinness films, *Barnacle Bill* ("not a very good idea of T.E.B. Clarke, for whom work had to be found"), and *The Scapegoat*. When he himself left Ealing feeling highly disgruntled at what he had not been able to do, he complained of Ealing's reluctance to deal at all seriously with sex, social problems or politics. He also felt it had "made" no actors of any significance, except for Alec Guinness.

28

The incommunicable part

As a schoolboy Guinness had sung hymns with images of twilight or geography, Greenland's icy mountain – either melancholy or rumbustious. When he was confirmed in Holy Trinity Church, Eastbourne, by the Bishop of Lewes, he had realised with a flash of insight that he had never really believed in God.

At the beginning of the war, on one Sunday morning, he had got up to bicycle to church in the dark for Holy Communion; but again his enthusiasm for Anglo-Catholicism had declined. He had had "odd, almost mad, phases of near-psychic experience, too"; once, in his search for a meaning in life, he had sought enlightenment among the Buddhists. In 1945 he had spent a leave weekend in Rome and met the Pope: "I felt for the first time in my life I had seen a saint," he said.

However, it had only been as he neared forty that certain professional and personal threads were pushing him towards a more extraordinary outcome to that crisis of middle-age that most people experience. Already, playing Father Brown in France had provided him with that strange mystical experience when he was mistaken by a child for a real priest. Then his son, Matthew, now aged eleven, was struck down with polio, and paralysed from the waist down. Walking back from filming one day in Hammersmith, Guinness had dropped in to a Catholic Church and made, as he said, a negative bargain with God: if Matthew recovered he would never put an obstacle in his way should Matthew wish to become a Catholic.

Matthew did recover and they had then decided to send him to Beaumont School, near Windsor: at the age of fifteen Matthew did become a Catholic. In the meantime the conversion of his father proceeded slowly: in 1955, having by now played in the stage success of *The Prisoner*, Guinness visited a Trappist monastery where he took a retreat.

John Russell Taylor identified, none too sympathetically, a feature of his subject in *Alec Guinness: A Celebration* (1985):

> It is well-known that in virtually all his major roles, and indeed major successes, Guinness has got cold feet somewhere along the way, and begged and pleaded to be released from his contractual obligations. So much so that it became a ritual, not perhaps to be taken totally seriously, even by himself.

Taylor then went on, with possibly unjustified logic:

> Though he is an Aries, he should be a Virgo, since it has to be rape every time, with someone else taking final, formal responsibility.

"Rape every time" was surely an extreme charge. But Taylor was trying to say that Guinness's professional character seemed often like that of a victim. Was this true or false? Certainly there had been a sacrificial feeling about the last time he played Hamlet. It had seemed then as if he was offering himself up to be mauled, inviting the world to participate in tearing him apart and causing him pain. But this, of course, was likely to happen to anyone who took risks, and playing Hamlet was an extreme form of risk. Yet it had been his own decision, while he had already, to some extent, bought an insurance against failure in the success he had made in *The Cocktail Party*.

The failure of *Hamlet* resulted in his abandoning all kinds of high-flying theatrical projects involving figures as variously distinguished as Edwige Feuillère and Tallulah Bankhead. He renounced also the ambition of playing King Magnus in *The Apple Cart*, a role for which he lacked the necessary Shavian brazenness or panache.

Yet that failure germinated in him, finally, the seeds of religious conversion. If he was a victim, he was now ready to embrace the idea that the greatest and most important man of all was helpless in his moments of victory. The readiness was all. And at least, in this production of Hamlet, he had crossed himself the right way round.

There are many forms of conversion. Some of these, as described in William James's *Varieties of Religious Experience*, are sudden and dramatic, impulsive and compelling – the whole of one's future life is revealed in a flash and the path which is to be followed is illuminated. This had occasionally happened to Guinness, especially during these years of uncertainty when he had not yet fully committed himself: for example, in the middle of one afternoon he was walking up Kingsway "when an impulse compelled me to start running, with joy in my heart and in a state of almost sexual excitement". He ran until he came to the little Catholic church (St Anselm and St Cecilia) which he had never entered before. "I knelt, caught my breath, and for ten minutes was lost to the world."

It was typical of the man's ever watchful intellectual censor that he should have to justify this deranged – or so he called it – excessive zeal some few lines later, by saying that the eminent Jesuit Ronald Knox also had such extreme lapses and had found himself running on several occasions to visit the Blessed Sacrament.

Without invading, I hope, Guinness's private spiritual territory, I will attempt to explain how I understand his conversion. In *The Cocktail Party*, as in all of Eliot's plays, as well as implied if not stated in much of his poetry, a single moment of choice, as in the Either/Or philosophy of Kierkegaard, confronts the main character. Eliot's plays are true to life and coherent because, in spite of their restricted scope, they were based closely on Eliot's own experiences, and these experiences shaped themselves into a pattern on which Eliot continually drew, and repeated in many forms. Central to his experience – in fact the main formative experience of his adult life – was his own acceptance of Christianity. From the time he wrote "Gerontion" (1920) and *The Waste Land* (1922), until *Ash Wednesday* (1930), this gradual commitment – fluctuating sometimes, at other times seemingly barely attainable – provided the main inspiration, in the widest sense, of his existence. In *Ash Wednesday*, after passing through what mystics call the dark night of the soul, as well as after reflecting in other works that terrible, arid, post-first-war despair and nervous exhaustion of society, he celebrated his sense of recovery, his turning towards life.

There were already certain parallels between Eliot's "voices" and Guinness's faces – the man, described to his own annoyance, of a thousand faces. So, perhaps, just as Guinness, twenty years later, after a similar experience of war, could find no identity at the centre of himself, and therefore of his acting, so also had Eliot only found a society of displaced, homeless individuals whose spiritual desolation was only compensated for by their need for stimulus:

These . . .
Excite the membrane, when the sense has cooled,
With pungent sauces, multiply variety
In a wilderness of mirrors.

In picking on the right words for the situation, the poet may be said to be mapping the unknown, and of course Eliot's words on the poetic method, in *East Coker*, are too well-known to need quoting again. But actors also make and define, and therefore help or hinder people to control the world in which they live or, worse, encourage them to coarsen or destroy their culture. At the same time powerful actors, such as Olivier and Guinness, have had a huge influence on the world in which they have become the mirrors held up to nature.

To some extent all religion has at its centre – and before it can become real to the believer – an act of conversion or at least affirmation. Eliot's own entry into the Anglican church happened at roughly the same age and over the same span of years as did Guinness's and, therefore, we may view it possibly as a similar, emotion-maturing process as well as a firming up of intellectual conviction. If *The Waste Land* was, as Guinness said, the "last great poem Eliot wrote before he became a Christian", *Ash Wednesday* marked his acceptance of the will of God. If you listen to Guinness's inspired reading of this poem which was broadcast in March 1974 (or to his recording of the *Four Quartets*) you can understand a little how Guinness identified with the finality of the emotions in the sense he conveyed that he had renounced something, made up his mind so that he would never, from that time forth, go back on this decision. But there was more to it than that.

Eliot, although he became an Anglo-Catholic rather than a Roman Catholic, underwent, or had undergone, during the time of writing *Ash Wednesday*, a profound change in his literary method and aspiration. This was as an effect of his reading Dante's Divine Pageant at the end of the *Purgatorio*. The scene where Dante for the first time re-encounters Beatrice, wrote Eliot in his essay on Dante,

> belongs to the world of what I call the *high dream*, and the modern world seems capable only of the *low dream*. I arrived at accepting it, myself, only with some difficulty. There were at least two prejudices, one against pre-Raphaelite imagery which was natural to one of my generation, and perhaps affects generations younger than mine. The other prejudice . . . [was] that poetry not

only must be found *through* suffering but can find its material only *in* suffering. Everything else was cheerfulness, optimism, and hopefulness: and these words stood for a great deal of what one hated in the nineteenth century. It took me many years to recognise that the states of improvement and beatitude which Dante described are still further from what the world can conceive as cheerfulness, than are his states of damnation.

Eliot may have been writing of Dante, but he was perhaps talking also of himself. And it was not long before, having travelled a long way from *The Waste Land*, he could move on to celebration of the Christian martyr Becket in *Murder in the Cathedral*:

Destiny waits in the hand of God, shaping the still unshapen . . .

only
The fool, fixed in his folly may think
He can turn the wheel on which he turns . . .

Ambition comes when early force is spent
And when we find no longer all things possible.
Ambition comes behind and unobservable.
Sin grows with doing good . . .

In Guinness's case the "high dream" he could now begin to enjoy as a result of his conversion was his greater ease in making those public transformations, those leaps, into men of genius, those notable leaders and heroic figures, instead of the "little men you do so well", as Gielgud had described them. He could identify on a higher plane, at the same time have a strong enough sense of himself to which he could return. It is perhaps also important to make it clear that Guinness's conversion, similar to Eliot's, was not an emotional conversion. Both had, by the time of this crucial moment, their own processes of work very much under control. Eliot defined his own, in *Tradition and the Individual Talent*, as a "continual self-sacrifice, a continual extinction of personality". Both became, as Christian converts, essentially explorers in the world of inner experience, while still, of course, rooting their observation in the external world:

Those to whom nothing has ever happened
Cannot understand the unimportance of events.

Guinness secretly received instruction in 1955 and was confirmed privately by the Bishop of Portsmouth early in 1956. In the *News Chronicle* of 31 March 1956, under the somewhat disparaging headline of "Guinness turns Catholic", Guinness was quoted as saying, cagily, about playing Father Brown and the Cardinal, "My research work for the parts certainly made me go into the subject of Catholicism a bit more than I had before." The inference behind the defensive answer was plain: there was something rather dark and shameful about becoming a Catholic. Guinness's "excuse" was that of being an actor and so he could not help it. When he had confessed to his superior officer in the Navy he was an actor, "You automatically got the sneer." Catholics, like actors, were a bit beyond the pale, decidedly outside the mainstream.

When, in *Blessings in Disguise*, he came to write of other conversions and fellow Catholics it was of upper-class literary figures such as Evelyn Waugh and Edith Sitwell, rarely of his old Catholic housekeeper at St Peter's Square whom he cherished and generously supported in her old age and who maybe had, in her way, as strong an influence over him as the grand old roués of conversion such as Waugh and Sitwell.

Merula became a Catholic convert a few months later when he had started filming *The Bridge on the River Kwai* in Ceylon. It came as a complete surprise to him: "I had no idea she was receiving instruction. If I had known I would probably have opposed it, for fear she was doing it only to keep me happy."

What practical effect did Catholicism have on them? "Deep down, our faith has made a great difference to our lives", Guinness told the *Daily Mail* in 1959. "Merula takes some cripples out in the car once a week. And I don't swear as much as I used to." A year later he would muse (in the *Standard*) that Catholicism "seems such an eminently reasonable way of living; it is so sensible. The very opposite of the puritanical."

Guinness has always felt that the actor's affinity with priests — "unfrocked" priests, as he wrote in *Blessings in Disguise*, "because clearly they were not priests, nor had they a sacramental role to play, yet there was still something priest-like about them, a sense of evocation and a sense of ceremony". He believed that Olivier and Richardson both possessed these qualities, and now several priests came to be numbered among his personal friends, among them Father Philip Caraman, the Jesuit historian and translator who had been a friend and confessor of Evelyn Waugh, Graham Greene and Edith Sitwell. Although Father Caraman also became his confessor he considered himself unworthy of the company of such converts, and reflected later that it must be quite a burden to "carry" that lot in his mind. He found Father Caraman sweet-natured, very sophisticated, as well as extremely determined. He had been at Stonyhurst College with Peter Glenville, a tough upbringing by any standards; a deeply read man and a Latin scholar, Father Caraman published several books chronicling the lives of Catholics during the reign of Elizabeth I, and also notably *The Other Half*, a compelling documentary of social–religious history in that era of persecution.

Later, in Rome for the canonisation in 1970 of the forty English and Welsh martyrs, Father Caraman showed his determined spirit in an amusing way. It was his job to present Pope John Paul II with a pair of doves, but having done this he felt he would like to have them back and breed from them. But the Pope had also taken a fancy to the doves. Father Caraman won – after three days of negotiation and, it was rumoured, by expressing himself rather sharply in Vatican high quarters.

But many priests remained for Guinness essences, their influence absorbed through the words they had written. Chief among them was Teilhard de Chardin: "The incommunicable part of us is the pasture of God."

29

Terms of loyalty

On Sunday 22 December 1958 Noël Coward noted in his diary that he was now fifty-eight and that in the previous week Sam Spiegel gave him and the theatrical company he was touring with a private showing of *The Bridge on the River Kwai*: "Really satisfying. I rather wish now that I had done it."

But it was better he had not. Coward was a fine actor, but he was made for essentially vain and self-regarding parts. He was the perfect King Magnus, a self-portrait of Shaw. His ship's captain in Lean's *In Which We Serve* was moving because of the loyalty to his ship he portrayed. That he loved his wife, played by Celia Johnson, with sharp, delicate yet steely upper-class fragility, was a patent absurdity, for in her presence he exuded frigidity. And he would never have been able to suggest that quality of *agape*, or disinterested love, for his fellow men that was in Colonel Nicholson. With hindsight it is now almost inconceivable to us that the part of Nicholson should ever have been offered to, let alone played by, any other actor but Guinness, but this was so. The casting did suggest that Spiegel, the producer, and David Lean, the director, thought of the colonel as essentially an obsessive, one in which eccentricity and the mad sense of duty element finally won over the extreme brutality and stupidity of the Japanese captors. Before Noël Coward they had offered the role to Charles Laughton, who was too unfit to be underwritten by the insurers (and also too plump). But the first choice had been Olivier: "Why should I go to Ceylon to play a martinet when I can stay at home and act [in *The Prince and the Showgirl*] with Marilyn Monroe?"

Kwai took a long time to make: shooting ran from October 1956 to May 1957. The bridge itself, 425 feet long and 90 feet high, consumed 1500 large trees, cost a quarter of a million dollars, and took five months to build. Certainly Nicholson was never

Guinness's favourite part. He told Godfrey Winn in 1970: "I refused the part three times." Spiegel took him out to dinner. Guinness told him he was wasting his time, but "At the end of it, I was asking him, 'what kind of wig will I be wearing?'"

Lean inadvisedly told Guinness that he wanted him to play a character who, if he sat next to him at dinner, he would find a complete bore. "You're asking me to play a bore?" Guinness riposted tetchily. Later Guinness remarked that Lean was "hoping that Charles Laughton was going to play it" and that, "far from liking his own performance he was over the moon about William Holden," who was cast as the American guerilla detailed to blow up the bridge. Holden secured a much better contract than Guinness did, a fee of £300,000 and 10% of gross receipts.

Lean and Guinness had their greatest clash during the making of *Kwai*. Lean had already taught Guinness a great deal about films. Guinness himself, as he said, had earlier been "like putty in his hands ... He had a brilliant eye for visual detail ... I'm very *neat* as an actor. I do things rather precisely ... David was very keen on actors being able to do things *identically* from take to take. If you aren't careful, the spirit can go out of your performance."

The trouble undoubtedly stemmed from the degree of control both men wanted over Guinnesss's performance. Lean wanted control for what he called "the will of the film". Guinness wanted creative flexibility and space – and scope to behave spontaneously. Lean's intention was to show that the military ethos on both sides, the Japanese and the British, was equally mad. What he wanted was a humourless performance. Nicholson was a nut and Guinness had to play him as a straight nut. This was, in fact, a rather coarsening departure from the subtle and universal theme of Pierre Boulle's novel, namely that both commanders are intent on "saving face".*

But not only was Guinness inevitably bound to invest the part with some of his subversive humour, but instinctively he shied away from intensity. The most obvious screaming neurotic in the world was more than likely to end up, as played by Guinness, as underlyingly sane and reasonable. Guinness almost took a delight in avoiding the obvious and in circumventing expectations. But Nicholson was real, filled out with observation of himself: that he had been only fourth choice for the role was perhaps a sad

* So was the blowing up of the bridge. Said Boulle, "For three years I fought them over this change. In the end I gave up."

indicator of the muddled perception of Lean and Spiegel. At times during *Kwai* Guinness so failed to do what Lean asked of him that Lean felt his film was being undermined. On one occasion Spiegel found him beside himself with frustration. This was the moment – subsequently perhaps viewable as the most affectingly ironic in the whole film – when the bridge is complete and about to be blown up. Nicholson reflects on his twenty-eight years' service: "I don't suppose I've been at home more than ten months . . . I wouldn't have had it any other way." But there are "times when you are nearer the end than the beginning". Guinness played this obliquely, away from camera: "It was pretty good torture for me. David wanted me to finish this long speech just as the sun tipped the tops of the trees on the horizon down the river." They spent five consecutive sunsets getting it timed to the exact second. Guinness complained it was "like doing it backwards". And, "I never got a word of thanks." Nicholson then inadvertently drops his officer's baton in the river.

Spiegel said that Guinness so refused to do what Lean asked of him that Lean "literally shed tears". In fact it was the undermining comedy of dropping the stick that fleshed out the unbuttoning moment. Spiegel acted for an hour as go-between to settle Guinness's and Lean's differences. "I couldn't totally believe in the man," said Guinness later. "I knew it was a good part, I knew the naval equivalents, a bit thick between the ears, a bit blunted . . . I wanted a bit more send-up and humour." Lean later went on record as saying that "Alec is one of the most fantastically knotted up men I know." But this would seem to have been true of himself. Guinness knew that, although he cut down the humour, ultimately Nicholson needed to awaken the sympathies of the audience, tilt them strongly towards himself and traditional British grit and obstinacy. His blinkered and humourless humour was merely the background "humour"; his not allowing his officers to work on the construction of the bridge alongside their men was narrowly upholding the letter of international law but had a wider significance. That the whole centre of dramatic effect should revolve around whether or not officers did manual labour seems unthinkable today. But in his portrayal of Nicholson's refusal to be broken, Guinness suggested limitless inner strength and broadened the conflict to make it universal. What he was also to show in his portrait of Nicholson was humility, for, in the words of his favourite poet,

> The only wisdom we can hope to acquire
> Is the wisdom of humility: humility is endless.

Sometimes his slightly shifty eyes clouded with unspoken emotion; sometimes, after devastated hope, a smiling pride seemed to break through pain. Guinness has revealed how he based the half-blind, staggering glide of victory with which Nicholson crosses the parade ground, after his humiliating punishment in the suffocating tin kennel, on the way Matthew, his son, attacked by poliomyelitis, used to walk. He also generously conceded that it was at this moment Lean's "strength of imagination" which lifted him up to the exaggeration necessary: "It's in rather a different scale, a larger scale than mine . . . I thought I'd gone over the top." Lean took him behind the camera. "What sweep it had: I could see how extravagant I could be."

Elsewhere mastery of expressing hidden feeling irradiated the flat, officer-code dialogue: to lines such as "You're a fine doctor, Clipton, but you've a lot to learn about the army," Guinness brought a dimension to Nicholson's whole existence. The Colonel grows out of being an inflexible British officer intent on saving face into the representative of order versus chaos, civilisation versus barbarism, echoing Shakespeare's

> Take but degree away, untune that string,
> And, hark! what discord follows —

although Guinness's performance, remaining within the narrow limits of Nicholson's mind and physique, remained the very opposite of Shakespearean. It seemed that Guinness may well have deliberately kept or needed the temperature kept high during the filming of *Kwai* to draw on some extraordinary, unearthly power. He and Lean were both upset and parted without saying goodbye to each other. He had never been happy during the making of the film and after it he was exhausted for several months. But with it Guinness achieved the status of an international film star. He won an Oscar for *The Bridge on the River Kwai* as the best film actor of 1957.* The film itself won seven Oscars. Fifty million Americans saw it and it grossed $20 million. Later it was reckoned that it was seen by more people throughout the world on television

---

* Charles Laughton later generously commented that he never understood Nicholson when he read the script, but did so when he saw Guinness play him. Olivier would probably not have captured as well as Guinness that sense of loyalty arrived at through suffering with his men.

than any other film ever made. *Time* magazine devoted its cover and six pages of text to singing Guinness's praises. "One of the most expert living masters of his craft," said the article, "he ranks with Olivier, Gielgud and Richardson as the big four of English acting, and he is recognised as the most gifted character actor of the English-speaking theatre". This echoed Ivor Brown, the theatre critic who, in 1954, in his book *The Way of My World*, wrote,

> All that can be said of the most eminent is that they have their particular excellence, Sir Laurence Olivier his persuasion of voice and rich poetic quality, and Sir Ralph Richardson his truth of common humanity in its humours and bewilderments, while Alec Guinness ranges over the multifarious oddity of mankind and drily etches the ludicrous and drives into the heart of the pathetic.

Time also compared Guinness to Chaplin – an actor whom Guinness did not like. Guinness had made seventeen films, some of them, according to him, "pretty lousy" partly due to having "contracts to fulfil". He regretted not being his own master: "It's a great mistake, the frightened thing of seeking security." He especially disliked that element of having no final control over his own performance – and often seeing something that he had been relying on disappear, so that he would have conceived the whole thing differently had he known.

Achieving a celebrity status did not make him exult, or feel triumphant. But it did allow him for the first time to reveal publicly what he had carefully guarded as a personal secret:

> His absence of identity is an official fact; no record of his birth exists. Last week Alec cautiously made a statement on the subject to a *Time* correspondent: "My father generated me in his 64th year. He was a bank director. Quite wealthy. His name was Andrew. My mother's name was Agnes. He was a handsome old man, white-haired. A Scotsman. I saw him only four or five times. I was taught to call him uncle, but I suppose I always knew he was my father.

It was of course a factual error on the part of *Time* to say "no record of his birth exists".

Was this revelation of Guinness's illegitimate birth the solution to what *Time* quoted an actor saying about Guinness, namely "the best-kept secret of modern times, a sort of one-man Tibet"? The article was undoubtedly true in its assertion that Guinness's "essential gift is not for creating characters, but existences". But what other secret, if any, lay behind the giving up of this secret?

The secret behind that secret was that Guinness had now become a Roman Catholic, and yet, paradoxically, it was not a secret because it was well-known. Yet all the time when writing about Guinness we have to confront this paradox that we know about him, yet at the same time he has the capacity to wipe the slate clean, to eradicate all former traces of himself in each new role he creates so that he returns to some primitive state of being unknown. The master of the blank canvas had given way to acknowledge the greater master of the blank canvas.

Just before and from the time of his conversion Guinness's acting had been growing in the direction of a fuller inner life, moving beyond the creation of character to that creation of existences. But, as if harking back to the golden age, the state of man before the Fall, he still had a nostalgic desire to return to playing Abel Drugger in *The Alchemist*, at one time entertaining the dream of making a film out of it. He was inclined to be dogmatic about acting, he told a friend, while he could never quite sort out what he felt about it. His dogma changed with lightning rapidity and now and then he comforted himself by thinking perhaps he could remain fluid and that in middle age his experience of life had crystallised and given him definition. Actors *had* to grow up as people. He was still remarkably faithful – and so would remain – to Hamlet's philosophy that the readiness was all, but to that readiness or desire for balance had now been added, perhaps as the effect of his conversion, a sense of sin, a sense that most people had what he called a "list". This was why he was not at heart a method actor, because deep down he felt he could not put himself at the centre of his acting; reduce, that is, everything to himself. He had to go out to other people. Above all, he had to show imaginative sympathy with the character he was playing. He envied young actors their relaxation and assurance, and he wished he had had this quality twenty years before instead of his shy, inhibited, and above all frightened and over-careful "niggly" self.

These thoughts were formulated to Peter Copley, with whom he had long been friends, just after he won the Oscar for Colonel Nicholson. The inner man was very different from what the world now celebrated as a success. He was fond of quoting G.K. Chesterton; never more did he need, in the flowering of what others would call worldly success, to hold on to the famous dictum of Chesterton's that "the Church is the one thing that saves a man from the degrading servitude of being a child of his own time". Yet what had Hamlet called the actors to Polonius, but "the abstract and brief chronicles of the time"? Here was the dilemma that the life he led constantly presented to Guinness. "After your death you were better have a bad epitaph than their ill report while you live," Hamlet went on. How could you avoid "degrading servitude" if you chose to be an "abstract and brief chronicle of the time"? It was Shakespeare's problem, as well as Guinness's and, like the actor, Shakespeare had continually to play Russian roulette with his soul.

Some years earlier, when Peggy Ashcroft, an actress of Guinness's stature and intelligence, had been playing Hedda Gabler, Guinness had been to see the performance at the Lyric Theatre, Hammersmith. He had experienced a fascinating insight into her acting of the role, especially as various people had told him Peggy could never play Hedda.

> They thought she would emotionalise it. In fact, she was wonderful. But usually after a performance she is drained of vitality and everything has gone. She will try and disguise it but if you asked her out to supper, she would say No or maybe finally Yes.

After this performance he did not suggest a meal, but was astonished to find her "as bright as a button":

> I congratulated her and said "It's very unlike you to be so up at the end of a performance." She said "Oh, it's wonderful. It's such a relief because there is absolutely nothing in Hedda at all,

there is no feeling. She's a woman of no feelings, everything is calculated. It makes no demands on me at all. I come on, I say the lines, I do what I think is the right thing and I feel years younger doing it." What particularly came over in Peggy's performance was Hedda's callousness and indifference: I always remember the comedy of the incident over the aunt's hat where she deliberately makes rude remarks about it. It was superbly done but so unlike Peg.

So unlike Peg in real life, he meant. But his own acting had moved in a completely different direction, away from characters who were caught in the search for the truth about themselves. As far as the present writer can ascertain he never once, in sixty years of acting, played a character of Ibsen, which is why this appreciation by him of Ashcroft's explicitness, as reported by Michael Billington in *Peggy Ashcroft, 1907–1991*, becomes so gripping. In his creation of existences rather than characters – and all the emotional investment and sympathy this involved – he would increasingly take more trouble to realise, then hide carefully more than reveal, what the personage he was playing feels. He was formulating a complex grammar of indirect discourse to master the invisible gesture and the unspoken word. These might seem to be the reverse of heroic or romantic acting qualities, such as Gielgud practised, but they were not. He had found, with time, the ability to interiorise all Gielgud's gesture and showiness, scale it down, make it show in the face's hidden yet manageable musculature, hint at it, shadow it into inferences of mind. The influence of Gielgud had therefore remained the strongest of all, but Gielgud had now been turned into Guinness.

There was now another element in his acting, which he disparaged, but which was now inevitably there. His Catholicism. But, of course, just as Graham Greene had said of himself as a writer, Guiness was not a Catholic actor, but an actor who happened to be a Catholic. Catholic writers and actors were not in the English tradition (as they were in France). Cyril Cusack, much admired by Guinness and himself an Irish Catholic, explained the function of Catholicism in Guinness's acting: "Somewhere amid the elaborate Guinness scenery lurks a spiritual watchman, somewhere a brand of Catholicism that was to flare through the portals of the Farm Street church". It had been there in his Hamlet, noted by Tynan as "a touch of the headsman, judicious and inexorable". The powerful presence, to be switched on and off at will. The ability, perhaps, to keep separate life from art.

In the New Year Honours list of 1959 Guinness, now in his forty-fifth year, only a few months short of completing twenty-five years as an actor, received a knighthood. Almost immediately afterwards he became nicknamed "The Knight from Nowhere". Even about the timing of this recognition there was a meticulousness, a precision which Guinness could not wholly shrug off modestly with his long account of how he quelled an anti-British riot in Mexico City when sent there by the Foreign Office to restore British prestige at an international festival. It was, although sincerely meant, one of his poorer efforts at modesty. There was no need to deflate the achievement by an enjoyable piece of make-believe.

PART FOUR

Sunlight on a Broken Column

Virtue is free, and as a man honours or dishonours her he will have more or less of her.

Plato

Who wants to embrace the daughter of the sun will never see light again.

Sartre, after Euripides

Flamboyance doesn't suit me. I enjoy being elusive.

Alec Guinness

30

Whisky for those that don't

You cannot really believe that the 1960s belonged to Guinness, but they certainly could be said to belong to his *Ladykiller* doppelgänger Tynan. They began with Christine Keeler and the shaming of the Macmillan old guard, the dissolution of the establishment, or at least that particular establishment, in an acid of satire and scandal.

Not only Kenneth Peacock Tynan was part of this new critical and satirical wave: but William Donaldson, impresario of *Beyond the Fringe*; Jonathan Miller, a director with whom Guinness was never to work and yet they both had Alan Bennett in close friendship; David Frost, Peter Cook, and many directors and producers. Sons of doctors, clergymen, professional soldiers, civil servants, these extremely clever – and indeed generally very attractive and presentable – pedlars of a new age were fiercely anti-traditionalist. Many were reacting against their well-established comfortable backgrounds, the security of their parental homes and incomes, and, in many cases, their absent, hard-working fathers. Not one of them had a quarter of the insecurity in his background that Guinness had had.

It did not seem to matter that English society as a whole and certainly many well-established institutions had long tolerated discreet sexual deviation so long as it kept a decent, low profile. This tolerance still had its outer bounds or limits defended by a law objectionable to many.

Tynan demonstrated against the prosecution of his close friend Peter Wildeblood who, with Lord Montagu of Beaulieu, was arrested and convicted of homosexual offences. The Wolfenden Report, publish in 1957, was still in the air. Aids had not yet been heard of. It was a glorious dawn of sexual permissiveness. Tynan uttered his four-letter word on television and conducted correspondence with Lord Annan and the Archbishop of Canterbury on the display of the sexual organs in public. He would have liked to have seen the carnal act itself take place on stage. Germaine Greer used four-letter words in a National Theatre programme. *Spring Awakening* was followed by *Soldiers*, and finally by *Oh Calcutta!* and *Carte Blanche*. Censorship was rolled back on all fronts: bare backsides, aleotic penises and *le triangle frisé*, were the London rage.

Guinness was all rather to one side of this fashion. His world of conversion, his visits to Rome, his withdrawal to a Trappist monastery, his quiet, persuasive love of Latin litany, did, from one viewpoint, seem rather remote. On 15 January 1960 he told the *Evening Standard* he had just turned down half a million dollars to play Christ in a film, saying he would not do it for a million. His bank balance was nine hundred pounds (although he had just paid twenty-five thousand pounds' income tax).

It's true he had played Gulley Jimson in Joyce Cary's *The Horse's Mouth*, the film he himself wrote and organised in 1958 on Merula's suggestion – he had overcome his early dislike of the book. This had been directed by his friend Ronald Neame. But the artist – hero of Joyce Cary's somewhat mannered prose – was essentially backward-looking, to the world of the Ealing Films except that, in the case of *The Horse's Mouth*, it was not the nondescript clerk or salesman, or even the modest inventor who was the creator of subversive anarchy, but the artist himself, Gulley Jimson. This is perhaps what gives the film its somewhat monotonous air today; authority is weak, while the "creative spirit" has firmly moved downmarket. Ealing presupposed a world where the boss who, however much he might be sent up, had real authority. Yet the film was a work of integrity: close to the novel its strengths and faults emerged as being almost the same, and much dialogue remained unchanged.

But it was above all the comic obstreperousness of the part which failed to catch fire, for the anarchy of Gulley's mind was perhaps more appealing on the page than was the physical expression of his ego in the film. Seeing his models made flesh did not really work either. It has to be said too that Guinness as Jimson was not wholly convincing: but as character impersonation, with white hair, unshaven stubble, gravelly, it remains impressive work: "Merry, rowdy, droll in one of the most exciting and searching character portraits to be found on the contemporary screen," said the *New York Herald Tribune*.

Guinness's other film made at this time, also directed by Ronald Neame, was *Tunes of Glory*, based on James Kennaway's novel, in which Guinness captured the nature of an unreflective egotist with superb self-assurance. The Acting Commanding Officer "Jock" Sinclair, he claimed on at least one occasion, was his favourite film role, and "perhaps the best thing I've done". Cast against type – Sinclair's disciplinarian replacement, played by John Mills, was the role Guinness had first been approached to play – Guinness rose magnificently to the task of crushing this stickler for form in a conflict which was again, like in *A Bridge on the River Kwai*, a conflict between two sets of military virtue.

The duel is to the death, and Sinclair wins. "Whisky for the gentlemen who like it – and for those that don't, whisky" . . . sums up his easy-going, paternalistic attitude to the battalion. It was, as Guinness said, madness to cast him as a drunken, heavy, boorish Glaswegian up from the ranks; but, "for all my reticence, now and then I like to take a big breath, and semi-explode." Note the "semi-". But the passion scenes with Kay Walsh as the Colonel's pet were not very sexy.

Of Guinness's profane, rabble-rousing appeal, there is no doubt, and the delight with which he got his teeth round phrases such as "a piece of cherry-cake", as he fired off scorn at his Eton and Oxford butt, makes the film of *Look Back in Anger* seem, by comparison, arch and dated. My own favourite moment comes when Sinclair notices how one of his junior officers in the mess is inept at smoking a cigarette: "Go on, laddie, smoke it, smoke it!" exhorts Sinclair, "Draw it in like a man."

The film of *Tunes of Glory* was almost not made at all: it was turned down by every major company. During the shooting, again with that absolute need to restore balance in his mind so that Jock Sinclair did not tip him over too far into coarseness and self-gratification, Guinness, after filming, would talk far into the night of his Catholic faith to John and Mary Mills. This became so affecting that, according to Mills, "Mary and I were within an inch of becoming Roman Catholics". If a young Jesuit priest who had spent ten years in the Gobi desert had not many years before "flung himself at Mary (Mills' wife was seventeen at the time) and bitten her lip, we would, with Alec's enthusiasm, have embraced the faith".

Tunes of Glory remains a superbly watchable film, but at that time (1960) the Cuba missile confrontation, pacifism, and the anti-Vietnam war movement were soon to loom. The heroes of the hour were Castro and Che Guevera. So was Chariman Mao, and his "Thoughts". Old-fashioned British military virtues were being swept away in what Macmillan had called "the wind of change". But such a wind was not yet affecting Guinness, whose next major theatrical venture centred around another, although less conventional form of military hero, but who was, unlike Jock Sinclair, also a scholar and a literary genius — Lawrence of Arabia.

At first *Ross* did not seem a promising venture. Terence Rattigan had just written his love story *Variation on a Theme* which had been critically ill-recieved, although it had, like the fringe satirists, the intention of "blowing up" the establishment. The reason for this play's failure, according to B.A. Young, Rattigan's biographer, was that "Terry had written with his heart rather than his head . . . He could not write convincingly about love between a man and a woman, because this was something he had never known at first hand." Shelagh Delaney had seen *Variation* on tour and wrote *A Taste of Honey* in a few days because she reckoned she could do something better.

"A human personality is many-sided," Guinness once said, so that one has to be "sufficiently balanced to know which side to bring out in a given situation — when to be reckless, and when to be cautious, when to be critical and when to be understanding, when to stand firm for one's rights and when to give way a little."

Rattigan's Lawrence was a complex, many-sided character, who had begun life in a film script, which, when the money was withdrawn from the film (in which Dirk Bogarde was to play Lawrence), Rattigan promptly salvaged and simplified. In his play he concentrated on a "dramatic portrait" rather than on the events of Lawrence's life: as he had worked immensely hard on the film narrative, perhaps the figure of Lawrence which emerged was not entirely clear and determinate. The dramatic centre of the play is Lawrence's torture when captured by the Turks: although it is understated in Rattigan's treatment, it is clear that off-stage Lawrence is subjected to homosexual rape and Rattigan's implication is that Lawrence found in this a secret pleasure.

Strictly speaking this seems not to have been true, for Herbert Wilcox, the film producer, recounts in *2001 Sunsets* that when the five-foot-three-inch Lawrence himself brought to him his book

The Seven Pillars of Wisdom, wanting to make a silent film of it, he described the homosexual advances of a Turkish chief, and "how in desperation once he fought him off with what he called a 'knee-kick', which resulted in the chief being uninterested in homo or any other form of sexual activity for a week or so, and the author being scourged and tortured for his attack". But of course there was no reason why Rattigan should not create his own version of what happened to Lawrence, or of what Lawrence felt, than Shakespeare had his view of Richard III.*

Guinness studied the role with immense care. Auden and Isherwood had based Michael Ransom, their hero in *The Ascent of F6* on Lawrence of Arabia whom Guinness at that time, twenty-one years before, was able to impersonate easily "by chucking a towel over my heard and twisting a tie into a sort of burnous". He still felt Lawrence was a fascinating enigma. He went to see Sydney Cockerell in Kew, who was now bedridden in his ninety-third year. Cockerell told him that Lawrence was a "terrible fibber" and when asked why he bothered to lie, replied "because my lies are more interesting than the truth". Other friends of Lawrence to whom Guinness talked, such as Siegfried Sassoon, Robert Graves and David Garnett, gave Guinness highly coloured views, tainted, Guinness thought, by their jealousy over his friendship: "like schoolboys who had a slight crush on the captain of the cricket team". He walked like a duck, someone else told Guinness, toes turned out, arms stiff at his side, straight down the middle of the road in the dusk. Guinness found this useful. But later, when taxed with sharing an intense privacy with Lawrence, he said he did not feel a great affinity with him: "I don't think I had a great deal of personal sympathy."

The exact power of Guinness's impersonation amazed critics and public alike. Herbert Wilcox, who had bought the film rights of *Ross*, saw it eighteen times and "never once lost the illusion that I was seeing and hearing Lawrence himself". Franco Zeffirelli was "overwhelmed". It was, he said, "wonderful, fantastic, one of the greatest emotional experiences I have ever had in the theatre. I went three times." Donald Wolfit, the great romantic actor-manager, was more circumspect. He wrote to Ronald Harwood, his dresser and later biographer:

---

* Shakespeare based himself firmly on the best historians of his age, including Sir Thomas More, not knowing or disregarding their political bias.

I set myself to do a theatre round. 2.30 "Ross" at the Haymarket where I saw some of the worst settings (by Motley) and some of the worst acting I have ever seen at the Haymarket. Dear oh dear – but Guinness redeemed all as I told him afterwards – it's a film scenario of a play, four good scenes. But the climax was buggery, you know.

An occasional night Guinness liked to "break out" – to redress the balance. He straddle-walked across the stage after the famous understated scene in the black-out giving an extreme impersonation of someone who had just been so violated. One can well believe that, if not actually on his face, then somewhere inside him was a grin.

Noël Coward's response to this masterpiece of acting was sour. Guinness looked very like Lawrence, he wrote in his diary, and played it well enough, but there was something lacking: "He has a certain dullness about him and his big moment seemed contrived. He also wore a blond 'piece' which was too bright and remained blandly intact after he had been beaten up and buggered by twelve Turks."

Ross opened on 12 May 1960 and the run lasted for 762 performances, although Michael Bryant took over after the six months that Guinness would only ever commit himself to. During the run Guinness again visited the bedridden Cockerell in Kew. On 2 June Cockerell wrote in his diary that Guinness came at noon and stayed an hour. "He was absolutely charming, as he always is. He brought a mass of beautiful roses and kissed the top of my head when he said goodbye." Cockerell gave him his old Arab cloak in which he was shipwrecked in the Gulf of Suez in 1900 and which he had once lent to Lawrence. Later Wilfrid Blunt, seeing the huge bunch of pink roses, asked jokingly if they had come from the Pope. Cockerell gave him a second guess, but Blunt could not find the right answer, so Cockerell told him.

The period from six to ten weeks was the time Guinness felt most happy during any play's run, "when I am at my least awful". Guinness did not play Lawrence in New York eighteen months later, when it opened at the Eugene O'Neill theatre, but John Mills did. In June 1960 the normally reticent Guinness revealed to the English press that, two years before, he had turned down an offer of £500,000 from a brewery company in America to introduce thirty-nine of their half-hour shows. Guinness told the *Daily Telegraph*, which described him as "the one star of the British screen who can be guaranteed to bring in the audiences in any part of the world", that he would have despised himself for accepting, and referred to his working in his youth, and against his will, as a copywriter in an advertising agency. He said he would "rather die in the gutter than go back to advertising".

In fact he had just appeared in the five hundredth edition of the BBC Radio feature, *Desert Island Discs*, during which he recalled he had played Macbeth at Sheffield when he was twenty-five, and would like to play it a second time. He pulled a cheque from his pocket and said, "Thirty guineas, not bad."

31

Unyoked humours

Guinness rarely showed any political passion. An exception to this was when on 12 January 1960 he saw the front page of the *Guardian* filled with a cartoon by Low. This depicted a spectral figure by a blackboard, against a cemetery of endless crosses, instructing a crowd of youngsters. "Alas! a New Generation", ran the caption.

There had been an outbreak of anti-Semitism and Nazi-like slogans which the government had done little to counter, and Guinness felt that Low's cartoon should be made into a large poster and placed on hoardings throughout the country, "which has always boasted of racial evil, 'it couldn't happen here'." He wrote vehemently to the editor that Low's cartoon should be seen daily by a larger public than the *Guardian* normally reached.

This apart – and recovering from a ten-day sojourn in a private London nursing home for the removal of varicose veins – Guinness for a short while seemed in the way his career was pointing him to be taking on a distinctly international flavour. On the eve of the most frightening confrontation between East and West since the war, Grigori Kozintsev, the outstanding Russian film director who some five or so years later was to become known through a resounding four-part *War and Peace*, mentioned him specifically with regard to making a joint Soviet-British film, "providing a common subject of interest for the Russian and British public could be found". It is interesting to speculate what such a common subject of interest at the time might have been.

Not very much later Henri-Georges Clouzot, the French film director, announced that he had agreed to make his first English-language film. Clouzot had made *Le Salaire de la peur* (*The Wages of Fear*), his supreme study of fear, and, more recently, the macabre *Les Diaboliques* in which Simone Signoret had acted. The principal

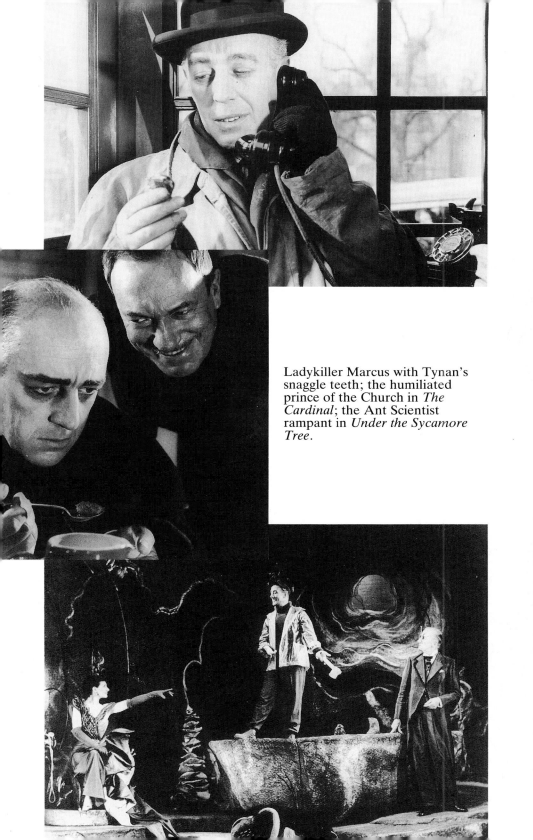

Ladykiller Marcus with Tynan's snaggle teeth; the humiliated prince of the Church in *The Cardinal*; the Ant Scientist rampant in *Under the Sycamore Tree*.

Colonels and seafarers: Nicholson with bloodied upper lip (Sessue Hayakawa as Saito) in *The Bridge on the River Kwai*; "Jock" Sinclair in a highland fling in *Tunes of Glory*; William Horatio Ambrose (*Barnacle Bill*).

Priest and transvestite:
Guinness as Chesterton's
Father Brown and as Mrs
Artminster in Simon
Gray's *Wise Child*.

Father of the Fatherland *Hitler – The Last Ten Days*; father of Amy Dorrit (Sarah Pickering) in *Little Dorrit*.

player was to be Guinness, and his part that of a painter living in Paris after the Second World War: *The Horse's Mouth* had clearly impressed the French, and they were arranging settings of a Modigliani studio, a Parisian police station, an art gallery, and a cheap Montmartre night club. Again, one cannot help speculating what the character Guinness was going to be called on to play, would be like: Gulley Jimson crossed with Father Brown crossed with Poirot crossed with Professor Marcus? It all sounded most unlikely. But shooting was scheduled for the spring of 1962, "after Sir Alec had completed two other films".

These two other films were, *HMS Defiant*, in which he played another naval captain, and *A Majority of One*, a frivolous Broadway success which was transferred to the screen with Guinness as Koichi Asano, a Japanese diplomat who has a holiday fling with a Brooklynese Jewish widow (Tom Conti as the Greek in *Shirley Valentine* is the 1990s equivalent). Guinness was paid £70,000 for this film, which received appalling notices, but it did not stem the offers to him of more parts of 'the Great Inscrutables', which now became something of a flood. Gandhi headed this list, for David Lean was hard at work setting up this project as a suitable follow-on to *The Bridge on the River Kwai* and, as with *Oliver Twist*, he undertook the most exhaustive preliminary work to make sure his casting was exact.* Guinness had only recently completed playing in *The Scapegoat* both a lonely English schoolmaster called John Barrett and Jacques de Gue whom he meets and who is his double, but – appearance apart – selfish, immoral, a French aristocrat of romantic fiction. Burdened by the impossibility of the life he is leading, de Gue ensozzles his English counterpart and runs off in his skin.

Daphne du Maurier had seen Guinness as The Cardinal in *The Prisoner* and sent him the manuscript of *The Scapegoat*. He liked it. When they met she found him very compatible: he seemed to suffer from the same shyness as she suffered. Du Maurier became the film's co-producer with Guinness, and she overturned the wish of MGM to have Cary Grant in the main double role. Guinness chose Bette Davis to play de Gue's mother, but they did not seem to click. She was his opposite. "My price for putting my name on that marquee is £200,000 and 10% of the gross. They're seeing

---

* Guinness had already turned down the opportunity to play Gandhi, telling the director Gabriel Pascal, "I think it should be played by an Indian."

thirty-seven years of sweat." The film was shot at the château of Semur-en-Vallon, but the director, Robert Hamer, was continually drunk. As Gore Vidal, who with Hamer adapted the novel for the screen, said, "I think Alec was flattered until [Daphne] began her monologues to all of us on Alec as the reincarnation of Gerald du Maurier" (her father). Because of Hamer's problem – ("gone back on the booze which I, out of loyalty to him, told no-one") Guinness had been handling most of the direction. Now he listened to her carefully. Vidal said,

> Poor Alec, in her presence, became very still and soothing, like an analyst with a potentially dangerous patient.

Guinness commented later, "I was fond of her and after the film we used to meet from time to time for a meal. But I don't think I ever felt I knew her well."

The Scapegoat fared no better with the critics than Graham Greene's *Our Man in Havana*, which Noël Coward, who also starred in the film with Guinness, said was a good script, directed by Carol Reed. The Guinnesses visited Firefly, Jamaica, to stay with Coward before filming began. In Havana Coward stayed with the Guinnesses in the Miami-American. It was just a few weeks after Castro had wrested the city from the control of the corrupt Batista. People were being rounded up and interrogated. On his way to the gents' lavatory in the Miami-American Guinness jolted a fat man who was loading his revolver, whose bullets then spilled on the floor and rolled off towards the *pissoir*. English supporters of Castro were also in Havana. Kenneth Tynan,* whom Guinness met in his hotel bar, suggested to Guinness he might like to join him at the Fort that night at 1a.m. when Castro's men were due to shoot a pair of sixteen year-olds. "A boy and a girl. I thought you might like to see it. One should see everything if one's an actor." Had Guinness gone along, perhaps his participation would have ended up being recorded in a piece that Tynan was writing. Guinness's instinctive refusal was wise although Tynan's widow later said that Guinness misrepresented Tynan when implying, in *Blessings in Disguise*, an unhealthy voyeurism in Tynan's attendance at the execution.

---

* His most recent contact with Tynan had been his participation in the *Observer* playwriting competition which the critic had organised for his paper in 1957 and 1958. Guinness and his fellow judges had awarded the prize to Errol John's *Moon on a Rainbow Shawl* which had then flopped in a lacklustre production by Frith Banbury.

They walked the streets, surrounded by thousands of "bewildered Cubans and surrounded, for protection only, by hirsute armed policemen". Merula went to have her hair done: "I was the only woman client. All the other chairs were occupied by Castro's boys, with their guns slung over their shoulders. They all had their beards in curlers. The girls serving these heroes were in ecstasies. But Alec and I could not fail to see the tumbrils going by."

One day they were hustled, together with Graham Greene, into a car to be driven off to a remote hideaway to meet Castro, but after ninety minutes of waiting for him he did not turn up. Guinness, on another occasion, did meet Castro: he was sitting in a small café drinking black coffee when Castro unexpectedly passed through this old *quartier* of Havana. Guinness was taken outside into a square to meet him, where he found him entirely surrounded by small boys who brandished daggers at Guinness – bodyguards unobservable from a distance. They had a brief, completely unremarkable conversation in English. Guinness also spent time in Havana with Ernest Hemingway, who had a house in Cuba, and who found Coward's chatter at dinner inane, expressing an urge to hit him "if he wags that silly finger once more". Not a comfortable man to be with, thought Guinness, who commented that the fact that his death, later, was self-inflicted, did not take him entirely by surprise. He also encountered Ernie Kovacs, who struck him, in a Goonish way, as "just about the funniest man I have ever met". He was apparently dreading working – playing the part of the Chief of Police – with all the "toffee-nosed Brits; Sir Carol Reed, *the* Noël Coward, Sir Guinness . . . but you're the one who laughs with me, not all those American broads and clapped-out bores".

Although Coward left the filming in Havana with a glow of happiness and had loved working with Guinness and Ralph Richardson who "although slightly boring, is a dear", when he saw a private showing of the film he felt that Alec played the whole thing in too minor a key . . . "A faultless performance," he wrote, "but actually, I'm afraid, a little dull." The reviews were in agreement with this. Quite tactfully, and much later, Guinness laid the blame for his performance on Carol Reed, who wanted him, he said, to play Wormold straight, and not as Guinness had envisaged him, as a shambling Ealing comedy middle-aged man with worn shoes who had bits of string in his pocket. What he was really saying was that Reed had inhibited him and should have left him alone to play the part as he wished.

From inscrutable oriental to Greene at his most light-hearted, to decadent Frenchman, to self-tortured Oxford intellectual, to tobacco-inhaling Scotsman, to ascetic Arab Prince, to anarchic artist: the most remarkable thing about Guinness during these celebrity-ridden years was how each of these roles was so easily sloughed off. If he could become another person, either a fiction or an historically founded character whom he could base with documentary exactness on the known evidence, would he so easily have extricated himself? There was, as far as one can observe and judge Guinness, never a trace of him being affected in himself by the character he was playing, of him being taken over, as was Laurence Olivier about whom it used to be said he never knew when he was acting and when he was not. Like a scientist or a clinician who could separate himself with total objective thoroughness, Guinness seemed to preserve himself, his private life, his marriage and his family life, from any incursion his work made upon them. This was remarkable if not unique. His professionalism, in a word, was complete, but the characters he played were not powerful, positive types, they were for the most part weak, or deficient, or victims in some way – subjects that easily fell prey to inventiveness. Whether they succeeded or not did not seem to bother him much either way, for he was inevitably, remorselessly, in demand from that other new factor of the rising, permissive sixties, the juggernaut of popular culture which soon created a supermarket commodity attitude to theatre and films. This was to ensure his being almost ceaselessly in demand for the next thirty years.

It has often been recounted that David Lean and Guinness had fallen out so heavily over *The Bridge on the River Kwai* that Lean did not want to work with him again. However, Lean had wanted him for Gandhi. As in most accounts of film and theatre events or incidents, there was at least one version of the story which entirely contradicted the well-known version. Legend, if so it be, has advanced the colourful notion that Lean had already started shooting Robert Bolt's version of the Lawrence of Arabia story with the tall, gangling romantic Peter O'Toole playing Lawrence as a self-deceived mystic, when Sam Spiegel, the film's producer, announced to Lean that he had cast Guinness as Prince Feisal. According to Andrew Sinclair, one biographer of Spiegel, Lean stopped work and said he was leaving the picture:

Spiegel fell to the ground, the apparent victim of a heart attack. Rushed away to the hospital he was put in an oxygen tent. The stricken Lean visited him, offering to give Spiegel anything he wanted, anything, if it would help him to recover. Spiegel immediately revived and smiled and said, "You're so nice. So we cast Alec Guinness."

True or not, Feisal was a near-perfect piece of casting and one of Guinness's most impressive film roles, in which he could display his whole-hearted and unreserved admiration for a gentleman, and his disdain for the self-centred virtues of Lawrence, who had once been an idol of his. He could also show again his uncanny genius for penetrating the mind of a foreigner, this time a wily Arab who yet had a code of honour in many ways superior to that of Lawrence.

Although the slant on Lawrence was historically unsupportable, *Lawrence of Arabia* captured a romantic image of the man with a breadth of vision and a sense of style which made the picture a complete success. Lean had created a nuttiness to match his own obsession with such figures, and it took him three years to achieve it; but in an oddly contradictory way, Guinness's performance emerges as the touchstone of sanity, gentleness and balance. Maybe this is basically a boring quality of maturity, yet it was one which, perhaps uniquely, Guinness could make significant and above all gripping. Feisal is intricate and complex and different – apart – a portrait of someone whom the ordinary Englishman, who identifies with Guinness, would distrust, yet Guinness also brings to him an ordinariness, an innocence, which makes him universal. For an equally intelligent portrayal of an Arab leader, and his relationship with an Englishman, one perhaps has to look to that of Saladin in *The Talisman* by Walter Scott. Scott had with words a similar gift for character impersonation.

But for *Dr Zhivago*, which followed on rather too quickly from Lean's point of view, Guinness was attracted, this time with Lean's totally reconciled and happy enthusiasm, into a major minor role, that of General Yevgraf Zhivago.* The result was grey and colourless.

---

* Guinness did not at first respond to the script, but Lean persuaded him that the role was both subtle and warm: "Don't let's argue about you being a bore. I seem to remember we've had that one before."

32

Close encounters with the anti-hero

Exit the King, the absurdist play by Eugene Ionesco – the Romanian exile who wrote in French and who tangled antlers with Kenneth Tynan in a ferocious but gentlemanly dispute over whether the theatre should be political or not – was an attempt on Guinness's part to do something different, and the nearest he ever came to performing in an avant-garde play.

Guinness declared: "When you look at the performers I most admire – Eileen Atkins, for instance – you see it's all done from the inside. You have to change yourself, alter your personality, to be the part. Of course that's far more difficult and it can be dangerous. You're playing about with your individual soul." What did he mean, in this context, by "individual soul"? Did he mean that which might be for ever damned, or saved for eternity? Did he mean that unique sense of oneself, or did he simply mean the rational self, and the ability to hold on to oneself? Out of the limelight these anxieties possessed him continually, although he played games with them. In a way there was something in him as apocalyptic as the lyrics of Bob Dylan, which were among the small quantity of genuine and lasting art that the 1960s produced. They gave the sense that at every minute of his life man was dicing with death. How else could any man, convincingly, in the very same year (that of 1973), act the roles of the Pope (in *Brother Sun, Sister Moon*), and Adolf Hitler (in *Hitler – The Last Ten Days*)?

Yearly, hourly, Guinness gave the lie to Aldous Huxley's absurdly unintelligent statement that "no actor could be a good man or lead a spiritual life". But Guinness – unlike great actors who were more histrionic, such as Gielgud or Olivier, or more poetical and fantastical souls such as Richardson – could not survive in bad material. It is difficult to imagine him filling Pinter's stylish pauses with the comic invention of acting rapport such as Richardson and Gielgud showed in *Old Times*.

Exit the King was as ephemeral a play as most of the so-called "theatre of the absurd" will most likely prove. At the time Guinness thought he was showing his sympathies were "entirely with new methods of putting over stories and characters". It also gave him the opportunity to work again with George Devine, to whom he had not entrusted his artistic soul since the days of *Great Expectations* at the Rudolf Steiner Hall. Devine, a touchy man, was now at the very height of his influence, for the Royal Court Theatre had, with the advent of Osborne, Pinter, N.F. Simpson and Wesker (playwrights in whose stage plays Guinness never once appeared), become the new powerhouse of the English stage.

Devine and Guinness had in fact last met professionally when both had been acting in Arnold Bennett's *The Card*, which Roland Neame directed. Devine had ruined a scene ten or dozen times by drying. Guinness had taken Neame aside and asked him to pretend to shoot another take without running any film and for this take he (Guinness) would dry to restore Devine's confidence. They did this: Devine's reaction, according to Guinness (who told this to Irving Wardle) had been instant derision: "Ah," he said, "it even happens to your great film star."

Devine chose Eileen Atkins to play the part of Juliette opposite Guinness: she did not expect to find him in "an avant-garde theatre like the Court . . . it didn't have film stars, it was for dedicated grubby actors who didn't care about money or fame". But there was dispute at once about the age Devine wanted Atkins to play Juliette: she wanted to play it her own age, that is to say about thirty, while Devine, on the principle that Brecht often expressed, namely that young actors play older characters better than older ones, wanted her to act about sixty, with a funny walk and a grey wig. Guinness, who had endeared himself to Atkins by asking her to drop the accolade of "Sir" — further won her gratitude by supporting her against Devine when the latter wanted her to leave the play:

George has told me what he said to you this morning and took me to one side. I think he's wrong and I've told him so. I think you're going to be very good indeed — and you're quite right, she should be young. So it's agreed you're not leaving. All right?

She stayed in the role and learnt a great deal about stage-craft from

Guinness, which she felt was ironic when she had thought of him as a film star, although he often said he saw little difference between acting on stage and on film:

> In *Exit the King* I was required to wheel him in a wheelchair for half the evening. It was the first time I was aware of finding the lights on stage because it was my responsibility to get the chair with him in it into the correct position each time. There were also tricky technical things when he had to start to fall and I had to push the chair under him at just the right moment without giving the back of his legs a whack. Alec would rehearse this business meticulously and I found I enjoyed the discipline of getting that chair in exactly the right spot all the time. George rather left me alone and Alec would occasionally, very tentatively, give me a note which I always found to the point and very helpful.

Guinness confirmed what Eileen Atkins said. Devine did not give him a word of encouragement throughout the production. He was sensible, a bit schoolmasterly and dispiriting, clapping his hands to get people back to work. Guinness believed that, having just directed Rex Harrison at the Court the previous month, Devine was suspicious of star visitors. When Guinness wanted sometimes, as he constantly did, to send up the whole play during rehearsals, Devine was intolerant. Compared to Guthrie, Guinness later told Irving Wardle, Devine was both lumbering and too meticulous.

Exit the King opened at the Edinburgh Festival in the summer of 1963 and ran for a short while at the Court: Guinness's performance was much applauded. Peter Brook came to see it and conveyed in no uncertain terms his feeling that the whole production sagged and could do with a lift.

After the rarity of the absurd, a descent into documentary coarseness. Guinness's uninhibited impersonation of Dylan Thomas, which Guinness opened in Toronto and played on Broadway at the Plymouth Theatre, and which enthralled packed houses for six months, was a concession to the vulgar, popular side of his gift. *Dylan*, by Sidney Michaels, was a subject full of dramatic possibility, but it was treated as little more than a series of flippant jokes interspersed with pathos. Guinness's performance won him the 1964 Tony Award, but he spoke the naked truth, namely that it was easy for him. "Of course, it's not really Dylan Thomas at all that I am playing: just an exaggerated Welsh version of myself if I had tow-coloured hair and drank a lot. I have no reverence for Dylan, or anything like that. He wasn't my kind of person at all. People go on about his voice, but to me it was the voice of a bombastic curate. I really have no interest in the man." Too true; but perhaps for Guinness it was all too easy to let himself go, but far more subtle and demanding for him to reach out to what he would like to be: to attempt to embrace the true quality he felt to exist inside him. As the *Times* critic wrote, he was

> not only giving us Dylan Thomas, but is able to stand aside and watch himself, adjusting his performance as if in a mirror. Every movement, every gesture is so real that competent portrayals by his fellow actors sometimes seem stilted beside him.

One might add, in that wry tone Guinness himself made his speciality, "I'm amused by people who stand apart and look at life; maybe I do that a little myself."

Guinness knew that it was only too easy to indulge oneself, let the "truth" hang out, let oneself go. Just think of the numerous, self-indulgent characters he could have played, but with an unerring instinct and an unintended enhancement of his own lasting reputation, did not. But of course, when T.S. Eliot, whom he really admired, died on 4 January 1965 and Guinness was asked to read from his later poems at the Westminster Abbey memorial service, he readily accepted.

33

The simplicity of Macbeth

What made Guinness a great English actor was that he never gave up his relationship with the live London stage, with Shakespeare – "God's gift to any actor" – and with the living audience. Actors are, by the very nature of their calling, and especially by the conditions of their work, incomplete and complex beings. Richard Burton lost touch with his roots by becoming an itinerant film actor, and, as if by some inward peculiarity or perversity of character, settled on having a home in Baby Doc Duvalier's Haiti. Part of the informal self-dismantling of Burton during his tragic break-up in drink and successive marriages was that he lost touch with Shakespeare. Guinness had been a great Shakespearian clown, and he could have been a great Hamlet and an unusual Lear, even, had he found a director he trusted. But he wasn't keen on the current fashions of presenting Shakespeare: "I'm offended at the sloppiness of it and directors trying to put over some particular theory of their own and not seeking after what's in the plays . . . I don't want to be involved in any of these." If not Hamlet and Lear, then he could most certainly have proved an exceptional Prospero. Perhaps one of the greatest shortcomings he had as a stage actor was that, after Tyrone Guthrie died, he would not entrust his gifts to the moulding power of Peter Hall who was in many ways Guthrie's successor. Tynan, during his literary stewardship of the National Theatre, tried to entice Guinness to act there. Perhaps it was acting under the aegis of Olivier that made him feel uneasy about accepting. He felt that Olivier sapped the energy of other people and lived off it. Certainly it cannot be disputed that Olivier was a great feeder upon others, a consumer of other people's talents as well as a great creative power in himself. Perhaps Tynan was the most notable example of how Olivier used the gifts of others and made them his own. While literary manager of the National Theatre Tynan unsparingly committed and spent himself in the glorification of Olivier's power. Olivier used him, played upon him, sucked him dry and ultimately repudiated him. But Olivier was so skilful in the wielding of managerial control that he would allow Tynan little autonomy of his own. When Tynan quarrelled, as he sometimes did with other members of the directorial administration – George Devine was a notable example – or with the governors on the Board, as over Rolf Hochhuth's Soldiers – Olivier made him feel he knew nothing about people of the theatre, and that – "dear boy" as he addressed him – he should come to him, Olivier, with all his troubles. "I know how to run the ship and if I seem light in my touch, or indulgent, it's because I am in touch", was Olivier's directive. Of course this was true, too, and perhaps temperamentally and because of his family background Tynan would always be a misfit in such an institution. But at the end of his tenure of the post Tynan felt extremely bitter.

In the ten years of Olivier's National Theatre, from 1963 onwards, Guinness was approached several times to play important roles. He was approached to play Danton in Buchner's *Danton's Death*. He was approached to play Shylock in *The Merchant of Venice* (*before* Olivier himself played the role in Jonathan Miller's memorable production). After 1973, when Peter Hall took over direction of the National, Hall was extremely keen to have him play Prospero. But Guinness did not want to become at all involved in this side of theatre work. He had parted company with the institutions of his country's theatre when he left the Old Vic in 1948, and he never returned. He was essentially the outsider who looked sometimes as if he was at the very core of power. Again it would seem that he knew himself, but he was the outsider with a gentle pervasive power and influence.

Guinness was always somewhat studied in his apoliticality. In the early 1950s he had sat twice on the Equity Council and, each time, had felt useless and tongue-tied. He had described his convictions as, "having no political convictions other than an old-fashioned brand of liberalism – I do not enjoy the situation of fence-sitting, which it seems to me I am so often involved in". He wrote an anti-nuclear sketch for Tynan who was organising a Sunday night at the Royal Court. This was, as Guinness told him, a "clownish mime thing", while Tynan responded in a sweet and flattering letter telling Guinness how well he wrote, but that the piece as such did not work.

Try as Guinness might, the identity, the *zeitgeist* of the sixties, was one that was alien to him. Yet in spite of himself he became, inevitably, part of the new rootless, globe-trotting confraternity of celebrities who were the new order of world aristocracy. Always meeting with one another, always moving on tomorrow, never sure where they would be at the same time next year. "Doomed nomads" was Richard Burton's phrase for them, and for himself.

For instance, in late 1961 Guinness was telling a friend that, in December, he would be taking a two-week holiday, then he would be off to Spain, in January, and that this would be followed by a year's exile in Hollywood and Spain for a Fred Zinnemann picture. This last film never materialised. In August 1962 MGM took over for him and his family an eighteen-room miniature castle outside Madrid, completely staffed from chauffeur to scullery maid, while he played, in *The Fall of the Roman Empire*, the part of Marcus Aurelius, a performance the *Telegraph* described later as "warm and foxy". That same year also saw him in retreat for a fortnight in the Benedictine Santa Scholastica in Rome, sleeping in a monk's cell in a wooden cot and eating simple food. A few years on, in 1965, he was defended by Roy Jenkins, the Home Secretary, who remarked during a speech that Alec Guinness was not responsible for Britain's formidable crime wave, and that Guinness's films contained "such an element of fantasy it was difficult to think they could be constructive to criminals".

In the summer of 1965, as Guinness himself reported in the *Spectator* in 1987, he was in Paris filming *Hotel Paradiso* with the old-timer Douglas Byng in the cast. Walking in Saint-Germain-des-Prés one day he spotted this figure, straight out of his early love for the outrageous bygone age of the music-hall stage, sitting at a little table outside Les Deux Magots. Byng, a familiar dapper figure in a grey Homburg hat, had once been Boadicea, Queen of the Keni, or Flora MacDonald ("bending the bracken with young Charlie Stu"), or another dozen dames. "Gay Paree," the old stager told him hopefully. "This is the spot to watch the cruisers."

In this flux, in this ever mobile and shifting uncertainty, Shakespeare had remained a lodestar for Guinness – but also with other stars to which the identity of Guinness remained attached and around which he would always revolve: "I like a line drawing, a very simple line, it pleases me, I love simplicity in acting. Shakespeare in the end is the Bible . . . In the whirlwind of your passion you must beget a gentleness," is how Guinness himself expressed it. But his stab at Macbeth, which he was to play next, was too gentle, while Shakespeare's great tragic figures could perhaps never be described as line drawings.

Ernest Milton had once performed privately for him, in his front room at St Peter's Square, both Lady Macbeth and Macbeth in the scenes before and after Duncan's murder: "It was as if blood had dripped on the carpet." However, when Guinness himself played the most guilt-ridden of all Shakespeare's tragic roles opposite Simone Signoret at the Royal Court in late 1966, no such powerful evocation of evil happened. Guinness was now fifty-three and he felt that opportunities to stretch himself would in the future become more and more rare.

William Gaskill's production, which opened in October, was stark and Brechtian, perhaps also unsuited to Guinness. There was virtually no set and the lights were blazing and so powerful that, as Guinness observed, "You cannot flick your finger without it seeming as significant as a pistol shot." But his main difficulty remained that of confidence, that kind of easy confidence he had with *Dylan* but which eluded him with Shakespeare's tragic villain: "I do find it hard to trust the flow of something and not be cautious. I'm far too cautious an actor very often or usually."

He did not regret the lack of lush scenery. He felt that the work he had been doing recently had been lazy work, and that Macbeth was not lazy work: as one person who talked to him noted, "Exhaustion had drawn pink lines round those pale lizard-lidded eyes." He also greatly enjoyed working with Simone Signoret, of whom he was very fond, and who was, with her husband Yves Montand, very left-wing. She had a purity about her which he admired. As Corin Redgrave said, "He liked actors who had more to them than just acting." Outwardly unperturbed by the appalling reviews, the worst since *Hamlet* in 1951 – one was sneeringly headed "Aimez-vous Glam's?"; another said his eyes were "as blank as contact lenses" – he claimed that he did not read the critics, adding, possibly a little waspishly, "It must be dreadfully annoying for them. But I learned that whatever they say, nice or nasty, is a distraction." Yet Kenneth Williams applauded the way he showed such vulnerability as to be deeply moving, while Irene Worth noted the walk he assumed on his way to the murder of Duncan as "frightful, blood-curdling". The production was completely sold out before it opened: standing room only. It bore, said the director Alan Strachan, an "air of civilised controversy".

Perhaps this was also the point at which Guinness started a little to enjoy acting less and less. He did not look forward to it quite so much, he did not embrace it as he once had, and each part became more and more of a mountain to climb.

34

Skirting the issues

Quite unusually, given that bisexuality and transvestism were becoming almost the norm, or so the politically correct newspapers would have us believe, the *Daily Express* asked in early October 1967 if a shortage of good parts had possibly landed one of our most distinguished and dignified actors in a situation he regretted. "I sat on the script in trepidation for a few months," Guinness said about Simon Gray's *Wise Child*. "No, I thought, not another of those transvestite things."

He was caught irritatedly wondering how to hang up his skirt in the dressing-room of the Wyndham Theatre. Rather like Guinness with his skirt, Simon Gray, for his first play, had also found himself with something he did not know quite how to handle. The fashion was for baroque nastiness: Joe Orton had set this fashion with a certain style, but others climbed on the bandwagon of unpleasantness for its own sake.

Guinness felt uncomfortable. He agreed to play Mrs Artminster. He had to appear first on the stage as a trim, grey-haired matron clad in a blue suit and a fur coat. The scene was that of a seedy provincial hotel, of the sort he was familiar with from childhood. He had then to delve into a handbag and pull out a small whisky bottle and take a manly swig. Guinness tried to reassure himself: "Do not worry. I change back into a man in the last moments on stage. That is the trickiest part – playing a man who is playing a woman who is not a woman really but a man. A complicated bit of technique."

Some of it, of course, he could carry off in the *Kind Hearts and Coronets* manner; different voices, seraphic smiles, and he was well up to realising every trick of stage camp. But for what? The intention of the play eluded him: was it merely black farce, was it vaguely threatening, ambiguity for its own sake? Was it a social play?

He tried to reassure himself by checking out Simon Gray, who had just written several successful television plays. Gray built another, slightly tart comedy upon this tentativeness on the part of the actor. The subject of his play, transvestism and bizarre sexual passion, was such that he wanted "every possible guarantee that the author himself wasn't a freak". So he was invited to Guinness's London pied-à-terre for dinner. "It was, needless to say, an immensely civilised evening, in which we quoted to each other from the poems of T.S. Eliot, he in movingly canonical tones, I in the brisk fashion of a respectably married university lecturer. But Gray had resorted to drinking steadily to calm his nerves.

> The evening was a total triumph . . . until the moment the door closed behind me, and I tottered down the path, across the pavement, fell into the gutter, and was sick. I had an impression that a curtain twitched in the pied-à-terre, and a compassionate face peered towards me through the darkness, but that may have been an illusion. And even if it wasn't, the sight of a respectably married university etcetera rolling drunkenly in the gutter was probably vastly more reassuring than that sight of a departing transvestite however sober. (*Dear Alec: Guinness at 75*)

The reassurance was only temporary. The director, Gray found, who was John Dexter, was an astonishing combination of the pragmatist and the magician, and revered "Sir Alec" too much while behaving abrasively towards the other actors. Gray found himself carefully segregated from Guinness; he discovered only one thing wrong, which he tried to rectify:

> At the end of the first act my text called upon the character played by Sir Alec, togged up as Simon Ward's surrogate mother, to recoil in disgust from a particularly perverted outburst from the Simon Ward character, and then in spite of him/herself – moved by the Simon Ward character's display of pain (jealousy) – to put an arm around him and cuddle him into comfort, in which image *lights down* and *curtain*.

Gray felt they were getting the disgusted recoil, but not the pitying cuddle,

> so that *lights, curtain* descended on an image of Sir Alec keeping a morally refined distance from the surrogate child I'd wanted him not to be able to withdraw from.

When he pointed this out to the director, Dexter impassively drew him over to Guinness

Sir Alec listened with seraphic gravity, and then the two of them retired for one of their canonically artistic conferences. After rehearsals John Dexter came over to me as I was about to head to the pub and put it to me that as we were only a few days off our first (of three, I think it was) previews, Sir Alec would prefer me not to attend any further rehearsals

When it opened Gray's play received good reviews, became something of a *succès de scandale*, and ran for six months. After one performance, recorded Kenneth Williams in his diary, he went round backstage at the Wyndham Theatre to Guinness's dressing-room. Williams happened to be rather drunk and in a state. "My hair is in a terrible mess," he shrieked. "Alec stroked his bald head. 'Oh! I so agree – couldn't do a thing with mine either . . .'"

Guinness's qualms about the modishly shocking piece deepened further. Something about it stirred him up at a deeper level, although of course he had no difficulty in doing what was required of him technically. Gray continued his account:

His initial affection for the piece was, I suspect, gradually eroded by the reaction of his long-established admirers, who doubtless expected from him, even in his comedies, a touch of the spiritual – failing that, certainly a dash of gentlemanliness. But there was no place for spirituality or gentlemanliness in the character I'd provided for him – an ageing thug who cavorts about in a wig, skirt, high-heels, squawking out gross indelicacies while tippling from a concealed bottle of whisky – simultaneously trying to have it off with the Cleo Sylvestre character, while being sucked into a deeply unhealthy relationship with the psychopathic Simon Ward character. At an early performance a gentleman of the old school rose in the middle of the first act, shouting: "I thought you were above this sort of thing, Sir Alec!" and led his family out.

Guinness insisted on a short-cropped ginger wig under the female wig, presumably for the contrast of butch manliness, and this made him seem even less like himself than when dressed up as a middle-aged woman. The fan letters, said Gray, must have had an unsettling effect on Guinness. Fetishists and weirdos wrote all kinds of strange propositional letters to the playwright, so one could hardly imagine what they must have been like to Guinness (except that he would have replied courteously). Sadly, sex was no longer camp fun, as it was in the old-fashioned days of the pantomime dame: it had assumed the murky, disturbing mantle brought on it by permissiveness, and this became even more encrusted with new baroque layers as time went on. The innocent vaudeville tradition of cross-dressing which Guinness at first had found in the play revealed itself as an evil monster: "Sir Alec seems uncertain exactly what proportion of masculinity should show through his Widow Twankey outfit," wrote Alan Brien in the *Sunday Telegraph*. By his own miniaturist standards this was "a coarse, slapdash performance".

Gray called in at the theatre during the run and found Guinness progressively more and more embattled in wrestling with his distaste. Guinness was in the last stages of preparation: "sitting in front of the mirror, in his wig, skirt, blouse and high heels, dabbling on rouge or stroking on lip-stick, his eyes briefly meeting mine in what I came more and more to feel was a kind of reproach". Gray could see that four months in the run of his play had been quite enough and why he was never once mentioned in Guinness's volume of memories, "even though it's called *Blessings in Disguise*".

Yet a very different reaction emerged for Gordon Jackson, who played Mr Booker. Once Guinness was checking all the props in the handbag and he told Jackson, "You know, Gordon, I may seem rather silly and sentimental to you, but I'm going to miss this old bag – " and walked on stage. Another time he remarked, ribaldly, before going on: "Oh! I can't play it tonight, my dear, I've got the curse!"*

In *Wise Child* Guinness dressed as a woman for the last time: but earlier in the same year he had played Major Jones in *The Comedians*, Grahame Greene's attack on Papa Doc Duvalier's Haiti. The major had disguised himself for a minute or two in drag "as a swivel-hipped cook in blackface", but that had been a much more conventional affair, directed by his old friend Peter Glenville. The film was poor. Duvalier sued the film in the French courts and was awarded one franc damages.

It was with relief, undisguised, that in early 1968 Guinness returned once again to his touchstone T.S. Eliot. Guinness, who was directing *The Cocktail Party* as well as repeating his performance

---

* Jackson visited Guinness at Steep where he was taken out to the meadow to see the new pony, called Gordon. "Call his name," Guinness told Jackson. He did so and the animal dutifully trotted up. Jackson told Simone Signoret this story, who exclaimed, "That's nonsense! When I visited, the animal answered to Simone." The trick was in the carrots Guinness held.

as Harcourt-Reilly, had in the meantime deepened his friendship with Eileen Atkins:

> An odd thing happened before Alec asked me to play Celia Coplestone ... I'd been in New York for eight months in Frank Marcus's *The Killing of Sister George* and I dreamed one night that I was doing a play with Alec on a platform surrounded by green fields and we were both dressed in evening dress and speaking verse, but I knew it wasn't Shakespeare, and out of the back of my evening dress I had a huge cock's tail and I said under my breath to Alec while we were performing "Have you noticed what's sticking out of the back of my dress?" and he said, "Yes, that's perfectly correct."

Guinness asked her to play the part at Chichester and later they transferred to London. She found the experience happy: Guinness's direction was firm and tactful: he told her, when she thought she had parts of this very difficult and complex play well worked out, "Yes, now you know exactly what you're saying but you're spelling it out to us – because *you* know exactly what you're saying you can now gather it up – the audience will understand". Atkins added, "Oh how often have I sat in audiences since saying to myself 'Yes, yes, don't spell it out to me – GATHER IT UP!'"

Guinness had created the part of Harcourt-Reilly nineteen years before. This time, directing it, he would make the play "Bloomsbury, literary, tatty". Harcourt-Reilly would become a "mentally Herculean figure". There was a lionskin on the floor, and he carried a heavy walking-stick. But Guinness still felt his production did not do the play, and its marvellous diction, full justice. At large in society there was a kind of reaction against the "parental" attitude of Eliot, as Irving Wardle called it. Wardle admitted the truer basis of Eliot's stripping away of illusions: ("in this respect at least the play has not dated: Eliot's 'hell is oneself' is a truer line that Sartre's 'hell is other people'"). As for Guinness, he played Harcourt-Reilly as a "white-bearded replica of Freud, and cultivates a manner of grave whimsicality (lying flat out on a tigerskin in his consulting-room), which seems the most satisfactory approach to a profoundly unsympathetic role." Wardle praised Guinness's direction which conveyed the spirit of intimate dualogues over the huge open stage of Chichester, and also lifted the atmosphere to somewhere near farce. He also liked very much the smooth transitions between party chatter and ritual exchanges, "when the guests whip out their dark glasses as spiritual guardians".

While playing the profane Gray, Guinness had liked to refresh his spirit with talk of T.S. Eliot; but now he was playing Eliot he seemed to need profanity. He did some wickedly funny things to make Atkins laugh. Before one show she had been saying how she liked sexy mouths with the lip rolled back (Steve McQueen, Jeanne Moreau, Mick Jagger). He secretly sellotaped back his upper lip, and then appeared facing upstage at the beginning of the play – they were all facing him – rapidly whipping the tape off before he had to face the audience. Atkins had great difficulty in not corpsing. Another time Atkins was losing her voice: Guinness was irritated by this, having the traditionalist (correct) approach that if you use your voice properly you need never lose it. Atkins consulted a voice specialist called Mr Punt who, to mollify Guinness, left him a note saying, "You must not be cross with Miss Atkins, she has difficulty because all her passages are narrow". During the performance that evening Guinness, as Harcourt-Reilly, handed Celia Coplestone a piece of paper on which he was supposed to have written down the name of the convent she was to leave for. He had written on the piece of paper, "*All* your passages are narrow?" At another time Harcourt-Reilly speaks of the affair Celia had, and the man she had had it with, and asked, "And what does he seem like to you now?" A member of the audience shouted out, "A cunt". Guinness and Atkins could not credit it. They worked out that the man who responded thus was a poor fellow who had been dragged to the theatre by his wife, who had had too much to drink, hadn't understood a word, but suddenly, during a moment of illumination after more drink in the interval, all had clicked.

It was a measure of Guinness's dedication to Eliot that *The Cocktail Party* kept going and going: first at Wyndham's, to which it transferred in November 1968, and then at the Haymarket (February 1969). And now he was signed up to play one of the film roles in which, in the opinion of this present writer, he excelled: another profoundly spiritual being, but also a victim. The only sadness was that, overall – and his performance in it apart – the film was a poor one. This was *Cromwell*, directed by Ken Hughes, in which the name part was played by Richard Harris. Guinness's film roles, as his stage roles, had in the 1960s been for the most part lacking in substance. Not surprisingly he now wanted to attempt "something impossible," or "something that would pull the best out of me".

Playing Charles I was a chance to do this, but the role of the martyred king unfurled in an interpretation of history quite unfairly loaded on Cromwell's side – and also this was not a story the director managed to elevate into greatness. When they filmed in early 1970, and with little help from his script, Guinness did manage, with stutter and prancing walk, and the variable shading of a Scots accent, to create a memorable existence of the doomed king who, like Colonel Nicholson, thought it his duty to uphold the law. He also showed Charles as having a keen sense of humour – which was more than could be said for Harris's hoarse-voiced Cromwell – and a touching sense of family feeling.

6 January 1970. "My next stint is to play a chemist – rather a special kind of chemist – the more I visualize the part, the more I see him with a moustache like this," he told the journalist Godfrey Winn. They lunched out of doors in Steep Marsh at the end of a very warm January under a cool green vine. "Oh, it never produces any grapes," said Guinness with typical self-diminishment. They ate Quiche Lorraine which Merula had concocted.

The chemist was in Bridget Boland's *Time Out of Mind*, a project which, although destined for the West End, never left the Yvonne Arnaud Theatre in Guildford where it ran for several weeks in July 1970. Guinness played this rather special kind of chemist, named John, who had lived for six hundred years, beginning life as a mediaeval alchemist. Having discovered the elixir of life John finds that death eludes him. Perhaps for Guinness it was the ultimate elusiveness. Matthew, his son, was also to appear in *Time Out of Mind*, as Paracelsus, the scientist of history who figures in John's imagination. Matthew was now thirty and had been acting for four years, mostly in northern repertory companies. He had just played a sizeable role in Solzhenitzyn's *A Day in the Life of Ivan Denisovitch*, which was filmed in Norway with Tom Courtenay in the title part.

Irving Wardle in *The Times* disliked *Time Out of Mind* extremely, calling John a "crass reptile" and the performance "seraphic". 1970 was a lean, slack year for Guinness, perhaps appropriately marking the end of a decade which for him ended with not so much a bang as, in Wardle's description of John's death, an "ecstasy of giggles".

PART FIVE

The Man Within

All I'm left with is me – and thirty years of cold war without the option.

"George Smiley"

Everything that is in agreement with our personal desires seems true

André Maurois

Is the disguise right for *him*? (*Him* being himself in his new persona.)

John le Carré on Alec Guinness

35

The secret service

Robin Fox, father of the actors Edward and James, and of the producer Robert, had been a solicitor before the Second World War, in which he won the MC. He was an old Harrovian and was, as an agent, a consummate actor who combined, or so Robert Morley said, "the lethal charm of a Prince of the Borgias with membership of the MCC." He lived in Cuckfield, Sussex, some three-quarters of an hour's drive away from Steep, and he and his wife Angela were close if not intimate friends of Guinness.

He "fitted his clients with ten-league boots and encouraged them," according to Morley, "to walk tall". But as the Sancho Panza who was at the side of many a Don Quixote in his profession, he was having his own problems. James was the main one, for after a well-publicised spell as a heroin addict (at the time he was filming in *Performance* with Mick Jagger), he had become a born-again Christian. He was now twenty-nine-years-old and his apparently self-destructive orbit was hurting and upsetting his parents, while an added complication was that the ever buoyant and apparently indestructible Robin was diagnosed as having cancer of the lung.

Guinness had known Robin and Angela for years. They would send telegrams to him on his first nights and on one occasion at least Guinness replied (this was when he played *Macbeth*) that the box office was booming – at least temporarily. Typically he would joke how he never read the press on such occasions, and then playfully sign himself off as the *Observer* theatre critic, Penelope Gilliatt – spelt with several extra "ts". At another time he wrote thanking them for a delicious supper, but apologising for carrying on about Graham Greene's *The Living Room*, and delivering ghoulish tales of his dear Martita Hunt. He didn't sleep a wink as he spent the night thinking up witty and stinging replies to a letter written by Michael Powell, the film director, to the press.

In August 1970 Robin Fox was undergoing radiotherapy, but stopped when they went on holiday. Guinness told Angela that he was relieved to hear they were no longer continuing the depressing treatment, and that he remembered Larry Olivier telling him how suicidal he felt at a similar time until they ceased the bombardment. Guinness then made to Angela an unusual declaration of his belief in the efficacy of prayer. He believed in it totally, or so he thought, yet it remained a very odd mystery. He was in those days discontented with that Church and what it stood for, and he would happily have broken away, and yet it had an umbilical cord of great strength and love, while he felt at his least mad and wayward when he submitted to its tug.

These thoughts prompted Angela Fox to ring up Guinness and express all her fears about William (i.e. James), and his conversion to Christianity which had really shocked Robin and her. Guinness invited the three of them to dinner and subsequently, on the morning of Friday 4 September, they had a long telephone conversation. Guinness told Robin that he and Angela should on no account mock James in his state of religious fervour and that he should, at this critical moment, be treated with a very special delicacy which is what they had done at the dinner. He gently admonished them, hoping he was not being in any way rude or censorious, not to lose their patience if they received some arbitrary New Testament text flung at them.

For, having been through it himself, Guinness knew all about the extreme moods that conversion could bring about in one's psyche. He told Angela of the famous "enthusiatic" group in the early seventeenth century who ran naked through the streets of Amsterdam shouting "We are the naked truth" – commenting that in 1970 they were again nearly full circle. He warned Robin and Angela specifically against the dangers of reaction in James, and how it might become bitter and dismissive of the earlier extreme commitment. But he spoke only from partial experience, for he himself felt he had never gone a hundred per cent full hog at anything, although he regretted the extent to which he felt he must have bored the agnostic pants off friends when he had a "wild" Roman mood on him. Like many present-day English Catholics he had an aversion to proselytising.

Finally, and this again was perhaps indicative of how the Church, in Catholic theology the Bride of Christ, had spiritually taken the place of the mother he could never respect, he longed to suggest to James books he should read as he felt that a sane attitude to Christianity must be grounded in history. In fact, James had just been offered two good parts, those of a tempter and a knight in T.S. Eliot's *Murder in the Cathedral*, which was to be performed in Canterbury Cathedral in October 1970 for the eight hundredth anniversary of Beckett's death. Guinness hoped that E. Martin Browne, the director, and the Cathedral itself, might be hard-headed, steadying influences. It turned out he was wrong, because, as James wrote later, in trying to combine Christianity with acting, "I only succeeded in becoming more and more frustrated. I wasn't exercising my talents in what I could do best, and I found that Christian drama isn't necessarily an aid to Christian development or even communication."

But the main confusion in the family was now the illness of Robin, which worsened. The family planned to take Robin to a famous cancer clinic in Germany, run by Dr Issel. Guinness was, one dry and damp Saturday afternoon in November, sitting at his desk with the trees facing him nearly bare and the ground looking as if it was rotting. He swam somewhat in fumes of sloe gin of the "Messrs Berry Bros" version, having taken a glass or two at lunch. He and Merula had just spent a disappointing five days in Paris where, on Marie Bell's invitation, they had gone to see her act in Michel Simon's *Le Contrat*. On his return he had received the postcard which Angela had sent him from Bavaria; he had been impressed by the recent programme on television about Dr Issel and he looked them up on the map. All he knew of Germany and Austria was a depressing three months he had spent filming in Munich, a few enjoyable days spent at Salzburg, while once he had got fairly suicidal in Berlin (his sanity had been saved by the zoo).

He replied to the card in a most careful, generous, and consolatory way, remarking there was nothing sensible he could say about Angela's distress at seeing Robin's deterioration. The nuns at Stanbrook Abbey — where he himself had visited in retreat, and where the abbess, Dame Laurentia McLachlan, had been the correspondent of Sydney Cockerell — had written asking him about Robin, for he had asked them to pray for him. He had reassured them that all appeared to be going fairly well. He had written a second time. He vigorously believed something could be done through prayer. No cures, of course. He might have echoed Gandhi, whom he so nearly played on film and who above all else in life valued prayer: "Without it I would have lost any reason long ago . . . It delivers us from the clutches of the prince of darkness." Guinness also wrote to Father Caraman, his Jesuit friend and confessor, who had said mass for both the Foxes the previous Sunday. He questioned whether it might be an irritation or a pleasure to Angela to hear of such things, but of course it was the latter.

He turned to written anecdote, of which, as ever, he was the master. He regaled them with tales of Waugh, Sitwell and Greene's confessor, and his own recent trip to Paris, creating for Angela the most exact and extraordinary image of Marie Bell who met them after her performance dressed as a rather stout Vietnamese peasant in mink, with a vast curved hat to match, from which dangled leather thongs. A leather miniskirt, a rope of pearls descending so low they clicked audibly on the heels of her lace-up boots, completed this apparition of the great French *tragédienne*. It almost made the evening worth while. But he got rather stuck inside her hat while having a friendly embrace. As Angela Fox would rejoin, "Even in the worst possible circumstances Alec could always make you laugh!"

The Dr Issel treament having been worse than useless, and, in fact, as Angela Fox recorded in her books *Slightly Foxed* and *Completely Foxed*, cruel and senseless, Robin and she returned to Cuckfield where Robin died on 21 January 1971. Legend has it that when Robin's agent partner moved out his personal possessions from his office and took his place almost straightaway, Guinness, who had left him ten years before to join Dennis Van Thal, organised with others of Robin's clients a demonstration in protest. Over twenty years later, in April 1994, on the death of Angela Fox's half-sister, Frances Donaldson – Guinness wrote again to Angela hoping that she rejoiced, as he did, that James had made such wonderful strides towards life. He had remembered everything.

36

Visible invisibility

In 1970 and 1971 Michael Noakes, the portrait painter, worked on a portrait of Guinness, which provided him with a curiously privileged glimpse of the private person. This was a daunting assignment because, showing what Stuart Freeborn, the make-up artist of Guinness's David Lean pictures, pointed out, Guinness's face, basically, was very ordinary: a "smoothish face which had no features in any overall development . . . not an outstanding face in any way". But just under the skin (and as George Lucas later found revealed about Guinness in an unusual moment during the filming of *Star Wars*) there resided the most amazing musculature. Guinness was able to become "so well into what he was going to do", that with just a "small amount of movement he was able to convey the greatest amount of emotional feeling". Of all this, Freeborn thought, Guinness was extremely aware.

But how does the portrait painter paint what lies just beneath the skin? How does he convey the invisible gesture and the unspoken word of which Guinness was the master? And how does he paint that power which, in the actor's face, lay in the control of movement? Further, who should the ontologically insecure Guinness *be* for the portrait? Actors are usually painted playing somebody. That is how people want to see them.

Both painter and subject must have exercised considerable thought on this problem. Noakes, for example, at once noted how Guinness could merge into a background, yet, when he wanted, summon up a powerful presence. He reported later that Guinness talked to him a great deal during the sittings; the subjects he raised were his illegitimacy, which he realised early; his decision to become a Catholic, giving the painter, who was also a Catholic, a sense of privilege (because, as Noakes said, this was before he wrote it up in *Blessings in Disguise*, so he felt complimented "that he chose to tell me about these important factors in his life").

But of course, as we know, these were well-known "public" subjects by now so Guinness was not really being revealing. If you have told *Time* magazine some secret you are not really granting much privilege to your portrait painter by telling him exactly the same thing. You were merely conferring on him the flattering illusion of intimacy. So Noakes was taken in by his subject at once, duped, one might say, in this particular feeling, which may cast a certain amount of suspicion on the clarity of his perception.

In fact it would seem from then on to have been, between sitter and subject, downhill all the way. Noakes related that Guinness (who was trying out autobiographical material he used later in *Blessings in Disguise*) recounted to him his near-psychic experiences of the early 1950s ("when he was preparing his notoriously disastrous Hamlet"). He had in his and Merula's bedroom a painting by Bernard Meninsky of *Two Irish Girls* – a solid subject of two females in shawls with a background of "bright green bushes and withered hedgerows") as described by Guinness – but which had about it something enigmatic. One night he was "seized" with a chapter and verse from Luke dinning in his head which, when he checked, he found to be, "For if they do these things in a green tree what shall be done in a dry?" When he looked at the painting closer he saw that while the greenery of the bushes was bright, the twigs which held the leaves themselves were "tortured figures", as Noakes put it, themselves, and so presumably reflecting some extreme state of the painter's soul. Guinness, uneasy at the ghostly M.R. Jamesian impact he felt, removed the painting from the wall. He learned later that this peculiar state of mind about the painting had overcome him on the anniversary of Meninsky's suicide.

The painter's rationalisation of all this material in the form his painting took was rather curious. Because of Guinness's "busy interior life" he decided to paint him surrounded "by more space that I would normally allow". He divided that space between a roughish terracotta floor and a pale azure wall (which had a blue-sky effect and increased the sense of space even more). He dressed him (or Guinness asked to be dressed) formally in a dark blue suit with a slightly short coat which was buttoned up fully and emphasised the chubbiness of his figure. His cuffs show just a little, so does his collar and an almost, but not quite, neatly tied tie in a knot that is just a little too large. But the most satisfactory part – the whimsical touch, one could say – are the shoes and feet. Clownish boots, socks which are flesh-coloured, the same tone as the pudgy fingers, and short, tight, drain-pipe trousers which have a ragged end to them as if they had been cut off short at the ankle. It was as if Noakes wanted to turn Guinness into the kind of type Guinness followed in the streets, although as he now said, "I can't keep up with people's walk any more . . . I long to play not a tramp but a down-and-out dotty character . . . My eyes go straight to them because their trousers are always four to six inches too short."

The chair Michael Noakes chose was also peculiarly although deliberately demeaning to the subject: a high-backed, white-painted Victorian kitchen chair with a very large and dominating back which curved round like a band behind the lower part of Guinness's head. It made him look not only clownish but completely passive, as if it was the white chair which held him together, enveloped him, gave him backbone, but also imprisoned him. The painting was that of a mollusc, a clown without backbone but with a shell; the face is sad, the eyes inward-looking – the nearest, one imagines, to what he conveys and then only perhaps, is a gentle, thorough police inspector who may have a somewhat secretive private life (note, too, the slightly pained, quizzical eyes, the ambiguous sensitive mouth, similar, here, to the make-up of Lawrence of Arabia). Indeed, if there was a secret person Noakes discerned in Guinness it was the, by now, cliché of Lawrence of Arabia. Lawrence, it was true, liked space around him – that of the desert, naturally. But the space around Guinness in the Noakes picture seemed to emphasise not so much the busy interior life but a loneliness, an isolation, and also, curiously enough, the sense of Guinness as a victim. How Noakes could then express the hope that "the lone figure would be read as shrewdly observing all that goes on around, whilst knowing it is all, the height and the depths, the beating of a gnat's wing", is difficult to grasp. The figure of Guinness in his portrait may be reflective but it observed nothing.

I suspect Guinness yet again chose to be "absent" from the sessions and, perhaps because he did not find the right rapport with the painter, the latter was unable to do him justice, although the painting has a strong and effective photographic likeness. At any rate he was not there.* But what a difficult subject. Noakes expressed a later view of Guinness which suggested a much stronger image. The actor was walking in St James's Street. The painter drove past in his car, stopped and offered a lift which was refused. Noakes remarked that Guinness was wearing a large floppy hat (it was summer), and an overcoat and carried a plastic bag in each hand. The interplay of intentions struck Noakes as curious. Guinness had chosen to be anonymous in his action – travelling on foot around a famous quarter of London carrying plastic bags – yet at the same time he deliberately wanted, with the floppy hat, to be eye-catching. Here Noakes probably drew the right conclusion from this observation: "He must surely have taken pleasure from the thought that everyone who glanced at him without a thought would have been tickled pink to have known who he was, had he decided to be less anonymous". In other words, Noakes was saying, Guinness enjoyed his fame, at the same time as wanting no part in it.

* Ralph Richardson, in Noakes's portrait of him (1963, National Portrait Gallery), is by contrast remarkably "present".

37

A noble tree has fallen

Guinness's affection for and gratitude towards Tyrone Guthrie was deep and lasting. When in 1971 the director died peacefully in his Irish home on his mother's birthday while opening his mail – having just received a rebate on his rates – Guinness delivered the address at his memorial service in St Paul's, Covent Garden, the actors' church. He recalled a dispute he and Guthrie had had during the rehearsals of that famous production of *Richard III*, perhaps exemplifying the overworked generalisation that there is no fire without heat, and no artistic event of any worth without conflict and tension of personality:

> Rehearsals were always immensely lively, with never a slack or unconcentrated moment . . . Personally I don't think I got through any production with him without a bicker somewhere along the line. But he was always the one who made the gesture of reconcialition – usually by some extravagantly absurd and funny statement. But once we had a row which, through my fault, reached proportions whereby we were non-speakers for two days. It all had to do with the severed head of Hastings in *Richard III*. Tony's gesture of reconciliation was to give me, very solemnly, a small brown paper bag of rather squashed cherries.

Not only a great man of the theatre, he was great in himself, the clue to his greatness being, as Guinness put it, that this lay in the fact that he was never "all things to all men. He never cut his cloth, or trimmed his sails, to suit other personalities, but gave wholly himself . . . He had great personal humility – and rather hoped for it in others. And riding above all else was his laughter – rich, ironic, kind and memorable . . ."

The address was a long one and showed how Guinness had become, and was to remain, a master of that neglected form, the funeral oration. This address ought to be studied in schools as a model of its kind. It summarised Guthrie's career and its inspirational moments, especially that moment in *Henry VIII* at Stratford, with Anthony Quayle in the name role, when Guthrie told the whole tale of the Reformation and the break with Rome in a piece of silent business which only took seconds to act. Guinness had most liked, among Guthrie's production, *The Cherry Orchard*, with Charles Laughton, Flora Robson and the Liveseys, *Henry V* with Olivier, *Peer Gynt* with Richardson, and *All's Well* at Stratford Ontario (in which he himself had played the King of France).

He also listed Guthrie's personal eccentricities with great affection. How he admired Victorians and cats, and had a streak of caring in him: "It was typical of him," said Guinness, "on a very cold night, surreptitiously to push a hot-water bottle across the stage to a shivering Titania."

His gifts also extended into welding communities together, especially divided ones, as happened in the case of the first season in Ontario, where there were Episcopalians, Presbyterians, Methodists, Catholics, Baptists and "including also that sect which feels it vanity to wear buttons". The effect of his six-foot-four striding about and smiling on all, had been miraculous: the result became that "strict teetotallers began to keep whisky and gin in their homes for visiting Anglicans, Baptists – not greatly given to colour – bought and planted geraniums round the theatre, and at the dedication Catholics deigned to join in the Lord's Prayer with everyone else".

Guinness ended his address with an account of the few minutes after Guthrie's death. He obtained Judy's permission for this "totally Guthrie-esque" piece of dialogue:

When the doctor arrived, just after his death, he looked at Tony and said, "Surprising humility." Judy replied, "Yes, surprising humility; but quite tiresome!" The doctor thought for a moment and then said, "Surprising humility, and – yes – quite tiresome!" William Tyrone Guthrie. May his noble soul rest in happy peace, in the God he trusted.

38

The guise of anonymity

"Biography is a convenient fiction," wrote Peter Ackroyd in his life of T.S. Eliot. "We cannot hope to understand Eliot as he knelt . . . in the presence of his God . . . We cannot reach into the mystery of his solitude." This last sentence, as the critic Barbara Everett pointed out in an essay on Eliot and his biographers, was decidedly odd because, as a poet, Eliot had often been trying to express just that sense of mystery through his verse. A comparable process always took place in Guinness, who, whatever the nature of the public mask he wore, tried to convey the inner life of every character he played by tapping into some inward experience or memory of his own.

Guinness had three times lent his prestige to *The Cocktail Party* and on each of these three occasions the play had largely been a critical and commercial success by virtue of his participation in it (although he himself felt the play had never been done full justice). Eliot held for Guinness a lifelong attraction, for Eliot was a reclusive and private yet famous man on account of his thinking and writing, and this was what Guinness would have liked to have been had he not been an actor. Yet it is also true that Eliot's authority in the intellectual Western world (both before and after he was awarded the Nobel Prize in 1948) had become almost grotesquely huge. This, although to a lesser extent, was what happened to Guinness in the world of theatre.

Eliot's "hollow" man was similar in some ways to the proto-typical little man Guinness had so often played, for it is, as Everett indicated about Eliot, often through a fullness that someone comes to think of himself or herself as "hollow" ("Socrates's ironic 'all I know is that I know nothing' is the oldest and toughest of philosophic underminings"). Both Eliot and Guinness had something strongly in common in that both wanted to undermine the biographers.

Guinness's elaborate modesty concealed – or lived alongside – an immodesty and sometimes rank and raw impatience. How often can modesty be pointed out as the public ritual of the defensive, insecure person? Everything in Eliot's life "not only supports, but supports with judgement, that expressed wish not to have a biography written . . . but this is far from the impulse of secrecy," went on Everett. And then, illuminatingly as far as Guinness was concerned, "Poets, like Hamlet's players, 'tell all'."

When Eliot died in 1965 Guinness had read from his later works at his Westminster Abbey memorial service. Again, once more, to express his love of Eliot's work, Guinness agreed in 1972 to read "Little Gidding", the last of the *Four Quartets*, on television.

At first, when they rehearsed the poem, it did not go well at all: "He just droned on a bit, all rather repetitive," said David Cellan Jones, the director who then suggested they take a trip down to the Huntingdonshire manorhouse which was the poem's setting, contradicting completely Ackroyd's lofty discovery of the "absence" of fact in Eliot's *Four Quartets*. "We look for a recognisable landscape and find it concealed," wrote Ackroyd of Burnt Norton. This was not at all true. What to Guinness sounded like strange abstractions in the poem became extremely clear. And as Eliot's poetry invited a kind of complicity in the reader ("No, I am not Lord Hamlet," was the knowing, self-mocking aside that would seem to have suited Guinness best), so Guinness was perfectly suited to this peculiarly modest/immodest mind of the great Anglican convert who shared with him the profound conviction that the self that lives should be separate from the self that acts (in Eliot's case "writes"). At the same time Eliot, paradoxically, could assert, "The experience of a poem is the experience both of a moment and of a lifetime. It is very much like our intenser experiences of other human beings."

One cardinal mistake Guinness made in his act of homage to Eliot was his wish, which the director wanted, to provide an introduction for the poem. "I don't want a script," Guinness told him. "It will be self-conscious. I don't think we should do it beforehand." But, as Cellan Jones remarked, Guinness was no ad-libber and the end-result was stilted and difficult to cut and edit.

But Guinness, holding a first edition of the poem reprinted larger than life on recycled paper, came into his own with the reading of the poem. One could well imagine that bombed street in the city just before the dawn light where the narrator meets the ghost:

> At the uncertain hour before the morning,
> Near the ending of interminable night.

39

Inside the mind of evil

"I want to be an artist."

"Of course you do. Everyone wants to be an artist."

The film Guinness had made of *The Horse's Mouth* had had a very coherent script, written by Guinness himself, a script moreover that had been nominated for an Oscar. It was an ambitious work and had more or less succeeded because at the time Guinness had just received his Oscar for *The Bridge on the River Kwai* (he had accepted his Oscar in the make-up and costume of Gulley Jimson and it made, in the press pictures, a telling contrast of faces with Colonel Nicholson). His performance as the half-mad, highly suspicious artist, when eventually seen, made also an impact wonderfully antithetical to the meticulous sense of justice Colonel Nicholson stood for.

"Who do you pray for?" someone asks Jimson.

"Me."

But in *The Horse's Mouth* there is no real adversary, no-one was making Gulley Jimson into a victim. Perhaps this was the problem too with the book itself, whose reputation at the moment is at low ebb. Perhaps now the artist's ego has become so monstrous and maniacal, that Gulley by comparison seems tame and old-fashioned. Indeed you could make a convincing case that society today has unconsciously manoeuvred itself into providing an outlet in art, popular music, drama, literature, even biography, for many potential dictators, sadists and violent criminals so that they may not directly express their destructiveness in political action or war. To want to play Hitler as the ultimate victim, therefore, was an adventurous move by Guinness. He felt he would be able to bring to the role his quality of objectivity.

While he studied this part he played John Mortimer's Q.C. father in *A Voyage Round My Father*. Just before it opened he was to be found at the *Oz* trial, conspicuously seated to the left of the dock. During the try-out week in Brighton, before the play came into the West End Mortimer felt, as other authors came into the West End Mortimer felt, as other authors were to feel, that Guinness was underplaying his role. "My father was an angry man consumed by inner anger at his blindness and I am not getting any of that." Guinness appeared to be astonished at Mortimer's reaction: "But surely you can see the anger in the breakfast scene by the way I hit my egg." This performance, which enjoyed a long and successful run at the Haymarket was completely, and unfairly, overshadowed later by Olivier in the same role on television. Olivier, with his much more direct and vulgar appeal for sympathy, turned the character into a popular hero, giving a huge and affecting performance rather than a well-observed study of a real person. And perhaps, while Guinness's sympathies with the blind, opiniated old lawyer were subject to a just sense of restraint, Olivier had no inhibitions which kept him aloof: he "blazed". He loved old Mortimer as he had loved Richard of Gloucester and every other villian he played because he himself had something of the dominating Machiavel.

Perhaps the same thing was wrong with Guinness when he came to film Hitler in Ennio di Concini's film *Hitler – The Last Ten Days*. The ten days in question were from 20 to 29 April 1945. They started with Hitler's irrevocable decision that he would remain in Berlin. Guinness spent ten months, or so he said later, researching and preparing for the role. At another time this became five months reading the records and seeing all the film. "My poor wife, my friends," he said, "have to put up with every new scrap of information I unearth. So I'm not depressed (by getting inside the mind of such an evil man). I'm obsessed."

But was he also prepared to strike out and declare anything outrageous or histrionic in the man? In fact the Hitler of the script, as well as being the more hackneyed maniac when, for instance, he threatens his own senior officers with execution, has quite a lot of sympathetic elements. And there is also his puritan streak which would recommend him to millions today when he boasts (this was a true and quintessentially Hitlerish stroke) how he stops everyone smoking.

For the most part Guinness took the line that Hitler was a Gulley Jimson *manqué*, that he sacrificed his vocation as an artist in order to restore law and order to his country, or, as someone in the film says, "What a pity for the world you couldn't have devoted your life to art." You feel quite sorry for the Guinness/Hitler, betrayed by the drug addict Goering, especially when his women, too, turn on him. ("The Germans are a nation of whores: destiny will punish them.") After all, as Guinness showed him, boyishly moving from foot to foot and with his extraordinary shy and shifty face, he was a moody anti-bourgeois and a misfit ("Nature is cruel, so I too must be cruel . . . They want to see me naked in a cage"). When at last he commits suicide the rest, the real villains of the film, as one might call them, celebrate by lighting up cigarettes and cigars, as if he were a pioneer of ASH and the anti-smoking lobby. (And, of course, his enemies Roosevelt, Churchill, and De Gaulle were all heavy smokers – as was Guinness himself.)

Guinness spent an inordinate amount of energy and thought in making himself into a rather close proximation of the man himself. As someone put it when meeting Guinness off the set, "I cannot quite account for the tremor of shock I felt when that pasty face, with its hooded mesmeric eyes above the little blot of the moustache, spoke with the amiable, relaxed musical voice of an English country gentleman." Amazingly, though, and this was where the research was important, the face was almost entirely his own. He grew a moustache and "gradually cut it down from each side. It's now a fraction too narrow – a sort of black postage stamp – but that is in order to make my nose look as broad as his." He also sought out someone who had seen Hitler in the bunker: Gerhardt Boldt, a cavalry captain sent with a message to the Führer who described to him elements of behaviour which he copied; how his left arm trembled, his left foot dragged, how he raised only one limp hand to his shoulder in a token Nazi salute.

Guinness thought it was his best work to date, but when he saw the film, he expressed disappointment. It was somehow a desultory picture and the performance, objective as it was in Guinness's new mood of paring away anything superfluous in a performance, totally lacked love and devilry. Where was the Hitler of Chaplin's satire, Brecht's Arturo Ui in his *Resistible Ascension*, or even Hollywood's big bad wolf? In fact he wasn't there at all, because of Guinness's deliberate holding back and desire to do something different. Guinness's reflective Hitler could never have swayed eight million people, a man who had, as Guinness said of him, "a great following outside Germany, in France, Italy, Spain, Sweden, Denmark, Norway . . ." Guinness blamed the script: "The film has been cut by half-an-hour and cut sensibly but I wish the script could have been cut before we started." This contrasted with what he said during the filming, namely that Concini had a "touch of genius . . . Hitler, surprisingly, had a sense of humour." And Guinness made another *ex cathedra* statement: "Let's face it, wicked or evil people are fundamentally more interesting dramatically than good ones. The other day I was asked why I didn't make a nice film about someone nice, like Nelson.* I wrote back to say I had no objection to playing Macbeth, who wasn't a particularly nice man either.† Failure perhaps produces weather-vane moods, for at another time he named Hitler as one of the four or five best performances he had given: "Although it was dismissed I thought the performance had something."

When he came to do some publicity on the Duke of York Steps in Pall Mall, and his car was parked in a forbidden place he was politely approached by an elderly policeman who wanted to book him. "I was going to pounce on you sir, but I don't want to end up in a concentration camp," observed the latter who knew that something was afoot. But on screen Guinness's performance did not terrify: the Israeli film censorship banned the film for representing Hilter "in a human light without giving expression to the terrible murders for which he is responsible".

He did not pursue the evil in the good man, as Chesterton might have done, when in the same year he played Pope Innocent III, a small part in *Brother Sun, Sister Moon*, a sumptuous film Franco Zeffirelli made about St Francis of Assisi. Olivier had backed out from playing this role. Of Guinness Zeffirelli said:

He was presented as a giant. His first appearance in the film was at the top of a gold-encrusted staircase with gold mosaics. Byzantine, embodying the glory of the Church. When he descended the long flight of stairs each step he took was a coming down to earth, as it were. All the glory, the paraphernalia, the accessories fell away. He came down to this group of poor young friars . . . One had the impression

---

* The author once thought Guinness would make a wonderful Nelson and sent him the script of his play about Nelson later performed in Oxford. Guinness thought the title splendid ("I Forgot How Nelson Died") and found the play intriguing and enjoyable. However, he continued, even if he was available, which he was not, "I do not think I am right for your Nelson. Too old and heavy now."
† But what awakens sympathy for Macbeth, surely, is that he has a conscience and a desire to be good which he allows to be crushed.

he envied them for their simplicity and poverty. There he was trapped in luxury and glory desperately wanting to begin his life again, perhaps on a different course, perhaps to be poor and simple like those young friars.

The director added: "I have a feeling Guinness is a bit like that himself." He worked one week on this film. "He is very withdrawn," concluded Zeffirelli. But "why should he be pinned down? You see, it's the tip of the iceberg again. The English would call him shy but I don't think he's really shy. He is, from my point of view, the exact opposite of the Latin temperament."

40

Cold feet (I)

By this time Guinness had a small London flat in Smith Square near Westminster Abbey Cloister. It was also very near to the Cathedral into which he would often repair for spiritual solitude. Even later he would stay at the Connaught Hotel, near the Jesuit Church in Farm Street. At Petersfield there was the red brick and green copper-domed Church of St Lawrence happily without "hideous plaster statues of brogue-ridden Irish priests". On 3 April 1973, the day after his fifty-ninth birthday, he sat at his small writing desk in the sober blue and white drawing room on the fourth floor: he was now studying the part of Dr Wickstead in a new play by Alan Bennett due to open in six weeks' time. In the small hall of the flat were hanging several framed costume drawings of roles played by Merula in the 1930s: the lean majestic Tiger, one from *Richard II*, another from *School for Scandal*. Guinness moved to sit in his sumptuous peacock chair. The silence was interrupted by the soft ticking of a clock. The draught blew open the door of the drawing-room.

The day before he had gone home to Kettlebrook Meadows to have the chance to walk around the garden and look at the fish in the pond. But it was pouring with rain. He had a slight gastric infection and felt irritable. Yet he was healthy, although the glowing face was now surrounded by wispy white hair. He was dressed in a dark "mod" shirt and a blue suit.

He thought that perhaps *Habeas Corpus*, the title of the play he was studying, was a bit misleading because it had nothing to do with legal affairs. It meant, in Latin, "You must have the body", a phrase Bennett chose to take literally.

"I play a doctor who is immoral, or is it amoral? He is inclined to interfere with his patients:"

I suspect [Alan Bennett] would be a bit tetchy if I described the play as a farce but it has all the ingredients of a farce. But it's also like a kind of Restoration play, some of it goes into doggerel verse and rhyming couplets. It is unlike anything I've ever been connected with before. The form is rather odd, but it is very funny indeed in places. Music is used but all played by cinema organ.

I was a bit scared about being in a sort of permissive play but there are no ordinary four-letter words and no-one is actually in the nude.

But Alan Bennett, an Oxford graduate, mediaeval historian and scholarly investigator, was just within the pale, just the right (or wrong) side of decency. As Michael Codron, who produced both *Wise Child* and *Habeas Corpus*, said, Guinness was much happier with *Habeas Corpus* probably because he seemed able, with Ronald Eyre directing, to voice continually his insecurities about the whole enterprise: "I don't think I'm quite right for it," he would keep saying, or "I can't do it, I'm not going to be any good, why did you choose me?" He worried about the Latin title and one day, when they were auditioning an actress for another part in the play he turned to Bennett saying "Cold feet". Bennett was impressed with this new idea. "What a wonderful title." "No, no, no," said Guinness, "I've *got* cold feet."

Codron related how Guinness suggested he should at the end of the play introduce a little dance of death. He had begun this fashion of a celebratory dance with Harcourt-Reilly in *The Cocktail Party*, continued it in *Time Out of Mind*. Olivier had taken up the idea, possibly unconsciously, in his exultant little dance as Shylock in the National Theatre production of 1970. Bennett disliked the idea, saying "That's not my play." Guinness begged him to let him try it. The dance he produced was, said Codron, "magical, haunting, just what was needed". When they played in Oxford prior to London, Guinness had another attack of cold feet. Cutlery fell noisily to the table in the Randolph Hotel as Guinness was overheard telling Dennis Van Thal, his agent, "I think you're going to have to get me out of this one." When the play opened in London it received excellent reviews but Guinness thought everyone else in the play was good except for him. Again, the distrust went too deep for any triumph to alleviate. One thinks of Yeats's self-styled epitaph:

> Cast a cold eye
> On life, on death.

Horseman, pass by!

The early years of the 1970s were slightly desultory in terms of new projects for Guinness although he read as much as ever. Approaching the age of sixty he seemed to be slackening off, although this may just have reflected that nothing very exciting came his way and that, since the intellectual vacuum of the war years when he was forced back on his own resources, he had not really thought of originating any idea of his own. He did have the notion to write a play about Jonathan Swift, which came to him out of a charitable enterprise at Aldeburgh in which he had read the *Journal to Stella*. Swift's description of taking a swim in the river at Chelsea during a hot summer had attracted him in particular. Adapting Swift for the stage seemed a fitting progression from his three previous adaptations. But if it was Swift's anger, his bitterness, his darkness and his wit which attracted Guinness, how would he handle these when he came to play them on stage, if ever he did? For the most part, now, he became involved in minor enterprises. In 1970, he claimed when talking to a journalist, he made only £90 and he underlined the insecure feeling all actors had: "Each morning it's simply a question of *How insecure shall I feel today?* One never knows, does one?"

Yet he turned down the superb opportunity to play Prospero at the National Theatre in Peter Hall's new regime (and with Hall directing). He still felt the scars of Macbeth, but perhaps this was an inexcusable rejection based on wanting to control everything and have, as actors tend naturally to want, everything on his own terms. Hall shrewdly commented:

> Bad news from Alec Guinness whom I had asked to do Prospero, a part he had never played. He has decided he dare not in such an exposed situation as the NT. Funny, everyone always agrees the propositions, and then gets out of them. At least in the theatre. I do it myself. Perhaps we are too anxious to be loved, or perhaps the basic insecurity about our work makes us agree to every possibility as something too reassuring to refuse. Perhaps we only contemplate something seriously *after* we have agreed to do it.

Here was a role in which Guinness could have excelled had he been prepared to work with Hall. Was it overweening pride or overpowering humility which made him say no? Opposites are sometimes equals. Probably it was just cold feet.

The year of his sixtieth birthday, 1974, passed with two television films, *The Gift of Friendship* by John Osborne, in which he played Jocelyn Broome, a largish insignificant part in a not too significant play, and Shaw's *Caesar and Cleopatra* in which he was cast as more of a grandfatherly potentate than a sexy old man, opposite Geneviève Bujold, the French star. They made a strangely incongruous pair without much of the right chemistry that is supposed to ignite their wit. While Bujold was not feeling very well during the rushed period of filming Guinness himself became openly fractious. He didn't like his performance at all.

He seems briefly to have considered at this time the idea of writing his autobiography. He owned up to writing three chapters but did not go on. "I do wish people would stop asking to do it for me." At fifty he had told the *Sunday Express*, "I have no ambitions left," but now he somewhat reluctantly admitted to trying to find new classics. On Wednesday 12 February 1975 he attended the Queen's reception for the media at Buckingham Palace with several other actors (Ustinov, Finney) and many directors, television channel controllers and the like. He tramped the reception rooms, drank the sweetish white wine and choked on the Lyons pâté. He would rather have been anonymous, but he was there. He reflected on the worst moment of his life, when he had been knighted in 1959, and the band at the Palace had struck up with "I'm Gonna Wash That Man Right Outa My Hair".

Now he was sixty-one he deigned to make one appearance on stage: in Julian Mitchell's adaptation of Ivy Compton-Burnett's *A Family and a Fortune* at the Apollo, a first directorial encounter with Alan Strachan and a last and touching acting partnership with Margaret Leighton, with whom he had acted at the New, who was by this time seriously ill with multiple sclerosis and had to walk with a stick. Pretending nothing was wrong he quietly insisted she receive top billing, and moved out of the star dressing-room on stage level so that she could make her many costume changes with the minimum of effort.

Guinness had first been asked to play the part of Dudley four years before and had read the book with a view to it being filmed. But it had been relegated to the back of his mind until he was turning out some scripts to send back to their owners when he came across this one. Dudley was the hanger-on of the family, one of those misled people who believe they can "edit" their own lives; as Guinness said, a kind of Chekhovian conception with a "bit more steel tucked into him". He was amusing, pleasant, had to sing for his supper and was aware of the "jealousies, and how that he's been hurt and how that comes through".

People were sometimes critical of how he fixed first on the externals of a part, said Guinness at the time, but "unless I can look like I would like to look . . . then I wouldn't tackle it". With Dudley he used a wig with a quiff at the back, to catch this most schoolboyish of men in his late fifties. Guinness brought out every last shred of irony in the character: it was, said Strachan, like "excavating the innards of a crab".

In May 1975, a month after the play opened, the more mischievous social side of Guinness was written up by Kenneth Williams in his Diaries, posthumously published in 1993. He reported that Guinness wanted him to play a small joke on some American guests at a dinner party. Rona, the wife of Gordon Jackson, at this time well-known for his role as Hudson the butler in *Upstairs Downstairs* on television, and Williams needed to arrive early and "had to hide in the kitchen. Rona was introduced as Mrs Rona Trossach, and then he clapped his hands and called out 'Hyde', and I had to enter with the tray and the Americans shrieked 'Oh my God, Alec.' — I said I thought it was a tasteless piece of vulgarity".

Guinness called his exploration of Jonathan Swift's work by the ugly, unpromising name of *Yahoo*. Swift's imaginary brute with the form of man had just been used in a speech by Harold Wilson, the Prime Minister, and Guinness believed it had acquired respectability. He wanted above all to get away from the received idea of Swift, underline the *saeve indignatio*, as well as the literary impersonator and entertainer. He asked Alan Strachan to help him devise the portrait and also to direct it. Michael Codron, who loved "marriage broking" with Guinness, was to present the evening while Nicola Pagett was asked to play Stella, and Angela Thorne Vanessa.

Guinness committed himself to the idea with enormous enthusiasm: there were only three minutes, he said, when he was not on stage. This was a far cry from Abel Drugger. Learning was something of an ordeal and he went through his lines with a young actor, telling him how once, when he and Merula were on a ship to America, he recorded an arduous part he had to learn on tape in order to play it over and over again to himself. To depersonalise the character he had read it in an absolutely flat tone, which he thought would make learning easier. But the result was disastrous: he could not bear to listen to it.

Although *Yahoo*, when it opened, drew good audiences and ran successfully for six months, Guinness gave more of a *pointilliste* than a barnstorming performance. Guiness did not focus enough on the ferocious side of Swift, while during the long sections from *A Modest Proposal*, for example, "A child will make two dishes at an entertainment for friends, and when the family dines alone, the fore or hind quarters will make a reasonable dish . . .", he wanted to show Swift's human face, which was perhaps impossible in the context of what Swift was trying to say. The main consensus was probably with Peter Hall, who wrote in his diary on 8 October 1976:

> Guinness appears to have at the moment a bad attack of "the lovelies". He seems to me to want, above all, to be loved by the audience . . . What we received tonight was a gentle half-smiling ironist about as far away from the ferocious misanthropic Swift as a duck-pond is from the Pacific Ocean.

John Tydeman, the director, then Head of BBC Radio Drama, felt it was not a success. He recalled being invited with friends afterwards to have supper with Guinness not at a restaurant, but at the flat in Smith Square. Edith Evans had just died, and Guinness wanted to watch a programme in tribute. Afterwards Guinness regaled them with his marvellous Edith Evans stories, especially of the extraordinary incident in *Cousin Muriel*, in which Guinness played the advertising agent son of a kleptomaniac woman. He had to say a wounding line to Mummy about stealing and financial fiddles and during one rehearsal, after pleasing his leading lady, as he thought, he gave it plenty of conviction. She stiffened, asking him if he intended saying the line in the way he had. He justified it in terms of how the character should say the line to his mother whereupon Edith Evans gave a great wail and flung her arms in the air screaming, "Alec doesn't love me any more! . . . He *hates* me!" and threw herself down on the stage, drummed with her feet and seized the corner of a Persian rug between her teeth.

41

How can a robot look upset?

Much in demand, Guinness had agreed to appear in a dramatisation of Evelyn Waugh's *The Ordeal of Gilbert Pinfold* at the Royal Exchange Theatre in Manchester. He recalled how he and Waugh had first met on their hands and knees collecting up hundreds of bangles dropped by an old lady at Edith Sitwell's inauguration into the Catholic Church. He now seemed to want to extricate himself from Waugh, for his Hampshire neighbour, Ronald Harwood, who had adapted the novel for the stage, found himself invited round to Kettlebrook Meadows one weekend to have dinner with Alan Bennett, who was staying for the weekend and who, it was made clear to Harwood, was working on a new play. Harwood said on his way home, "I smell trouble."

But the extrication was not at all open. Guinness telephoned Harwood some weeks later and told him he had to go into hospital in early 1977 for a hernia operation (he had already had an operation for a double hernia some five or more years earlier, caused by flying about as Marley's Ghost in the television film *Scrooge*). Harwood felt that Guinness had engineered the operation as an elaborate way of getting off the hook, whereupon the "diplomatic hernia" became something of a cult. At any rate the operation took place and *Gilbert Pinfold* was cancelled as far as he was concerned, although it was eventually produced in 1977. At this moment he was also about to be relaunched into international stardom with the release of a film which became as famous as, if not more famous than *A Bridge on the River Kwai*.

Two years before, a film script had arrived at Petersfield:

It came through the door and the moment I saw a sci-fi sticker on it I said to myself "Oh crumbs, it's not for me." But I started to read and I had to turn the page.

Guinness compared the script of *Star Wars* to le Carré's *The Honourable Schoolboy*:

> It had vigour and I finished it at a sitting. Was that normal? No, not at all. But it's a jolly good sign. I don't apply any professional "technique", if that's the word, when I read scripts. But if I'm held then I think there's a chance the public will be held too. Probably the last time I went through a film script so swiftly was when James Kennaway's *Tunes of Glory* came into my hands.

Guinness agreed at once to meet the director, George Lucas, with a view to playing the master warrior Obi-Ben Kenobi. He thought the part difficult because Kenobi was good. There was a danger of becoming "a bit smug, a bit know-all". Kenobi had to have an "extra sense of what's going on". A short man, as short as Guinness, Lucas was very vulnerable, very nervous of people, and shy. Anthony Daniels, who was to play the robotic character C3P0, said Lucas carried a little black book in which he wrote everything down. His own part of C3P0 was full of "terribly corny lines", such as "Curse my metal body, I wasn't fast enough," which were, in an odd way, reminiscent of Victorian children's fiction.

After discussion with Lucas, Guinness agreed to play the role. But they at once had a crisis because, a week or so before shooting, Lucas changed the script which in its previous version had Kenobi appear on page twenty, when he became leader and tutor of a small band of rebels. He then led these on their series of adventures that "culminated in a giant space battle that destroyed the evil empire's principal weapon, the 'Death Star', and ended with Ben Kenobi giving everyone medals".

Lucas had to inform Guinness of the important plot change, and as he did, grew nervous. "Although Ben is the leader," he explained, "I think it might be better if he . . . Oh, like kinda died halfway through the picture." Guinness was upset. Understandably so. Actors do not want to play a character that dies halfway through the film; nor did they want to be informed of their premature demise over lunch.

Although he remained extremely civil Guinness later told Lucas he no longer wanted to do the picture. Lucas had a major anxiety attack, which led to another long meeting with Guinness. "I went on and on," Lucas said, "about how important the change was in order to make the story work. And how important it was to have a powerful actor play Ben, especially now that he had so much less screen time. As a writer, he was easily convinced."

As an actor, too, Guinness eventually came around. But he became more than an actor in the film: "an incredible blessing", Lucas was to call it later. The preparation for the filming was on a Herculean scale: what especially endeared Lucas to Guinness was that he himself brought the costumes to London to see if Guinness liked them, while he came to all the fittings.

Daniels spent six very undignified months preparing for C3PO, which sometimes entailed "standing naked in a cold room at Elstree" while they "faxed" his body for its robotic role. When Guinness and Merula arrived at Heathrow in 1976 for the flight out to Tunis, where they were to film on location, Daniels first saw him as a grand figure whose limousine drove right up to the plane. However, in the course of seeing much of them over the next weeks, he found Guinness extraordinarily approachable while Merula was "a living saint". Guinness worried over whether the young actor was being paid proper expenses and offered to advance him some. They spent two or three weeks on desert location on some salt flats in windy and grotesquely hot weather on a hotel diet of unremitting veal or chicken – at one point the Guinnesses went down with food poisoning while there were often long frustrating waits while the ailing special effects had to be sorted out.

Incarcerated in metal, at one time having to lose an arm (torn off in a fight), Daniels found the waiting horribly painful, while he was generally rather embarrassed about the whole restriction of being a robot. Guinness helped his confidence greatly, he was especially clever at indirectly paying him compliments, while his calm and interest permeated everyone, including Mark Hamel who played Luke Skywalker. The image Lucas had of Guinness was of him sitting in a chair with a relaxed, approachable elegance, as if on the deck of a ship on some exotic cruise floating down a celluloid river. As for Guinness, Lucas in his total concentration reminded him of the young David Lean. But, unlike Lean, Lucas did not dictate or impose. During the actual filming he had little to say although able to sense when Guinness was uncomfortable and would walk across and "drop a brief word in your ear". Others found him not all that interested in the actors as such: "Very retiring, he doesn't enjoy directing actors very much. He would invariably say, after a take, "Terrific; can you do it again a bit faster?"

The heat and the waiting while they tampered with the machines was too much for Daniels but grimly he stuck it out: then, "One day Alec blew up ... Gosh I'm not wrong," thought C3PO. Guinness quickly returned to serenity: "a whirlpool of serenity" was the phrase Daniels used. During the laser/sword fight between Guinness and another actor his assailant lost concentration and failed to keep to the pre-arranged numbers with the result that Guinness "hit the wall and the floor. They ran towards him. He was all right but everyone was shocked. It was the fact he didn't lose his temper made me realise how angry he was."

"His presence," said Lucas, "lent so much credibility that everyone finally believed that giant furry aliens and talking robots made perfect sense." It was even more than a presence, however. Familiarity breeds contempt. The machines such as R2D2 ("Reel Two Dialogue Two") and C3P0, ("an euphonic accessory"), as well as the hirsute monsters, were often treated as they looked, or relegated to a sub-human plane and ignored. But Guinness would enter this world of weird creatures and adapt entirely to it, yet he remained well-centred in himself, and kept exactly within his own brief. As such he helped the cast and the production team to treat the menagerie as real, sentient beings. He brought to *Star Wars* and its two sequels (both written by Lucas but directed by others) in which Kenobi returns as a ghost (or as an underlying deity of "The Force"), its human identity and at a profound level helped the film to communicate its sense of the good (conceived of as an energy source) triumphing over the bad.

During the filming on location Merula, Guinness's own saint, would be all this time out sketching in the local town or market: on one occasion she was drawing a mosque when some of the gendarmerie stopped her, threatened arrest, and wanted to confiscate her sketchbook. She gave them a few pages, but kept her own drawings tucked away.

One moment during the filming was of special significance to the director. In the cockpit of Han Solo's spaceship where the area was cramped, and when Han was at the controls – with Chewie, the giant furry alien, next to him, and Luke and Ben standing squeezed in behind them – they played a scene during which Chewie had to reach up and hit a switch above Kenobi's head. In one of the takes Chewie reached up to flip the switch for the "umpteenth time and accidentally hit Alec right square in the face".

He was unhurt but taken completely by surprise, so he fell out of character. When Lucas looked at the film the next day in the editing machine he noticed that when he took the film from the moment Guinness was hit and studied it one image at a time he saw Guinness's face go through a series of different characters, "all in a split second, starting with Ben and ending with Alec, with about a half-dozen completely different characters in between".

Lucas then came to understand more clearly what he called

the incredible physical nature of creating a character; how a truly gifted actor is so concentrated, so thorough that even their facial muscles are transformed. Like a chameleon, Alec has a lot of different shades, different colours and different characters. Every frame of film from the moment he was hit was a different character . . . until he finally arrived at Alec Guinness.

42

Of spies and inner space

The play that Alan Bennett had been working on still had to undergo what the playwright called "its elaborate wooing process, like a formal dance", before Guinness would agree to be in it. The subject of this play, *The Old Country*, in which Guinness agreed in the end to play the part of the Philby-inspired Hilary, was treachery. This was a subject which may today seem historically innate in the European character. Maybe it had a spiritual source: if so, this must go back to the Reformation when many powerful, present-day institutions were created in an atmosphere of betrayal to what had gone before. But perhaps the dichotomy of European spirit, its torn, rent quality, has always been there and instead of the British Empire expanding, as someone once observed, in a fit of absent-mindedness, it was a neurotic compensation for some deep division in the nation's psyche.

Whatever the truth of this, the means by which the modern state came to power and held on to its power had suddenly re-surfaced in the England of the middle 1950s and especially in the flowering of spy mythology. The cold-war techniques of subversion, betrayal, blackmail, concealment of motive and manipulated misdirection of affection became as current and fashionable as they had been at the time of the writing of *Hamlet* and *Othello*. This was perhaps why Shakespeare, presented in a hundred different ways, became so overwhelmingly popular. There was a big difference, however: this was an England in decline, not an expanding and buoyant new young country. In the late 1970s there would have seemed to be little by way of a fundamental soundness of spirit left in the English character which gave new hope for the future. "There's something rotten in the state of Denmark ... all is not as it seems." Treachery now so seemed to permeate English public life that one almost suspected that the country was back in the days of Mary Queen of Scots.

Hilary's brother-in-law, Duff, has travelled out to the Soviet Union to persuade Hilary, who had defected just before he was due to be arrested, to return to his homeland. The pair engage in a massive duel of mind and emotion, but Hilary can no longer feel, or can hardly even remember, the reasons that caused him to damage his country so many years ago, while the interrogator of his motives, Duff, has also emptied his soul of principle and virtue.

Bennett shows the thinness of aspiration, the rootlessness of middle-class English society. As he said himself the characters are discovered "seemingly in the English countryside . . . but it emerges they are outside Moscow". For Hilary loyalty can be bartered without a shred of shame, and crime expiated in a kind of affected cynicism (Hilary is perhaps more like Blunt than Philby). For Duff life is a game where the self-seeker may win honours for his ego. He is perhaps the new Englishman signalling the launch of the coarse materialism of the 1980s. Neither of them can feel, and neither of them has a soul. It sounds a bit like a variation on the theme of *The Prisoner*. This was not middle-Europe, however, but comfortable England. So here was Guinness yet again, perhaps more significantly than in other popular plays of the period, holding the mirror up to nature. As Bennett said later, "He made it like his own life."

They rehearsed in Cheyne Walk in Thomas More's Old Church Hall where a splendid statue of Henry VIII's Chancellor looked down the Thames in the direction of Westminster – as if to anticipate having his head removed soon as a penalty for his integrity. Guinness arrived – he had never before worked with the director, Clifford Williams – bearing Russian vodka and caviar. The cast included Rachel Kempson (behind whose back Guinness would on occasions, in black joke mood, pull scurrilous faces, as if to say, "Look at her" – this shocked the director), Heather Canning, Faith Brook and John Phillips, who was playing Duff.

Bennett continually worried about whether Guinness was not underplaying the whole part, and at one point stormed out of the rehearsal in anger, whereupon Guinness remarked drolly, "What's wrong with him? Something I did?" Williams found it very hard to make a judgement on his performance, while Guinness was anyway, he thought, not an actor he could direct. It was a case of finding "somewhere for him to perch on" and otherwise, as

Williams put it, "arranging the traffic". Guinness stuck to his under-energised guns and the performance finally turned out as great a success as that of Dr Wicksteed in *Habeas Corpus*. Bernard Levin described it in *The Times* as played by Guinness with "an infinite weariness of the soul", while Duff was "played with a no less consummately polished emptiness by John Phillips".

But there was a price to be paid for all this outer projection of inner emptiness. Guinness maintained his innocence by being what the director could only describe as "vitriolic" to Merula when they went out to dinner together. "What sort of life would it be if I couldn't grumble about the missing coffee-pot, the dangerously exposed electrical appliances, the burned potatoes, the oil paint on the door knob, the barking of her dog, or the forgotten arrival of my train from London?" He would take out the tension on the person closest to him who just, while he was being waspish, froze and said nothing. For, of course, Guinness was not really "under-energising", he was seized and active with a secret life on which he kept the lid well battened down. Or nearly so. He would allow nothing to "blow the lid off his closely guarded privacy" as Simon Callow has put it. But he needed – as who wouldn't? – a few safety-valves where he could hiss and bubble in full view of the public.

As a result of the production Bennett noted that Guinness was inimitable: "There has never been a satisfactory imitation of him. Peter Sellers had one," Bennett recalled, "but it wasn't very good . . . He doesn't leave anything spare for the public outside his acting."

When Guinness was performing in *The Old Country* in 1978 speculation about how much he made out of *Star Wars* grew to its height and like most reports of the earnings of actors, reached exaggerated dimensions. "*Star Wars* takings are already $100 million. Sir Alec gets 2% of profits", ran one *Daily Express* headline. The truth, apparently, was that his contract was for 2.25 per cent of the director's profit, which was only 20 per cent of the film profits. Of course this was on top of his fee, but let us say the profit was $100 million (which was absurd at that time, anyway, because the film itself was expensive to make), then Guinness would have received $450,000. Of course there were still *The Return of the Jedi* and *The Empire Strikes Back* – "I will do them if the lines are sayable" – so ultimately the return must have been exceptional. Yet the idea that Guinness had, overnight, been turned into a multi-millionaire was false.

"I would keep more, if I went to live in America. But living in Los Angeles I'd go completely mad" (Guinness momentarily closed his eyes at the painful thought). He decided to stay in England. "As I pop through the stage door every night, I think, 'This is what I wanted to do as a kid: going to the dressing-room, reading my correspondence, taking my time putting on my make-up . . .'" But he did add: "You think Denis Healey (the Chancellor of the Exchequer) might send one a letter of thanks for staying. I don't suppose he will."

Guinness was pleased with *Star Wars*: "It wasn't smug," he said. But he was a bit puzzled at some reactions: "It's funny how people identify." One person, perfectly sane, or so he said, wrote to him, "I wish to be a Jedi knight. I wish to come to outer space." He wrote back saying, "I earn my living as an actor at the Queen's Theatre."

43

A savaged saint

Tinker Tailor Soldier Spy, the first of John le Carré's Smiley novels in which Guinness was cast as Smiley, was filmed in 1978. About that time and just later there were at least two newspaper articles which claimed that le Carré based the character of George Smiley upon Guinness. This ignored the fact that the first appearance of Smiley went back to le Carré's first novel, *Call for the Dead,* published in 1961, and by the time he came to write *Smiley's People* Smiley had already appeared in five other books. In the very opening of *Call for the Dead* Smiley was described as "without school, parents, regiment or trade", and as "a traveller in the guard's van of the social express".

Yet was the idea so fanciful? Could it be that le Carré had found all those extraordinary films which Guinness made in the 1950s, formed the idea of a hero which was a composite, or perhaps the essence, of all those different characters Guinness had played? Smiley and Guinness certainly had much in common.

The name itself had a Guinness ring to it. It was neutral, ironic. Almost anonymous. Like the name Abel Drugger* for the tobacconist, the character was almost the opposite of the name. Smiley had little to smile about: "We are not speaking of pleasure." Although he far surpassed Drugger in intelligence, and although he was a major, huge character as opposed to a tiny, minor one, they shared one vital characteristic: both were dupes. Of course Smiley was not only a dupe, but somewhere deep inside Smiley was the cuckold, the betrayed, the essential Drugger; above all the innocent. He was victim and hero at the same time.

Smiley did not stand out in a crowd. Neither did Guinness.

---

* The minor character Guinness played in *The Alchemist* in 1946 and the part which he sometimes said he would like to go on playing for ever.

Smiley was plump, myopic. Guinness had to fatten out to play him, gathering several stone in weight, but even so Guinness was becoming more and more a short, barrel-shaped man. If Smiley had no look-alike face in an actor of stature – after all he was a creature of imagination – the famous English spy Maurice Oldfield bore an uncanny resemblance to Guinness. Le Carré had no George Cruikshank to create caricatures that would become so powerfully embedded in the mind that, when Dickens's characters came to be played in films, actors and directors would base their impersonations upon his drawings (as had happened with Guinness's Fagin). Another, more complicated process had to take place with le Carré.

Another striking quality which suggests that le Carré might have drawn on Guinness's past performances was Smiley's saintly quality, albeit that of the battered or savaged saint.* A sense of professional failure may often have substituted a sense of spiritual failure, but there was also a strong vein of the metaphysical in Smiley's isolation. The superintendent in *Smiley's People*, who looks at the corpse of the emigré Russian general, notices that Smiley, engaged in similar contemplation, has an oddly moist face. The policeman sees this as a kind of sympathetic horror in the presence of death which he knows only too well, so that it becomes for him as if he and Smiley were sharing a spiritual perception: "You wondered what the hell Christ bothered to die for, if He ever died at all." Even when he had first flashed his torch on Smiley's face he had remarked to himself, as if le Carré had Guinness specifically in mind when he wrote these words: Smiley's face was, he observed, "unlike your face or mine. It was not one face. More like a history of the human face." Le Carré, who is a much more flamboyant artist in words than Guinness is in gestures, went on to a baroque elaboration of the idea. But the point had been registered.

Saintliness, although in run-down or distorted form, also pervaded le Carré's depiction of the spying service as a closed order. The jargon, in the Smiley novels, was often that of celebrants or self-denying ascetics. Smiley gives the phrase "distant churches" to those aims in life that people find to substitute their spiritual

---

* Le Carré has claimed that his Smiley novels were about "national falling standards ... almost to do with meanness, mutual consideration and gentleness; the shameless adjustment by politicians of their position".

hunger, their deprivation of the wholesomeness of divine worship: "Party", "Circus", "marriage", "children". Smiley, too, has much of the philosophy of Chesterton's Father Brown with which Guinness was so conversant: to detect the criminal in the world you first found the criminal in yourself; to know one's adversary was to know oneself. Victory, when it came, brought no satisfaction. The image of Father Brown, with his round "Norfolk dumpling" face, his clumsy hands, and his similarity to our underground friend, the mole, took us from spying back to Hamlet's search, also, for his own identity. "Well said, old mole, can'st work i th' earth so fast?" asks Hamlet at the re-apparition of his father's ghost. In *Smiley's People*, as in *Hamlet*, religious imagery abounds, while Smiley is in many ways a Hamlet in reverse: his low-key, unglamorous pessimism does not tempt self-destruction. As le Carré said of Smiley, "He's also very understanding of human fallibility; he knows that most of life is led below the water's surface, and that people are very secretive creatures – secret even from themselves."

There were also many psychological similarities between le Carré himself and Guinness which were the more striking when considered in the light of the possibility that le Carré based Smiley upon Guinness's previous performances and something unconscious perhaps that he picked up from them. First of all both shared a deeply insecure family background. While Guinness knew no father and spent his childhood with his colourful and curious mother, le Carré passed most of his childhood living like a millionaire pauper. "We all knew," he said, "there was absolutely no money – the bills hadn't been paid, the staff hadn't been paid – we knew there was a lot to hide: women, the past, the present." Guinness wrote that he was born to confusion, he lived in thirty different hotels, lodgings and flats, each of which was deemed home until he and his mother "flitted", leaving behind "a wake of unpaid bills".

Le Carré, like Guinness, was turned into what he called "fake gentry", arriving in educated middle-class society feeling almost like a spy. He grew up feeling ashamed of himself: exactly similar to Guinness's state over his illegitimacy. He turned to story-telling as Guinness turned to acting: to organise narrative (in Guinness's case, identity and character) out of chaos, to "make an art" as he put it, "through jungles of confusion". But both also had a very staid, conventional side to their personalities. Le Carré joined the Foreign Office, Guinness the theatrical establishment.

So daily, too, le Carré and Guinness had shared the lonely outsider's sense of looking in. But both had from their fathers an imaginary, confused and yet somewhere deeply real sense of power. Both, in their childhoods passed in private boarding school privilege, felt at an early age what it was like to lead a double life. It was hardly surprising that both, much later on and when they were famous, felt alarmed at any intrusion into their privacy and grew extremely reluctant to discuss – except in their own time and on their own terms – anything of a personal or family nature. Recently, on hearing that someone planned to write a biography of him, le Carré took legal action to forestall him. In a more gentle manner Guinness also did all he could to discourage books about him being written.

Le Carré admitted that the double-life of his childhood introduced him to "familiarity with the sources of duplicity ... if I would knowledgeably about gothic conspiracies, it is because I had knowledge of them from earliest childhood. And is it surprising that I write about people who are emotionally exhausted?" Le Carré came nearest to creating an autobiographical portrait – or so it may be speculated – in the character of Magnus Pym in *A Perfect Spy*. As C.P. Snow the novelist once remarked, closely aligning le Carré with the actor, he was "putting on another of his disguises ... Le Carré is a good deal of a chameleon".

Yet and yet – and here we must beware of finding too much the same – there was also a remarkable difference between the insecurity of Guinness and that of le Carré. Guinness was given the stigma of illegitimacy and rejected by his father and, for some of the time, his mother; le Carré's father was always there, involved with his son who was unsure whether to love him or hate him; was it surprising, then, that le Carré should have created the "Circus", which someone once called "a chorus of male hates" but which le Carré himself felt, while doing "terrible things for a good cause", contained an element of nostalgia and redressed a sense of balance? Guinness's aggression towards others, especially men, had always been carefully sublimated, expressed in deliberate courtesy and politesse, and a disarming kindness. But sometimes, when I interviewed friends of Guinness, I was told that they did not really know if he liked them or not: he made them wary, watchful, on their guard. They loved him, but they feared his disapproval, a withdrawal of his favour, a silence in response to a letter instead of the unusually alacritous reply, the absence of the usual Christmas card.

It had been Guinness's mother, not his father, who was for some long periods the constant presence: mother with her "trashy constant muddle and minor dishonesty" always embarrassing and disappointing him. The father was unknown. Stiven, the stepfather, providentially vanished before Guinness was eight.

If, however, there was enough unusual parallelism in their backgrounds for the claim that le Carré based Smiley on Guinness to carry some weight, the truth of Smiley's birth went back to beyond the time when le Carré may have had any knowledge of Guinness. Smiley came out of le Carré's own past, his background, and his own unique imagination. "I naturally warm to this abstraction of myself . . . He's flawed enough, obsessed with the enemy."

There was a good chance that some of Guinness's quality was directly absorbed into the texture of *Smiley's People*, which was written just after the filming of *Tinker Tailor*. Just as the actors who played in Shakespeare's plays had many of their own characteristics, even unwittingly on the part of the author, incorporated into the characters they were playing, so some of Guinness found its way into Smiley. As Alan Bennett said, "He's written it as if Alec Guinness has always been Smiley."

Le Carré experienced great delight in the casting of Guinness as Smiley. He confessed that he had great trepidation in adjusting to the idea that Smiley was to be acted by someone, for while a novelist's characters lived in him as his intimates, and he had "shared his cell" with them, so to speak, they remained "*undefined* for all that, because, for the novelist, to write about them at all is to hunt them, to pursue an abstraction which, in order to lure him, must remain always a little bit beyond his reach".

Le Carré said he wrote to Guinness and never seriously considered anyone else. After meeting him it was Guinness or nobody. At first, working in rehearsals, Guinness seemed to find the part formless, which was not very encouraging. "So hard to be a sort of geriatric ear," he commented to the author. He seemed, according to le Carré, worried that everyone he spoke to had a different notion of who Smiley was. Le Carré found it strange to feel Guinness hunting for Smiley as once he had hunted for him, and to realise that "the journey was as intense for him in *his* medium as it was for me in mine".

This journey took him on an outing to meet Maurice Oldfield, the former head of M16. Le Carré had "wondered", said Guinness mysteriously, "whether I wanted to meet *someone*" (i.e. Oldfield). The three of them had lunch together at the Athenaeum Club. No-one has reported their conversation. Guinness noticed Oldfield's cufflinks, his tie-pin and his flamboyantly cut suit. "Perhaps that was his cover," Guinness later told a friend. Anyway it did not help much. He denied that he based his interpretation of Smiley on what he called "that man", not mentioning him by name. Nor did the body of the rest of le Carré's work help much: the illustrated editions which showed a pudgy Smiley with hands in pockets; the heavy spectacles, the many comparisons to other animals, in particular to the mole of course (but to owls, toads and frogs). The mole was something of a dead end when it came to acting a character: a character must always be visible, while the distinct quality of the mole was his invisibility. Konrad Lorenz, the naturalist, discovered when he tried to keep a mole in captivity that, apart from its astounding tunnelling ability and its skill in locating earthworms exactly, it proved most disappointing. It never grew any tamer and never remained above earth longer than it took to devour its prey. Lorenz grew tired of procuring the huge amount of worms it required and when he let it free it sank into the earth as a submarine sinks into the water. Perhaps this underlines the true nature of Guinness's so-called "invisibility" – it is always visible. The mole is actually not. Unlike Smiley, as le Carré noted. Guinness was not plump in build, and that worried him too.

But it was the remarkable toing and froing nature of Guinness's mind that le Carré found awesomely similar to his own idea of Smiley. He could think and read and worry and assimilate all at the same time: "He has a power of response that is like an open wound, and to protect himself he is capable of a sort of social duck-dive which is an almost physical act of self-obliteration." (Here was perhaps a dramatic resemblance to Lorenz's mole.)

When he wishes it can be exactly the way I once described Smiley; one of London's meek who do not inherit the earth. He can affiliate like nobody I have met; a moment later he can be luckless, inconsolable and utterly alone.

So le Carré found, too, that in the absolute and final reckoning it was the intelligence which counted: Guinness's authority, his powers of deduction, were never in doubt. "We had a Poirot; we had a Father Brown; but we also had a man searching for his own lost innocence among the sins of his companions . . . Seeing to the heart of his adversary Smiley—Guinness *becomes* the heart; his interrogations ennoble as well as reveal."

After the transmission of *Tinker Tailor* Guinness received a note from Oldfield which said, "I still can't recognise myself." He knew what the game was, but Guinness had not tried to mimic him or impersonate him: "It's just that you nearly always pick up some little thing when meeting a person like that if you are going to play something in the same area." In fact most people thought there *were* remarkable resemblances physically and in manner between Guinness and Oldfield, but only "maybe". Guinness ended by wearing glasses which were exactly like Oldfield's; his wig was an exact copy of Oldfield's hair.

Something of Smiley rubbed off, too, on Guinness, or so he heightened it for the *Sun* newspaper (one might think that Guinness would never grant an interview to the sensational *Sun*, but on this occasion he did). He said he thought people were following him all the time and when he went to a restaurant he would choose a table, "where I could sit with my back to the wall". He noted entrances and exits for a quick getaway. He would be thinking, "how do I get out of here?" This was what Guinness said, as if playing up to what he felt was required of him.

Overall, though, with the part of Smiley, Guinness was continuing his habit of refusing to fall into a rut; he was again avoiding the permanent, comfortable role. Smiley has to "be a blank and stay a blank", and never give away to the person he is interrogating what he wants to know. In this role of the interrogator turned martyr inscrutability was all-important. Now and then, as these two serials unfolded, someone or other asked Smiley a question. The answer might clarify. But Smiley said nothing. As le Carré put it neatly:

I don't know what Guinness does then. Perhaps nothing, perhaps a lot. His arts are quite as arcane as Smiley's. But the effect of his silence is to make you feel, not that Smiley is dodging an answer, but that such questions of him are in rank bad taste. I was reminded, the first time it happened, of myself as a small child asking my father whether God had a beard. He simply affected not to hear. It never crossed my mind that he did not know the answer.

Shylock at Chichester: study by Alistair Muir.

Guinness and David Lean filming *A Passage to India*; John in *Time out of Mind*; Obi-Ben Kenobi in *Star Wars*.

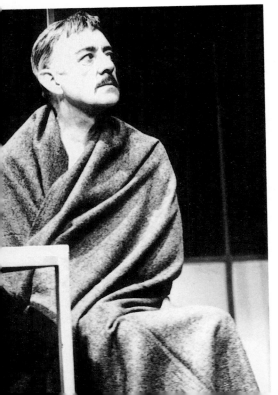

Elisabeth Frink's bronze (1984, from the National Portrait Gallery); Sheriff's Punch cartoon for *The Scapegoat*; Low's cartoon from the *Guardian* (below right).

Ultimate priest – as Graham Greene's Monsignor Quixote; "One simply refuses to put on a performance of one's private personality" – Guinness outside St Paul's after David Lean's memorial service in 1991.

It might seem unexpected of le Carré to reveal how Guinness did, at the peak of his professional prowess, remind him of his father, but this revelation only serves further to underline the uncanny closeness to each other not that they exactly shared but which they reflected in each other. The skill of Guinness was that he could maintain that ability to be real to himself and think along the right lines, yet much of the acting as Smiley was submerged, so that all one saw was a periscope gliding swiftly through dark water. Smiley's greatest gift, said le Carré, was "the gift of quiet . . . to be silent and to make others talk". Some, such as Hugh Carleton Greene, the brother of the novelist and a one-time Director-General of the BBC, could only see the dull dark water and thought it was tedious and boring. But this was a submarine mole with a periscope, and the periscope signified danger.

"We are among false biographers, born for the shifty life, the triple personality, sellers of false information and fantasies, sketching their way along, living by the gamble," wrote V.S. Pritchett. It was Smiley's ambiguous motivation, his introspection, his obsession that would seem to make him so close, as a fictional creation, to Guinness in real life.

44

Cold feet (II)

Smiley took up many hours of film, but it was never a feature film in the Hollywood definition and therefore did not quality for nomination for an Oscar. In 1979, the year *Tinker Tailor* was shown on television, Guinness was awarded an honorary Oscar for "advancing the art of screen acting through a host of memorable and distinguished performances". This now joined the list of awards Guinness had received: an Oxford Honorary D. Litt. in 1978 (and he was to receive the coveted Hamburg Shakespeare prize, awarded to a British citizen for outstanding success in the arts, in 1985, and to be made a Companion of Honour in 1994).

His own history of Oscar nominations began in 1952 with a nomination for Henry Holland in the *The Lavender Hill Mob*, although that year the Oscar went to Gary Cooper in *High Noon*. In 1957 Guinness learnt of his Oscar for Colonel Nicholson from his driver who heard it on the radio. In 1958 he was nominated as writer for his script of *The Horse's Mouth*, the only Oscar-winning actor so nominated. In 1977 his Obi-Ben Kenobi was nominated for best supporting actor but lost; in 1988 William Dorrit was also nominated and, with even less excuse than the Jedi Knight, lost. On receiving his Honorary Oscar Guinness said he felt fraudulent but was grabbing it (from Dustin Hoffman who presented it to him), "while the going's good".

A Passage to India (1985) saw David Lean's return to filming after fourteen years. When he had made *Ryan's Daughter* the American film critics, led by Pauline Kael, had so savaged this romantic story (in which Guinness had turned down the part of the Priest, which was played by Trevor Howard) that Lean had withdrawn deeply hurt from film-making: "One's awfully easily shaken", he said later. After his recovery Lean then spent years of preparation on *A Passage to India*, which became in some ways his own Kwai Bridge, the ultimate gesture of his uncertain monomania and tunnel vision. In it his desire to control every aspect of the film's creation turned almost into a parody of itself. Although Lean's location manager was looking for something that "couldn't be built, only by God", Lean had a whole Indian city built in India.

But perhaps the real shortcoming of A Passage to India was to stem first from its having no romantic hero and was itself, as were Forster's other novels, a work of flawed vision. The real hero of Lean's A Passage to India became manifestly outside the film – the film-maker himself – which was why a South Bank Show film about the making of the film emerged as possibly more gripping than its subject. "I'm fascinated by these nuts," Lean had said of Lawrence of Arabia and Colonel Nicholson; but sweet and kindly Aziz, the Muslim doctor, could never quite equal this pair; while the distorted rape vision of Miss Quested had hardly the right possible qualities for visual inflation on the Lean scale.

"I'm not sure that actors like me very much," said Lean. "I've got to make them measure up to the imagination" – by imagination he meant the script which in his Quaker-like sensibility, came to wield, when fixed upon, a kind of literal inflexible authority like the Bible. Some actors accepted such authority without complaint. Charles Laughton, who played in Lean's Hobson's Choice, never balked at his control. Lean preferred "no-nonsense" people.

Yet Lean always wanted the same faces; he needed the same sparring partners. How would he fit Guinness into A Passage to India? Here we go back to shades of Guinness's earlier skill of impersonation, to his grotesque Fagin, no less. The answer was the most unlikely role of Professor Godbole, the Indian sage and teacher who befriends Mrs Moore and becomes some kind of strange mystical chorus, commenting obliquely and enigmatically on the whole disclocation of soul and body in British India.

But again, as in Kwai, although with a less successful result, the actor and the director had an uneasy time together. Guinness, as viewed in the South Bank Show of the making of the film, grew almost visibly up in arms when being moved around by Lean as a pawn. (With typical understatement he reported at one moment, "It's not a problem, but I've just got to make up my mind.") This time the difficulty was over filming Godbole's strange and startling appearance at the railway station when, just before the trial of Aziz, Mrs Moore departs on the train. Guinness had to be placed exactly, and then move "two foot to his left". His rebellious spirit rose. "I hate being fixed like a specimen". He conceded, perhaps in not altogether good, or convincing, faith, that Lean's genius lay not in what he said to you but "when he is stuck - visually stuck, and he will say 'Come and look through the camera' – you see his vision".

Godbole was supposed to end the film with a bizarre Hindu song and dance, part of the muddled eclectic baggage that Forster carried with him all his life. As Peggy Ashcroft described it:

> There was an evening when he danced on an enormous stone circle (of perilous narrowness) clashing cymbals of over four feet circumference. The dance was partly rehearsed, partly extemporised, it lasted well over any expected limit, when finally "Cut" brought it to an end, the Indian 'crowd' of some hundreds, who had watched breathlessly, burst into applause.

But, when he had seen Guinness's rendering of this dance, Lean cut it. "Only some of the mystery of Godbole was revealed in the final version" commented Ashcroft sadly. Guinness complained that it was not there, at the same time thanking Lean for taking it out: "probably good judgement on his part, even if it left me presenting Professor Godbole as a comic-cuts character without the oriental mystery". But how could this be good judgement?

However, *A Passage to India*, or in other words Lean scenery without Lawrence or Nicholson, was a muddle anyway. Lean, as a man and a film-maker, needed certainties and down-to-earth realities: formed as an editor in the early documentary Balcon regime at Ealing, he had felt initial panic at the ambiguities, hints and half-defined characters. He could not cope with the central incident of the novel, the incident in the Marabar Caves: "The rape is *either* a man, or the supernatural, or an illusion. And even if I know! My writing mind therefore is a blur here," Forster wrote to Lowes Dickinson. This was not the stuff of a David Lean picture. Nor was Forster's later and sounder assessment: "I tried to show that India is an unexplainable muddle by introducing an unexplained muddle – Miss Quested's experience in the cave. When asked what happened there, *I don't know.*"

Apart from both the incompatible Lean and Forster, Guinness was sensibly trying, with sound dramatic instinct, to inject some humour – which was also one of Forster's saving qualities – into the film's ponderous, elephantine progress. If his performance did sometimes border on Peter Sellers caricature, so much the better for that. At least someone was viewing the proceedings with a measure of subversive wit. The ironic attitude of prayer adopted by Godbole on Mrs Moore's departure was one of the film's most memorable moments.

"David is a man of genius cocooned with outrageous charm." Guinness's summing-up had the ring of Antony's words in *Julius Caesar* just after the murder of Caesar: "For Brutus is an honourable man." Yet it was to this man, Guinness also admitted, that he owed his film career. Such were the hostile yet paradoxical feelings towards the authority, or father-figure that Lean represented. Guinness disliked the film. He rang up Peggy Ashcroft, who was in New York, in the middle of the night: "It's a disaster and I'm a failure," he declared; but American critics and public loved the film; it was a slow-moving feast to the eye and it echoed the hollow anti-British-colonialism sentiments of *Gandhi*; it also focused on rape and upon racial issues in a very simple-minded and even muddled way that somehow and unintentionally seemed to mirror American attitudes. Yet the end was an unforgivable travesty of the novel.

One of the last social contacts Guinness had with Lean was when they were both invited to 10 Downing Street with a "great flurry of showbiz and media folk" to a pre-dinner drink. Lean had been next to him when they both were propelled towards their hostess whose effect on Guinness was mesmeric. Lean, he said, "kept plucking at my sleeve in a state of high excitement, hissing between clenched teeth, 'She is all woman, all woman, all woman'." Guinness added, "And, heavens, with his experience he would have known."

In 1984, now seventy, Guinness played his last major Shakespearean role on the stage, one he had hankered after often but never attempted. "Shylock wasn't my idea. I've never been ambitious to play the role. There are very few roles that I have been ambitious to play in recent years", he said in 1984, when almost in the same week he reported saying to his wife, "I wish I'd played Shylock". But when the director Patrick Garland had suggested it for the Chichester Festival of 1984 it turned out to be an astute and highly mature choice. Guinness had to face the reality that he was getting on. Even so he refused to disguise himself as he had as Fagin. He made up for the role with only a beard, some eye-liner and the spirit-gum that flattened and sleekened his ears against his

skull. When, in the summer of 1981, he had visited Israel with
Merula he remarked upon the strange characters in Jerusalem with
black and silver embroidered robes and red, fox-fur hats. This
became his mental image for Shylock. He felt worried over the
racial implications of the part but then thought, "What the hell,
Shakespeare is bigger than any temporary racist issues!" In terms
of its length Shylock is a small part. Compared to other great roles
in Shakespeare he is an enlarged character part, for he appears in
only five scenes, one of which is little more than a fragment.

As Shakespeare's best-known character Shylock is in many ways
like Fagin: he has acquired in the popular imagination a life of
his own. Both sprang fully formed, one may speculate, from the
nightmares of their progenitors' family shame and financial loss.
Shylock undoubtedly emerged from the unquelled fears that were
once the centre of reality for the son of the prosperous Stratford
burgher and town Mayor fallen on hard times.

But, as with his earlier attempts at Shakespeare's more uninhibited roles, Guinness again went for one aspect of the character
which he could control intellectually. He went to round out a
"humour", as in the form of a comedy character devised by
Ben Jonson, rather than for the whole, many-sided disruptive
creation. He was true to form even now, at the age of seventy,
and in bringing what Simon Callow calls his "huge mental force"
to bear on Shylock when he was thinking himself into the character
"he eschewed orchestration of all the emotions".

In Guinness's Shylock it was the Hebrew which he singled out for
close attention. His experience of his race's suffering has become a
deep and wide scar. This Shylock incorporated the enormous chip
Guinness once had on his own shoulder and set it bemoaning the
Jewish money-lender's lot. Shylock's identity *is* his money-lending,
just as the black girl out of the ghetto becomes a blues singer, and
this becomes her identity. The same could be said of Guinness: his
deprivation, his sense of shame over it, had *made* him into an actor.
Deprivation casts its own inescapable mould.

When Guinness sat cross-legged on the carpet on the set, when
he took the weighing machine, he had assumed the essence of
the Jewish money-lender. It was an "extraordinary revelation of
extreme despair", one critic called it, full of telling details such
as the way he would shape curious little pursings or pouts with
his mouth when he wanted to make a point in argument. "The
central element in Guinness's performance," wrote Irving Wardle,

was "its sense of exclusion". He noted how, externally, Guinness showed the Jew's social affability and modesty while only at danger points did his face turn stoney and his eyes burn into the enemy. As with Hamlet's revenge, however, the rage was muted: the "huge powers" invoked were somewhere else. He allowed himself one fearsome gesture: placing his ear next to Antonio's heart before plunging his knife into it. But all agreed that the "crack" when it had come after the departure of Jessica, was tremendously effective. He hugged himself, wailing.

Guinness had been moved on his visit to Jerusalem by the scenes at the Wailing Wall. For Simon Callow he himself became "a weeping wall". A wall is static: it moves the feelings by what it suggests and symbolises. The thoughts, memories, intellectually have to be there already in the mind of the beholder. But after the breakdown he returned to his mask. And even in the expression of the extreme despair there was an indirectness, a subtlety, which disguised it: as Polonius tells Reynaldo, "By indirections find directions out." This was a performance of indirections.

There were also points of contact with that first production of *The Merchant* in which he had appeared as Lorenzo not far off fifty years before. Directed by Gielgud and designed by Motley it looked wonderful, "because every sort of kitchen rag was dyed and used", as Guinness had said later. Although, now, he had temporarily stopped smoking three weeks before rehearsals began, he started again. As Garland observed, "his cigarette was balanced, as always, on a slightly Pisan course and several centimetres of ash tenaciously held their ground." He worked with enormous concentration: how else does an actor of such name and stature, contrive, as he did in this production, to enter unnoticed in the most important scene of the play and discover himself to the audience by the sound of whetting his knife?

Guinness did make another late attempt at Shakespeare tragedy, although not a fully exposed stage attempt, but on radio. John Tydeman had first wanted to do a Welsh Lear with Richard Burton and surround him with Welsh characters: perhaps on the principle of what Elizabeth Burton once said to Burton – "Trouble with the Welsh is that they think everybody's Welsh, even Death" – Burton might well have made a wonderful Lear. But this did not work out. Next Tydeman managed to persuade Guinness who demurred, saying he had not got the weight. Tydeman persuaded Guinness he did not need the power to rant and rave and in the end Guinness agreed, reluctantly.

Gloucester was played by Cyril Cusack. He and Guinness had first acted together fifty-five years before at the Globe Theatre for the Michel Saint-Denis production of the *Cherry Orchard* which never opened. Guinness turned up for the first rehearsal with a "frightfully smart Gucci bag", according to Tydeman. He waddled over to the piano, put down the bag, opened it and took out a pair of extremely chic Gucci slippers, removed his shoes, put on the slippers, all this done meticulously. From the corner of the room Cusack was watching.

Next morning Cusack arrived at rehearsals carrying a Marks & Spencer's bag. He arrived before Guinness and came into the rehearsal room. Then Guinness arrived, stopped, watching Cusack who crossed to the piano, put down his M. & S. bag, reached inside for a crumpled and dilapidated old pair of bedroom slippers, then, having removed his shoes, put them on.

"Ah-h-ah-h" said Guinness in the slightly perplexed tone of exhalation, as this peculiar exercise by two non-upstagers in not upstaging each other came to an end. In fact both actors had the same weight and admired each other enormously. They were natural brothers and were later to play brothers in *Little Dorrit*. Cusack once said he recognised in Guinness his "familiar".

The radio Lear never worked for Guinness. Tydeman tried to encourage him to "let go" in the storm scenes but he held back in a very circumspect way, "playing it from within a safe perimeter". He had created a hedge around him, especially in the expression of Lear's sexual disgust which was unfeeling and strangely vocalised. One found it hard to believe that Lear ever had these feelings. Guinness said he loved working with Tydeman but only heard the last fifteen minutes: "It slightly shocked me. I'm always a bit shcoked at hearing myself. It just doesn't sound what one quite intended".

At another time Jack Gold, who had directed Guinness in the film of *Little Lord Fauntleroy* as the Earl of Doricourt, the boy's guardian, asked Guinness to play Lear on television. But Guinness had been disappointed in the film, which had not, he felt, been the fault of Gold – or only occasionally so – but the effect of the ridiculously tight schedule of shooting. "I haven't seen one frame of it," was his public comment; but he had seen it, and now and then was a bit embarrassed, or so he informed an intimate.

The Lear idea went back to 1982. Guinness heard that Graham Crowden was performing the role at the Bristol Old Vic, and he travelled to Bristol to see it. Peter Copley, an old friend from the days of the Old Vic Company, was playing Gloucester. After the performance Guinness took some of the cast out to supper: they had a table at Renatos and here, shortly after they arrived, Danny La Rue, the transvestite review artist, also playing at Bristol, came into the restaurant with his entourage and sat down at an adjoining table. "Suddenly," said Copley, "the atmosphere was electric. These two extravagant personalities at proximate tables, ruffling their feathers and competing."

"I'd like to play in *Lear*," said La Rue, "I'd like to play *all* the daughters."

In the end Guinness decided not to play Lear: he felt he could not match what was required. And afterwards he went into what Copley termed "a strange withdrawal".

The next film in which Guinness appeared was *Lovesick*, a light-hearted film which also starred Dudley Moore, and in which Guinness acted the part of Sigmund Freud. He was back to the safe bet, the portrayal of genius, although one suspects that in real life he may have made a more tentative and sensitive psychiatrist than Freud. He posed for a photograph in one of Freud's most famous poses and the impersonation was truly astonishing. Perhaps what was even more remarkable was the difference. The real Freud had a more aggressive tilt of the head. The man was clearly more of a monomaniac than ever Guinness could be. Freud's eyes were more certain, almost messianic, his brow unfurrowed. Here was the dogmatist of sex that Jung found so disturbing. Guinness's eyes as the great psychiatrist were shifty, cautious, his pose more passive, his forehead worried, with deep frowning. By nature he probably inclined more to Jung than to Freud.

45

Father of the Marshalsea

Guinness as a schoolboy had read *Great Expectations, Oliver Twist* and *David Copperfield*, and in the Navy *Bleak House,* but his enthusiasm for reading Dickens had for many years died down. In late middle age he became more an Anthony Trollope man and an admirer of Edith Wharton. When Christine Edzard approached him to play William Dorrit in her film of *Little Dorrit* he liked the script but found it very difficult to read the book; it took him three or four attempts to get into it although the idea of the debtor's prison appealed to him as an apposite image for our own age. As he joked, "We all might be sitting in the Marshalsea."

Dorrit is the most complex of all Dickens's central figures. Comic and tragic at one and the same time he is shifty, distraught and above all without shame, continuously reminding us of his own peculiar brand of self-delusion. It was in this, judging by the biographies, that he was closest to being based on Dickens's own father who, when Dickens was twelve, was imprisoned in the Marshalsea for debt. As the whole novel revolves round this central scarring experience, as reflected through Dorrit's daughter Amy, one might be looking for bitterness and anger, qualities that Guinness had never shown himself powerful at portraying. Yet Dickens, with affecting compassion, presented the character of Dorrit as a helpless victim rather than as agent of the awful circumstances which have been inflicted upon his family. Dickens's aggression went into dealing a dreadful satirical onslaught on the powerful social influences that affect the lives of his characters: religion and the law, using the popularly distorted idea of Providence – "Nobody's Fault" – as a particular target.

In playing Dorrit, therefore, it was the mobilisation of the passive sides of Guinness's gift that were especially called for, above all his ability to show the set of weaknesses revolving round a particular form of deception. Christine Edzard said, "William Dorrit is all about self-delusion." And, as Guinness commented:

> William Dorrit is a very complicated man. To start with . . . I couldn't make head nor tail of him – he was so up and down: he could have been an actor, he could have been all sorts of things. What appealed to me was the variety of it – some of it amused me very much.

Edzard gave him confidence in the grasp she showed of the character, and pointed out he should remember that Dickens was a reporter and had been a journalist: that what he wrote was what he saw and what he heard. This became a good lead, for although Guinness realised how Dickens exaggerated and "tipped things up", to understand that there was a reality behind Dorrit brought him the key to the character:

> Of course it's supposed to be one side of Dickens' father, in the way that Micawber is supposed to be another side, but I imagine that William Dorrit is the closer picture, because it's a more varied character, and not so comic. He's a very monstrous man in some ways.

To show the different viewpoints of Amy Dorrit and Arthur Clennam, Edzard conceived the film in two parts and she intended to shoot some of the scenes twice with two different versions of the script. For instance, to Clennam the Marshalsea Prison would be no more than a slum and Dorrit an old faded failure giving himself airs. But for Amy, in her view of her father, the beauty and pain were first and foremost apparent, so she would see the family room in the prison as much bigger: the geraniums would be in flower, the curtains much brighter and more elaborate.

This approach at first puzzled Guinness: as he pointed out, "saying the same lines with some missing, or words slightly altered, is very difficult to hold in the head". But they rehearsed it all carefully, and always shot the differences in sequence, and then Guinness fell "into it in the most natural way". The important thing was that Guinness retained complete trust in his director. Christine Edzard made him feel very secure in precisely those areas where other directors, perhaps especially David Lean, could upset him. He called her, with her tactful, easy way, "a joy to work with". She used little camera movement, so the camera gave him a unique scope for showing how important small things could be. Guinness knew, Edzard reported, "exactly where his little finger would be in relation to the edge of the frame. He knows exactly where he is and how much you see." He was content to leave this entirely to the director, although sometimes he might wander over and ask, "Where are my knees?" Edzard also noticed that she knew no actor who could switch off so quickly and conclusively as Guinness did at the end of shooting a scene when she called "Cut".

Not only did the director and her collaborators inspire his confidence (and like most actors he refused to watch the nightly "rushes" of the day's filming) but he found himself loving the atmosphere of this unusual enterprise, most of which was filmed in tiny studios in Rotherhithe in south-east London. Everything here was originated by the director, her producer-husband Richard Goodwin, his partner John Brabourne and their staff – "the crew they have around them", Guinness called it, "and the whole ramshackle oddity of it: the fact that it's on the Thames, down from Tower Bridge, with the river flowing, the tide coming in and out – that gives it all a curious life – I think that has something to do with it. I've never enjoyed anything so much."

He also respected the authencity of what was created, something he said he had never felt so powerfully before in a film. This impressed him particularly in the detail put into everything, so that all the costumes, to take one example, were hand-sewn. "Walking into the Marshalsea Yard, for a moment I had an uncomfortable feeling that I had walked back 150 years, into something which was actually there and like that". Three and a half months was a long time and so it became something of a way of life. But it had its exacting side, as Guinness expressed it: "In the part of William Dorrit I probably explored unpleasant things in myself – faced up to my own fecklessness and weakness and shelving important decisions, which is part of the character." Here, as at other times, Guinness owned up to small faults as a kind of propitiatory ceremony performed in public so that, as always, the inner core of privacy could remain untouched. This is not to say he was covering up from himself, because one feels he never was. It was how he had learned to deal with himself.

"It's very easy to caricature Dickens's characters into kind of papier mâché figures, and great fun to do. But to find the reality in them, and the reality he observed," Edzard said, "is quite salutary – and once something is real you've got to find it in yourself — "

Edzard gently, and with careful perceptive objectivity, encouraged this process. She found the dialogue lent itself incredibly well to his needs and to his "discreet type of diction – his very slightly precious way of putting things in a tiny space". He asked her for images and suggestions – "What Dorrit made me think of," she told him, was Chaplin eating his boots in *The Gold Rush*. "He was by nature the essence of forever seeking inside himself to find the truth of his character. I've seen few actors do it as honestly. He had to be autobiographical – uncomfortably close to himself – and he did it with real respect for truth and sometimes with such anguish."

The grandiose vision of the self-deluded man, his bafflement at reality, all was perfectly handled by Guinness – from within. But were they by now a part of him, as they were part of everyone, perhaps especially more as he grew older? Possibly so, as he later sometimes unguardedly revealed in some self-reassuring pieces he published later in the *Spectator*. But if he clothed and hid himself in words, he could still safely explore the deep insight and empathy he had with the victim. Dorrit is yet another of those helpless people who are life's casualties, this time writ extremely large and flamboyantly. But also this time and in essence Dorrit is the dupe of himself. He is Abel Drugger multiplied by a hundred.

The truth Guinness revealed in this performance was perfect because it was so uncomfortably close to what had been inflicted on him by his own mother when he was young. There was an extraordinary, unconscious femininity about the whole performance. He may not have wanted to know this himself, but he wanted to draw on and reveal unconsciously what his mother had done to him without any inhibition or restraining factor imposed by his intellect, by shyness or by self-awareness. His mind was entirely in the work, feeding it with everything from the past he could muster:

> It's been very swift on the floor – we haven't had to hang around for much lighting changes – that's been marvellous. I just sit and daydream and wonder if I know my lines for the next scene. The most I've ever done is look at scenes ahead and revise lines. I always learn the whole thing before I start. That's what I've done on my journeys here in the car, learning lines. Nothing else, I can't read – I can read newspapers briefly, but I can't concentrate on anything else. At least in a film that's as long in the making as this you become familiar with certain people who are constantly here, and you fall into each other's way of working easily if there's plenty of time . . .

If his imagination and his sense of shame and his mother's self-delusion and all those personal qualities were so carefully focused on revealing Dorrit through his own experience as broadly as possible – and especially in a kind of muted narcissism, a pantomime-damish sexual self-sufficiency which Dorrit often seemed to exude – the actor's intellect was also working at full stretch during the filming on the practical, technical aspects of the character. Edzard found Guinness very controlled in everything he did. He timed everything with complete precision so that he would know, for instance, when eating, when to put down his fork, when to swallow a mouthful. Everything was remembered, nothing left to chance. Of course something might occasionally throw him, such as a sudden noise off or on the set. But Edzard discovered that everything was used. Curiously enough, too, he never blinked in front of the camera. "Very few people can do that. He knows everything is switched on, and his concentration is total. It's like playing a finely tuned instrument."

With the other actors, Edzard observed, he was very courteous, but not "someone who gets a lot out of other actors", and not some-one who would pick up a spontaneous movement or gesture and do something unexpected with it. With him every little effect had been worked out, then created with the know-how and skill to become spontaneous. "Never is he doing things that he doesn't know about or doesn't want to happen. And if he did, he wouldn't have it." She found him quite remote, and that he could put people off, but although it might seem to be, it was not selfishness on his part or lack of generosity to others, it came more from the intensity of his concentration. He didn't give the others advice. Of Sarah Pickering who played Amy, he said, "She was determined to help me."

It was Guinness who suggested that Cyril Cusack play Frederick Dorrit, William's brother: Cusack was four years Guinness's senior, and as the two brothers they got along famously. As Guinness commented, "There's a kind of similarity in the shape of our faces". It was perhaps unbelievable that Guinness should now have been seventy-one years while Cusack, whose performance in this film was also outstanding, was seventy-five. Each of them appeared to be, or acted, men in, or barely past, their prime. Guinness as William Dorrit had a brief but moving death scene. As he commented, "I can't think how many times I've died . . . Never very well. This time, earlier in the year, I was *at* a deathbed – the first time ever, and, it's awful to say this now, but I couldn't help absorbing it for future use . . . I'm never going to be caught out again . . ."

All actors have their particular vanity: Derek Jacobi, whose performance as Clennam in *Little Dorrit* is no less than towering, betrayed on occasions to their affectionate director a tremendous need to please visually, to seduce, to be loved. He worried constantly about his hair, or whether or not his trousers were too tight. Guinness's over-riding vanity was intellectual: his mortification on losing a line, something which would never bother the Cambridge-educated Jacobi in the slightest. A particular obsession of Guinness's became how he would manage the great and final speech of Dorrit towards the end of the second part when, in the midst of his wealth at the Merdles' dinner table, his over-burdened mind suddenly reverts to the former life he led in the Marshalsea:

> Welcome to the Marshalsea: The space is-ha-limited; but you will find it apparently grow larger after a time, after a time, ladies and gentlemen — and the air is, hmm, all things considered, very good. Blows over the Surrey hills, over the Surrey hills . . . Those who are habituated to the-ha-Marshalsea are pleased to call me its Father.

Every actor's fear when they get on was "stumbling around for words. Pray God they'll shoot me before I get to that stage." When filming, too, there was so much to distract you, a different set each day, a different situation. Each morning in the car from Steep he spent polishing his lines for the day's "take"; each evening on the ride home learning them for the next day.

Dickens had "never dared tell anyone, not even his wife and children", wrote the academic critic John Carey, "about his father's incarceration in the Marshalsea, or his own childhood degradation as a 'little labouring hind' in a boot-blacking factory". When William Dorrit lets out the shameful secret of his past at the grand banquet he succumbs to a nightmare that pursued Dickens, too, for years.

"One finds things in oneself," Guinness had said many times when asked if he thought of the character he was playing as someone else. Maybe the shame and secrets of his early life, however well guarded for the energy they could supply, were well past their prime. He had spent fourteen happy weeks of 1985 filming *Little Dorrit*; it formed a natural background camouflage to merge himself with during, that same year, the publication of *Blessings in Disguise*.

46

The man within

Graham Greene talked to Guinness about his book: "I'll give you one tip," he said, "sit down to write in the morning. It doesn't matter how long you write and when you stop. But before you stop you must have the next sentence in mind." Guinness had to sigh: the advice was too late, the book was written. "If only he'd said that eighteen months ago."

Guinness claimed that, being an amateur, he worked swiftly for three or four days, then became stuck and abandoned it. This was a little *motif* he whistled aloud many times and could orchestrate into, "brief suave chapters ... finding a sentence, oh heavens, there's a paragraph, and then I would stop for three months ... I was terribly nervous, etc ..." Or, "I found it a pretty frightening experience because I didn't realise what extraordinary recall I had ... I'd set off on a chapter about something thinking I'd known the basic things I wanted to say and suddenly yards of dialogue which I know is pretty well authentic or little incidents came whizzing back from the past, from thirty, forty, fifty years ago and that I found alarming."

Typical also was the genesis of the book. He had been a writer: he had adapted Dickens and Dostoievsky for the stage; his script for *The Horse's Mouth* had been nominated for an Oscar. *Yahoo* had been his acerbic and lurid assemblage of Swift's life. He had written up his landing on Sicily several times; likewise his first theatrical encounters with Gielgud, even his failure as Hamlet, had long before found their way into the public domain. He was a perfectly competent prose stylist.

But he had, naturally, over the years resisted the advances of publishers, taking cover under the shelter of Hamish Hamilton, his friend, by asking him, "Could I say I've promised a book to you?" This eventually, and perhaps predictably, turned into

Hamilton saying to him, "Look, we've protected you, so where's the book?"

Anyone looking at Guinness's record of writing, and also setting aside his many roles of public heroes and geniuses, would at once remark that here was a born biographer, albeit on a small scale. Given his desire for mystery and anonymity, the problem would be how to make his gift for observation, as extended to others, seem like an autobiography? He must often have pondered on this as he looked through his scrapbooks. Typically, he had also taken pride in having once started his autobiography and abandoned it, using as authority a quotation from W. Watson: "I have not paid the world the evil and the insolent courtesy of offering it my baseneness as a gift."*

His solution was again judicious and in keeping with himself. He wouldn't write up his own career and, if he mentioned it at all, this would be by way of passing, the backcloth so to speak. Against this backcloth he would parade his friends. They would all come on, carefully arranged in a pecking order (as well as being carefully and compositionally placed as in a Franz Hals multiple portrait) – with due attention to their star status and gifts, and do their act. Their "act" would be Alec Guinness filling them with life, a life of his own.

Again it went back to Graham Greene. Your bank balance as a writer, Greene once said, was your childhood. The happy, glorious thing about Guinness's childhood were his visits to the variety and music-hall stages. So he would build his whole book like a wonderful, suave and magical variety show, with incursions into the world of pantomime which he didn't like (his family, that is), and with himself as Master of Ceremonies: here was, for himself, the perfect disguise in autobiography. The first turn would be Guinness himself, coming on to the stage, a few pages of childhood, a few juggling acts, a little tap dance (a "Totentanz?") of early misery, and then the master-magician would withdraw but remain in full view of the audience. He would sit down on stage in a comfortable, ducal chair and introduce the rest of the acts with comments in his own special brand of humour, "a curious mixture of the fey, the sly

---

* "Gift" and "blessings"(the word of Guinness's title) are synonyms. The interviewer (Bel Mooney) on this occasion noted that "to abandon your autobiography is the final proof of privacy, that the actor's 'real' self is nobody's business but his own." Guinness never gave that final proof.

and the marginally macabre", always clear that he was more after "the secret grin than an open laugh". His mother would occasionally erupt on to the scene, the evil Godmother or wicked fairy of his life, while there would be no end of eccentrics and curiosities, of good fairies and influences, beginning with Nellie Wallace with her parrot-like movements of the head, Martita Hunt – the Mrs Havisham of the story – Sybil Thorndike, and on and on ... It was an ideal method for Guinness: he was the perfect impersonator – you had only to hear him mimic Gielgud or Oliver on the radio to know that he could not only catch their accents and intonations perfectly, he also understood exactly which were the right words to put into their mouths, words that they would actually say. Although Guinness called it memory, it was much more than that: it was the invention of genius.

But his method of presenting his turns, as well as those others who had influenced him, as items on a variety bill, also had respectability. It even had a snobbish or fashionable appeal, just as the Royal Family in the old days mixed with the stars of variety, and T.S. Eliot wrote up the virtues of old music-hall performers such as Marie Lloyd. It would appeal to all classes of reader. Above all, this method was authentic and truly autobiographical because it enacted what had moved and involved him as a child, providing his escape and a route to his future. With a nugget of realistic narrative at the centre of the book – the superb account of his life at sea during the war – he could again return to re-creating his biographical sketches of friends and peers, making them live through their own words and actions. Then a final, sudden, few dark pages on the mystery of his birth: after the merriment of all the stars letting down their hair, giving us glimpses into their secret selves, with a little gentle pricking of their foibles and other quiet but firm debunking – all of them brilliantly impersonated by Guinness – the air grows chill. "I am sorry, madam, for the news I bring". The finish was perfect. Here am I, at heart a lonely illegitimate child, with no father that can be traced, or if a father then one who just on a single occasion confessed the sin of my birth to his legitimate daughter. But what I am most proud of all is that I never lost a friend. The entertainment is perfectly rounded off, as Shakespeare rounded off *Love's Labour's Lost*:

The words of Mercury are harsh after the songs of Apollo.
You that way, we this way.

Now, we all have to leave the theatre. The reassuring entertainment is over.

But where did this leave the actor Alec Guinness? One thing *Blessings in Disguise* did not demonstrate is Rosaline's statement from that same early and mischievous comedy of Shakespeare's, which was perhaps also more direct autobiography than some of his other plays:

> A jest's prosperity lies in the ear
> Of him that hears it, never in the tongue
> Of him that makes it.

The book was superb for those who read it: polished, accomplished, amusing, witty, but did it, or could it really satisfy its author as a frank and honest confession of what he was? Well, of course, finally we do not and cannot know the answer. But, as I have attempted to show, he was always revealing himself, otherwise he would never have been what he was: "There are lots of things I don't wish to admit, but come through willy-nilly . . ." and, "In my views of most things I'm swayed like a very busy weather-cock". So, in fact, his flaws and vanities *were* purged in the main portraits he painted of others, but again they were disguised. As in his acting he revealed himself indirectly through other people.

One thinks, for example, of the way he found himself in Sybil Thorndike's presence at the age of fourteen, tongue-tied at her larger-than-life presence, and that of her husband Lewis Casson. He had just seen them in Ibsen's *Ghosts*. Describing this production he made a strange, private, veiled reference: "I rather warmed to the feckless, handsome Oswald. (Ten years later, at the Old Vic, the Oswald played, quite excellently, the enigmatic, priggish Tibetan Abbot in Auden/Isherwood's *Ascent of F6*, in which I acted the even more priggish hero, Ransom)". Leaving the Thorndikes, still aged fourteen, he stepped outside the stage-door. He found nobody in the street. "Only Oswald, who emerged from the stage-door in a camel-hair coat and full make-up-Leichner sticks numbers 5 and 9, a red dot in the corner of each eye and a lot of mascara. In my puritanical way I was rather shocked; also perhaps a little alarmed. There was something ambivalent about him which I couldn't grasp, but which also *glamorised me*" (author's italics).

Perhaps even more explicit in indirectness was Guinness when he wrote up Ernest Milton whom he had invited round to give a piece of his Lear in front of the young Richard Burton . . . "he could scarcely take his eyes from the beauty of Burton's head." Milton then performed miserably, telephoning the next day to say he was sorry: "I was *distracted* by such beauty. Ah, the breasts (pronounced 'braasts") and the eyes of the young men are *damning*". Guinness continued, suavely, "Not long after this his wife, Naomi Royde Smith, died . . ." He celebrated Milton's great love for Naomi in the most affectionate prose. Then Milton confided to Guinness that the only woman who ever roused him physically was Lilian Baylis, yet she was, as most people described her, an old "battle-axe". He wrote, similarly, of his mother, his search for his father, the birds-and-the-bees talks in his early school dormitories, at all times swiftly moving on the next subject, not lingering on anything, the most skilled of raconteurs.

Certain of those critics, perhaps masters of the same game themselves, who reviewed *Blessings in Disguise* found this method slightly irritating and, perhaps also not being Christians themselves, thought his later faith may have been the cause: "No wonder, perhaps, that the inner serenity which his faith and his marriage have given him," wrote J.W. Lambert, for example, in *The Times*, "should, at least to this outsider, have seemed to produce in his acting a sense of a man with a built-in halo, a look, whether in an Alan Bennett play or in a John le Carré creepie on television, of an Ineffable, not to say patronising, Something". John Mortimer, while admiring his style and ease, believed "he and his book are clearly happier when describing other people . . . rich and strange enough to allow the central character to slip out of the limelight." Yet for him one passage alone was worth the price of the whole book:

> Coming off the stage as Yakov the butler in *The Seagull*, Guinness had won a laugh and a round of applause. In the wings he met Edith Evans and looked at her proudly. The next night there was no laugh and no hand on his exit and he asked Miss Evans, who was again waiting in the wings, for her explanation. "You're trying too hard", she told him. "You didn't know how you got it in the first place. But it's natural to you, one day you will find it again. Take it lightly. But when it comes back make a note of what you were feeling *inside*".

Blessings in Disguise was deservedly a bestseller and nearly ten years on from its publication remains remarkable. While it does descend at times into an orgy of self-effacement, the lasting impression it creates of its protagonist – his wonderful imitative skill apart – is that he is a model of attractive self-doubt. He wants to make friends, dispel hostility, be accepted; and, after all, is not making friends a perfectly reasonable and normal aspiration?; as one reviewer wrote, his book will make him many more. But was there not in him still, as Hamlet says, "that which passes show"? Perhaps he was really showing us that autobiography was the ultimate disguise.

47

The most important subject
in the world

On Monday 20 June 1988 fell the Golden Wedding anniversary of Merula and Alec Guinness. Many of their joint friends went back to even before that. They had met Peggy Ashcroft fifty-three years before in Gielgud's production of *Romeo and Juliet*; Margaret Harris, the designer of Motleys, a year or two earlier; Gielgud himself. The strength of Merula's family background had always been also a great support to Guinness, his much-loved father-in-law in particular, whom Guinness would often quote on growing old and not being 'past it'. He might reflect now on the past, such as how, when a young actor, he had often thought of old actors, "Oh God I wish some of them would die off. Now I'm an old actor I don't feel quite the same about it."

Rarely had Merula been photographed but she had occasionally been described as "an intensely shy woman" who had been for many years "behind the Guinness boom". It has not been this writer's intention to enter the privacy of their relationship. But it may again be noted that it has always been a close one, while Guinness's affectionate and grateful references to his wife have with the years increased. His only book, *Blessings in Disguise*, was dedicated to her. It may be fair to say that she has been content to remain in the background, painting and tending to pleasures quieter than her husband's public life, while that it is her more gentle virtues that have always shone through him and which he has continually celebrated. "I think reclusive is a bit strong", she said of herself:* "I am simply a quiet person who prefers to stay in the country. I've been like that since I was a little girl. We only like to see a few people at a time." Her painting studio had by now

* *Daily Mail*, 30 October 1992.

become her private territory where her husband did not intrude. But did he encourage her painting? "He usually comes round to it. But I think he'd prefer me to be cooking." (Pause) "Well, I don't particularly like cooking". More guilty laughter.

In 1992 she published *The Kingdom of Heaven is Like,* a book of twenty-four of her oil paintings illustrating Christ's parables, an enchanting collection revealing a sweetness of vision and a child's innocent eye for landscape. John le Carré said of it, "Her paintings are full of magic, comedy and love", while Alan Bennett wrote the introduction. She painted them mostly when Guinness was in India making *A Passage to India.*

Guinness has never had any reservations about the judgement she makes of his own work: "She doesn't have to be critical. She is very, very tactful and knows when comments might be injurious. But I know what she is thinking, and when she finally tells me I half listen, half resent it. But maybe she only drops one word about the whole performance and she is usually right."

In their long married life one is left perhaps with a picture of them having grown in some ways but not at all similar to their mentors Tyrone and Judy Guthrie, radiating on visitors an easy and gracious eccentricity. Always attentive to the needs of others they would depart for mass on Sunday morning and tell their weekend guests "Back in an hour". The guests might notice an Oscar casually tucked away on the mantelpiece, so that one saw it if one wanted to see it. Later they might be asked if they would like to take the goat for a walk. The mild gentle evenings would be loved most of all. Merula and Guinness have been a most devoted and loyal couple, and she has clearly possessed the breadth of spirit and quality of resolution to embrace the complex and not always easy nature of this actor of genius. "One of the few really good people I know," said Eileen Atkins of her, "who is also huge fun."

> There's no vocabulary
> For love within a family, love that's lived in
> But not looked at, love within the light of which
> All else is seen, the love within which
> All other love finds speech.
> This love is silent.

Can we reach into Guinness in his solitude? His garden, his modest acreage of Kettlebrook Meadows, its remote, buried quality off the beaten track and yet its very cosy, familiar and still English quality, also can tell us something. Lately there has been an increasing roar of traffic from the new A3 dual carriageway cutting through the hill only a few hundred yards from the garden. "The river is within us," wrote Eliot in *The Dry Salvages*, and this itself echoes the Tolstoy quotation in the first chapter of this book.

In late 1988 Guinness agreed to appear in *A Walk in the Woods* by Lee Blessing, an American two-hander based quite closely on certain aspects of the arms control treaty recently signed between Russia and America. The play had been successful on Broadway earlier in the year, receiving two Tony Award nominations and an Outer Circle Critics award. Indeed, it was a warm-hearted, almost sentimental germ of a play about that most elusive of subjects, reconciliation between enemies: it took, or rather pre-supposed, its dramatic power from outside, from the threat of nuclear annihilation, just as certain classical Greek plays assumed for their malignant and dramatic impetus the mindless destructive force of some god's passion.

But how do you anthropomorphise the threat of a nuclear holocaust? Greek plays showed gods on the stage, and while Peter Sloterdijk might write, as he did in his *Critique of Cynical Reason*, that the atomic bomb was the "real Buddha of the West, a perfect sovereign apparatus without bonds. It rests unmoving in its silos, purest reality and purest possibility," yet this was difficult to turn into a Dramatic Presence. By now, anyway, the fear of nuclear death had lost some of its urgency or thrust, and while the programme for *A Walk in the Woods* had its usual quota of the apocalyptic citations that are the fashionable hype of the day – "There is no doubt that art . . . is in radically altered circumstances if the future is placed in doubt . . . Masterpieces cannot be timeless if time itself stops . . . Without confidence that we will be followed by future generations . . . our life is impoverished" – there was a certain post-coital mood about the whole evening.

The events on which *A Walk in the Woods* was based had happened six years earlier, when Paul Nitze, the American diplomat who was only two years Guinness's junior, had entered into a covert and unauthorised negotiation-within-the negotiations with Yuli Kvitsinsky, his Soviet counterpart in the Intermediate-range nuclear forces (INF) talks. They strolled together in the wooded Jura mountains outside Geneva, "sat on a log and sheltering their papers from the rain", according to Strobe Talbott, put the finishing touches to what they called a joint exploratory package. Tentative compromise had been reached primarily by breaking through at a human level to make contact with each other.

Later when the compromise foundered in a series of complex, fractious and prolonged "deliberations" on both sides they met again, this time in a Geneva park, to try and resurrect the original "walk in the woods" formula. Their new deal also failed to go through, although as one State department official complained, Nitze was "still off there in the goddam woods with Kvitsinsky, cooking up deals to kill the Pershing II". Still, it was an inspired move on the part of the playwright Blessing to write up what *Time* much later called "one of the most extraordinary episodes of creative insubordination in the annals of diplomacy". What Blessing did was to reverse the roles, making his Russian, Andrey Botvinnik, the elder of the two men, and his American, John Honeyman, forty-fivish and a rising star (as Yuli Kvitsinsky actually was). This showed, of course, a certain pandering to popular taste (America youthful and temperamental, Russia old, tired and traditional), while the text was cliché-ridden and full of generalisations, but then politicians are cliché-ridden people. But the Russian realist and the American idealist (again quite the opposite of what Nitze was) were beautifully and persuasively underplayed by Guinness and by Edward Herrmann, whose earlier triumph as T.S. Eliot at the Royal Court in London in Michael Hasting's *Tom and Viv* gave the pair plenty to talk about off-stage. The whole evening, indeed, distilled a meditative state of mind not far from that of the *Four Quartets*.

Guinness's timing, as ever, was perfect. In a discussion, for instance, about boredom (always a tricky one, this, on stage), the way he said the somewhat banal line, "There is a difference between frivolity and boredom," had the audience hanging on every half-syllable. It was amazing, now, how Guinness, as a veteran performer, could inspire worship and affection simply by the accomplished way he paced the whole play and displayed the good man at the interior of this essentially passive, state stooge. Yet while it was exquisite and memorable – in the manner, for example, which Guinness received the gift of a pen from the American with a little nod of his head and the gesture of the hand over his heart over the pen which he had put in his pocket – there was little that could stir the passions. When acting in his last role, past the age of eighty, as Don Alberto in *Inner Voices* by Eduardo de Filippo at the

National Theatre in 1983, Ralph Richardson had shown not only great power but passionate comic frenzy. Guinness's last role was not that of a subversive, he had abandoned all disguise in favour of a calm, meditative centre. He was still a giant. But perhaps he was now a giant with nothing much more to hide.

And by now it would seem he had become a little unhappy at appearing on the West End stage; an old friend came round to visit him after the show and recalled that Guinness had a terrible cold. He greeted him in his dressing-room and he was now "like a barrel, but still chain-smoking. 'We're going out to supper,' Guinness told him. 'It's very plain. You may not like it. It's by the river.'"

When they arrived at the restaurant the friend was struck by the number of elegant Italian ladies with fur coats over their arms. Guinness suggested he take a dish with six different kinds of pasta and six different sauces. When they were leaving Guinness tipped everyone and the friend noticed he gave the manager as well some enormous sum. "Do you have to tip?" the friend asked him. Guinness replied to his amazement: "I'm so terrified of them all – I have to buy my way through".

Alec Guinness was not much pleased with the birthday tribute of essays collected by Ronald Harwood for his seventy-fifth birthday in April 1989. When Ion Trewin, the book's publisher, first wrote to Guinness suggesting such a book, Guinness replied testily. They had a sticky lunch at the Garrick. Guinness did not want it done at all, but said, with somewhat ill-concealed bad grace, he would try to tag along.

Graham Greene, unfortunately, could not contribute, replying from Antibes that he was very fond of Alec and would have liked to have written something. But the essay had never been an easy form of writing for him and now he was approaching eighty-four it was a nightmare for him to promise anything. Peter Glenville, Guinness's godfather and directorial architect of some of his best performances, agreed enthusiastically to write but, mysteriously, nothing arrived; John le Carré also agreed, planning to do a 3,000-word essay on "making a spy of Alec", but was chary of abandoning work on a new novel. Among those who said no straightaway were John Mills, who needed what he called his brilliant writing time for himself, and Anthony Quayle who would find, he said, Alec, as a dear and close friend, extremely difficult to write about. Snowdon made his pictures available, saying he had more admiration for Sir Alec's work, both on the stage and in the cinema, than anyone he could think of.

The reviews were characteristic (and echoed those of his own book). More than half said that the volume gave a surprising number of insights into what he was and who he was; the best picked out the constant reminders in the book to his qualities of stillness and quietness: a value compared to the "stabiliser of a great ship". The most repeated story was the self-told tale (perhaps always a little suspect) repeated by Harwood, of the cloakroom ticket. Invited to a grand luncheon at a West End hotel he handed his hat and coat to the attendant, and asked for a ticket. Oh no, smiled the attendant reassuringly, this would not be necessary at all. Guinness was secretly rather pleased at this gesture of recognition and departed. After lunch was over he collected his hat and coat and on his way out he reached into the pocket where he found a piece of paper. On this were written the words, "Bald with Glasses".*

The most repeated piece of gossip (in the reviews, that is) was Coral Browne's account of how she was served breakfast in bed by "Sir Alec" when staying at Kettlebrook Meadows, who then left immediately. Coral Browne turned her attention to the three books on the bedside table, which she called an unmistakable touch, carefully selected and inviting, they spoke for him:

'I thought you might like these!' Indeed, the only problem was which to tackle first. Alec reads a great deal and his choices, while off-beat and unusual, always have been right and have never failed to divert me. It would be heaven to have him always – not only this day – as my own, special librarian, infallible and challenging.

But the other half of the reviews, on the question of the number of insights the book supplied about Guinness, said it gave absolutely none. Some reviewers said it was too expensive. At least three reviewers commented on Guinness's postcard to Harwood, printed

---

* Telling jokes against oneself became something of a competitive game. Guinness and Merula were one night dining with Ralph Richardson and his wife Mu when, unaccountably but characteristically, Richardson got up from the table and said, "I'm going for a walk," then just left. Later they found him sitting all alone on a bench. He had found this old tramp and sat down next to him. The tramp said nothing. After a while looking at Richardson he said, "I know you, you're John Gielgud." "Fuck off!" said Richardson.

as an epilogue: "Wouldn't it be good to call the whole thing off?"
. . . Why not wait until my (unlikely) 80th? I would be gaga by then
and not notice and no-one who knew me in my twenties likely to
be alive. So there you needn't do it at all" – using this quotation
against the book. "You finish this slender volume," wrote Sheridan
Morley, "knowing even less about his private persona than you did
at the outset". Another critic dragged up the ghost of Tynan: "He
exists in a histrionic air-pocket, isolated and circumscribed by his
own eccentricity."*

But it is Guinness's impersonality, his withdrawal of ego or his
power to withdraw his ego, which lies at the very centre of his
creative process. As Alan Bennett observed, in another context,
"He doesn't leave anything spare for the public outside his acting."
One of the reviewers of this book, Douglas Dunn, in the *Glasgow
Herald*, expressed this reaction: "Impersonality is an ambivalent or
contradictory objective in a form of art as physical and humanly
present as acting in the theatre or a film. Yet it is tempting to
think of it as a goal that Guinness has made into an incontestable
virtue." Dunn then compared him to Eliot: as Eliot delineates how
the calm remains at the centre of being, so Guinness finds "an
actorly equivalent of a poet's grace and its imaginative withdrawal
of the ego from the centre of the creative impulse".

The greatest actor at impersonating others was also the greatest
actor at dissociating himself from others – of seeing where he ended
and the parts he played began. This, which is ultimately a spiritual
power, is at the very centre of Guinness's uncanny ability.

Yet, this having been said, one has to be fair to those critics – and
there were some of them – who had been feeling that Guinness, in
the pursuit of his inner serenity, had been detrimental to his art, as
J.W. Lambert had summed it up – resulting in a "built-in halo, a
look . . . of an Ineffable, not to say patronising, Something". The
contradictoriness was captured in another resounding phrase used
about Guinness – "sultan of self-effacement". There is something
smug, self-satisfied, even exhibitionist about the word "sultan".
Did the phrase ring true?

---

* Five years later, in April 1994, an eightieth birthday book, its forty-eight pages as
minimal as a late Guinness performance, was published to thank Guinness, "the private
man", as the editor wrote, "for all the large acts of remembered kindness, and generosity on an unprecedented scale". Most contributors vied with each other to redress this
imbalance. But, as John le Carré pointed out, in his own honest contribution,
Guinness "loathes [the adult world's] flattery and mistrusts its praise".

48

Dream's death kingdom

Since he played the Fool in *Lear* with Olivier in 1946–7 and carried off better notices than his principal, Guinness's relationship with Olivier had been a distant one. Olivier had tried to secure him several times for the National Theatre, but he found, always, some reason to extricate himself.

It is hard to believe he really *liked* Olivier. But Guinness, like Richardson, had a residual comradely affection for him, possibly a less warm one than did Richardson. Olivier, who brooked no rivals and was jealous of anyone who might be considered his equal, once told Ronald Harwood that Merula was the most talented actress of her generation that he had encountered. Alec had told him, Olivier said, that she was more talented than he was and gave everything up for him. This has a ring of truth.

After Olivier's death on 11 July 1989 it was natural that the acting profession should turn to Guinness to deliver the address when the memorial service was held in Westminster Abbey, and this was in spite of the fact Guinness did not seem to entertain all that high a regard for Joan Plowright. He was browsing in a bookshop once in the mid-1960s when he came across an edition of Shakespeare's sonnets which had been edited, and also signed, by Samuel Butler – quite an exciting find for him. He gave away this treasured edition, he could not quite remember why, to Joan Plowright, but was then rather disappointed and regretted it: "I don't think she was very interested in Shakespeare," he commented.

Being called upon to deliver an oration for Olivier was an honour he felt he could not refuse. "I am terrified of making the address about Larry," he confided, "with two ex-wives in the audience" (as well as Joan Plowright, Jill Esmond would also be there). "I have been to the Abbey to test the acoustics. They are so bad you have to speak very slowly."

The address had to last eight minutes. "I've written my piece. I am not going to make a single reference to any contemporary." But there would be more than two ex-wives in the audience. As he spoke about Olivier, he would allow his eyes, from between their now rather yellow eyelids, to circle the room and then swivel round on the listener, while he would occasionally sweep back with a hand the ash of his cigarette from where it fell:

> You know . . . Larry, I liked him and he was very nice to me but I knew how to survive him . . . He completely destroyed Redgrave. He tried to destroy Scofield, not deliberately but by animal cunning, instinctively. Also he could be very pretentious, do things quite unnecessarily, silly things to show off.

When it came to the memorial service the British nation seemed to go right over the top. The pomp was almost up to the scale of a coronation. Olivier, a mere performer, an "actor-laddy", was turned into something enormous and portentous on the American scale of treatment for its nation's fantasy life. 2,000 people attended. Some thought, especially after the grotesque ten years he had spent playing in highly paid but bad films, the ceremony was much overdone. His Order of Merit was carried in procession by Douglas Fairbanks, Jnr, a film award by Michael Caine, and the sword once owned by Edmund Kean by Frank Finlay. It seemed more like idolatry than ceremony. John Gielgud's perfect voice sang out Donne's "Death be not proud" over yet another of his great contemporaries.

To many on this occasion Guinness seemed to be the one person who was not unduly overawed and sycophantic. After giving a generous appreciation of Olivier as an actor and as a person, with a precisely tactful sense of weight he gently deflated him, telling how, when Olivier played Malvolio interrupting the midnight riot of Sir Toby and his companions, he changed the line:

> My masters are you mad, or what are you?

into

> My masters are you mad, or what? *pause* Are you?

He delivered this so perfectly it brought a great, relaxing sigh of laughter to the Abbey. He went on to say that, if you were on stage with Olivier and there was something you were doing and he did not quite approve (the suggestion being that you were being perhaps a little too good at something) he "could go very still and give you a steely look . . ." Thus Guinness indicated, very slightly, that the worm could turn. This brought, as one actor remarked, a sense that this god was a fallible creature. The occasion became real.

Guinness has allowed himself to be photographed by Snowdon in his garden at Kettlebrook Meadows. But when he appeared with Melvyn Bragg on the South Bank Show, as carefully guarded as he has ever shown himself, he made Bragg feel "unaccountably nervous", the reason for which, surmised Bragg, being "because I wasn't being allowed to find a rock to which I could anchor myself".

Bragg, noting he had "never been a tall poppy, never been slashed down", commented on his studied personality and on how difficult it was to get near him: "Is that the way he is – or the way he wants to be?" He inclined to the former view and ventured to suggest it may have been due to him being at cross purposes with himself, part of which was due to feeling the "inclination of intellectuals", while "he doesn't move among intellectuals". Having agreed to do the interview Guinness, Bragg found, gave him no help at all and he felt they were playing "a silly superficial game", while under his breath Guinness was saying, "you're not getting anywhere near me". He responds, said Bragg, to Alan Bennett's breeziness: "If I saw him again I think I would be much more jolly and buffeting." There was only one "thoroughly unbuttoned moment"in the programme, Bragg considered. When Guinness was playing with his and Merula's puppies near their outbuildings he voiced yet again his sentiments over acting as something you can't explain, "like an empathy with animals".

Some of Guinness's recent statements and jottings have a slightly snobbish or evasive, sometimes both, air about them. He contributed several diary pieces to the *Spectator* in 1992–3. On 17 July 1993, for example, he wrote about how he sat one lovely summer morning lolling in a newly acquired steamer-chair set up on his patio at Kettlebrook Meadows, pretending "it is the sundeck of the beautiful *Mauretania*", his favourite of the old Cunard liners, and tricked himself into believing we "are in mid-Atlantic and in the mid-1950s in time. But there is no charming steward to bring beef-tea or chicken-broth". Although he went to prick this little dream – with the bottled iced lemonade which tasted of the smell of gasworks – this was well away from the image of the ordinary little man which he spent much of his time in the 1950s conveying to the public. His remarks brought forth a stern rebuke from a reader who had been a Cunard crew member at the time and had no such fond thoughts about the ship; Sir Alec, he said, had not slept in a crew cabin sharing with seven others, smelt the "farts, the smelly socks" or seen the "uplifting sight of underpants hanging up to dry on a line slung across the cabin" – "I'm afraid I missed the charming steward."

Nostalgia for the vanished space of the past was extended also to the Sistine Chapel, now a "horrific experience" to visit. It had not been the same in 1939 when he found only one other visitor, an elderly lady in tweeds. We are, he wrote elsewhere, "throwing ourselves like lemmings into some overcrowded, over-publicised cultural sea".

But between the cherished privacy and the public urge to exhibit oneself fell the shadow. Perhaps sometimes the conflict and/or the dichotomy was too great for him to contain, for in October 1992 he had an "outburst" about the West End theatre which was widely reported on the front pages of newspapers. Yet the "outburst" was well-timed, just conveniently before the screening of his new role as Heinrich Mann in Christopher Hampton's *Tales from Hollywood*. The statement the reporters claimed he made was that he would never again act in the West End because he "hated" the "blank faces" of the uncomprehending tourists. "It's so hard to respond when the audience doesn't respond because they don't understand." He was now seventy-eight, and his last stage performance had been in *A Walk in the Woods* three years before. "I'd rather go to the provinces where they still speak English and not Japanese". He conceded that tourism helped put "bums on seats" and thus kept the London theatre alive, but the expense involved made him now seldom tempted to see plays in the West End. "I do go occasionally, but only if my pockets are sufficiently full", he grumbled. This must have struck a chord of approval among those people who loved the theatre and found it too expensive. Possibly he could recall that, for his 1938 *Hamlet*, twelve gallery seats were provided free by the *Sunday Pictorial* for those who could not otherwise afford them.

Irritated at what he had said, or had been reported as saying, Guinness again used the *Spectator* to air his views. "Thirty years or so ago, the West End theatre was self-sufficient; the audiences were almost entirely home-grown (as they still are in the provinces)" . . .

But are these claims true? In the 1960s London was flooded with foreign visitors and often plays were presented, during the summer in particular, purely for tourist appeal. *Wise Child*, for instance, attracted a large percentage of American tourists who flocked to see it because of Guinness. And many provincial theatres today are packed with foreigners, especially foreign students.

Guinness went on, "Recently, in answer to a sudden question about all this while being interviewed about something else, I replied tactlessly (not for the first time in my life), and this was treated as if it was some *ex cathedra* pronouncement from the Vatican. The flippant tone in which I spoke was entirely misjudged."

Here Guinness was claiming praise for the "truth" of his remarks and by "tactless" he meant "from the heart", at the same time not being entirely accurate about the kind of reports he got. The *Daily Telegraph*, for instance, did not at all treat his statement as if it had been made by the Pope. Guinness went on to say the point he laboured was "that it is hell for actors to play light comedy to an audience if there exists an acute language barrier. It is nothing new." But were West End comedies full of blank, uncomprehending faces and was there less laughter than in the 1950s? My own impression is that audiences laugh and respond much more easily than they used to, perhaps with less discrimination, especially in Shakespeare, while many foreigners, especially the Japanese whom Guinness singled out, have a greater comprehension of the texts they are listening to than the English themselves. Guinness then told a story which had no relevance, at least as far as one could see, to the point he was making: about a comedian playing to an unresponsive audience who came forward to the front of the stage:

"Anyone here speak English?" he asked. "Yes I do," came a voice. "Well, f— you for a start." The point of this story, was that the whole audience was English and that the comedian could not make contact with them. In fact the joke was being made about the deadness of *English* audiences, especially in former days when they were purely English.

Ralph Richardson's experiences of audiences before he died in 1983 was more warm. He saw them all, every night, as different and as unique as the people who composed them. He called the audience for Pinter's *Home*, for instance, a "hand-fed, pet audience" while for *Lloyd George Knew My Father*, at the Savoy, it was like "going into a cage of lions. You can frighten them, but you mustn't let them frighten you. Give them half a chance and they'll chase you out through the stage door . . . You mustn't fool yourself there are five hundred people keen on you. If you're lucky you've got five." The National Theatre Cottesloe audience he described more like a club. "You try to take them aside separately . . . You're in the end speaking to one person." Perhaps an attitude similar to his view of audiences was taking place in Guinness's last screen performances which had become more minimal and honed down.

When Guinness performed the unlikely role of Heinrich Mann, a victim part, in *Tales from Hollywood*, a play about the German literati in exile, Mann, who wrote the original story of the *Blue Angel*, was continually humiliated by Nelly, his wife. Mann's passive and exploited state was established over and over again by Guinness whose performance seemed both timid and wafer-thin. It seemed unconvincing that Mann had ever been full-blooded enough to have been attracted by Nelly (played by Sinead Cusack as an attractive tart: Nelly had been the original of the Blue Angel and so of Marlene Dietrich's fame). Yet, according to Benedict Nightingale in *The Times*, "the weariness, the sick misery, the increasingly debilitating attempts [of Mann] to sustain his self-respect and disguise his inner disintegration: they were all there, understated yet overwhelming". It needed Dominic Lawson in the *Spectator* to restore Guinness's observation to its full stature. In a diary piece he pointed out how Guinness astutely observed of John Major, during his first term of office, that he always followed Neil Kinnock's physical mannerisms. "If Mr Kinnock asked a question with a sunny beam, Mr Major would reply with a similar expression on his face. If Mr Kinnock led with a scowl, Mr Major's face would darken in turn." This meant that Kinnock was the more decisive character. Major should look carefully at Kinnock's expression and do the opposite, Guinness prescribed, to make Kinnock appear either pompous or flippant by turn, at the same time impose his own different character on the proceedings.

Opinion was more mixed about the last television film that Guinness took part in, namely *A Foreign Field*, Roy Clarke's film about a group of, mainly, ex-servicemen returning to the landing beaches of Normandy to re-capture that moment of greatness, or feeling of something, anyway, in which they had participated. It was severely trounced by one critic as similar to war in that it consisted of "interminable periods of brain-numbing boredom interrupted by brief moments of excitement" (*Daily Mail*). In fact it was a rather quiet and still piece, with a tenuous story line, and huge, empty-headed gaps to be filled with awe and the viewers' own memory of the celebrated players who took part. These included, as well as Guinness, Lauren Bacall, Jeanne Moreau, and Leo McKern,* who played the gruff but benevolent minder of Amos, the Guinness part, who was, but for five words, entirely silent. His brain had been irreparably damaged by mortar fire on D-Day plus whatever it was – where Brigsy, the comrade he asked about, died.

Amos enabled Guinness to give a quite touching display of that early Pierrot-like charm in this sketch of "second childishness" and "mere oblivion". He explored hotel-room appliances with the skill of Jacques Tati, and often reminded one of Chaplin in his sense of loneliness and rejection (and even of Jean-Louis Barrault as Baptiste, the clown of clowns in *Les Enfants du Paradis*). But brain damage was a bit of a misnomer here, holy innocent would have been more appropriate.

Will he be tempted on to the stage again? Both Patrick Garland, who directed him in *The Merchant of Venice*, and Alan Strachan believe he might. Garland offered him the part of Lob in *Dear Brutus*, while Strachan wanted him to play Father Keegan in *John Bull's Other Island*. But he declined both.

Near the end of the film of *Dr Zhivago*, there is a moment where General Yevgraf Zhivago, acted by Guinness, learns that his niece plays the balalaika well but is completely untaught.

"Who taught you?" he asks.

"No-one."

"Then it must be a gift," he calls after her and her boyfriend.

No-one could adequately describe the spiritual feeling which, in one way impersonally, he manages to convey in this line. It is in this power of differentiating, in switching off, in ceasing to be one thing and becoming another, that the gift of Guinness has reigned supreme.

---

* McKern and Guinness also played together in the television adaptation of Greene's *Monsignor Quixote*.

49

Actors tell all

When Tynan wrote his description of Olivier as Othello in 1968 he attributed greatness in an actor to "complete physical relaxation, powerful physical magnetism, commanding eyes that are visible at the back of the gallery, a commanding voice that is audible *without effort* at the back of the gallery, superb timing which includes the capacity to make verse sing, *chutzpah* – the untranslatable Jewish word that means cool nerve and outrageous effrontery combined – and the ability to communicate a sense of danger". To go through the list with regard to Guinness would be to find that he makes a poor showing by comparison.

He almost falls down even with the first one. He does convey complete physical relaxation, this is true, but one wonders if he really does have it? He has often asserted that he is not at all a nervous man, but there has always been something too measured about his need to assert how cool he is. Interviewing him in 1958 Alan Brien summed up the true Guinness manner: "the voice cool, smooth and soft as a Polar bear's fur, the style as measured and impersonal as a bulletin from Buckingham Palace". But when Brien asked him if it was true he never looked anyone in the eye except when hiding himself inside one of his favourite eccentric roles, Guinness replied (untypically) in the first person, while, as Brien wrote, "his eyes kept sweeping restlessly across me like the beams of a lighthouse": ". . . I find that I only look somebody straight in the eye when I am about to tell him a lie. All the biggest frauds I have ever met have been men with that steady, unwinking gaze."

Perhaps Guinness has never been an actor who *at heart* has relaxed and therefore could allow an unpredictable inspiration to take over and change a performance. Pre-planning and calculation: they have always been supremely in control. As Melvyn Bragg said of him, he wishes to have control not only of himself but of everything about him. Every effect has been meticulously staged. But perhaps Tynan's notion contains a slight contradiction in the first place. What actor has complete physical relaxation any more than a finalist at Wimbledon has complete physical relaxation? What is meant, surely, is supremely relaxed confidence and physical *control* i.e. a controlled relaxation, not a complete one.

The commanding eyes, the powerful voice, the powerful physical magnetism . . . although Guinness has the potentiality of calling on all three when the work demands it, they are not rich, superabundant endowments. Superb timing he does have, but again within the context of himself, for he has never been an actor who loves playing off against others on stage. Certainly he has plenty of *chutzpah* – panache might be a better word, although it has none of the knowingness the Jewish word conveys. But the sense of danger is limited to that of thought and implication: he has mostly found symbolic or minimal ways of conveying threat or anger.

But Guinness does have qualities which Tynan omitted from his list. Guinness may not have had the courage of Olivier, the wayward contradictory force which has a timeless, Kiplingesque appeal of risking everything at one go, but he does have a commanding intelligence which makes him a giant. He has always shown what Komisarjevsky considered the first essential of the good actor: imagination. He also has the ability to communicate an understanding of the human heart as no other actor has been able to do. But he has never been the conventional idea of the great stage actor. He has never had a larger than life stature, he never wanted to be stretched, pushed to the limit. Balance, to him, given his background and the lessons a very difficult early life taught him, has been much more critical: "The most important thing in life is a sense of balance: Oh, I don't mean spending one's whole existence on an even keel, daring nothing. But to be conscious that a human personality is many-sided and to be sufficiently balanced to know which side to bring out in a given situation". (And, typically, when he said this he smiled sadly and shrugged his shoulders: "Not that I have it myself but I know several people who have and how I envy them . . .") (*Evening Standard*, 2 October 1957)

Choosing the play or the film may have seemed sometimes like the substitute problem Guinness has found for solving some of, or keeping abreast of, those dark and potentially destructive elements inside him. But the quality of his choice has been in a different category from that of most. He spurns the idea he has played too many eccentrics:

> In a sense everyone is an eccentric. One can be eccentric by being enormously dull and normal. It would be truer to say that one's parts are people with a fixation – people in blinkers like a horse. Journalists who say I am insecure and ill-at-ease just do not know me. One simply refuses to put on a performance of one's private personality. (*Daily Mail*, 7 March 1958)

Yet the continual crisis of his career, with its temporary, joyous release in hope inevitably followed by a mixed sense of success and/or failure and, inevitably where he is concerned, sense of shortcoming, has been the pattern.

Sheer terror – with the ability to deal with it – is perhaps also a necessary component of great acting. Although hardly ever showing it Guinness had always suffered terror and panic. Perhaps nothing could make up for that desperation which lies at the heart of the supreme performer except for some extreme form of release, the darkness of which is an integral part of its attraction. Guinness has been in his emotional insecurity compared to Maggie Smith, another supremely vibrant, comic performer. Both have sometimes lived on the edge, desperately: "Alec has to surprise us all the time," was how another intimate put it, "he is the supreme actor laddy."

It is Paul Scofield who has expressed this terror of performance best:

> What is the worst sensation you can have in your life – worse than pain, worse than cancer or bereavement? . . . It's sitting in front of your dressing-room mirror with perhaps flu coming on, or a bad headache, looking at yourself in the glass and then suddenly realising "I can't do it, I can't do it, I can't do it."

This feeling is common to many great actors. It is, as one of them commented, the second-rate ones who know it is easy.

Humility in an actor is another quality omitted from Tynan's list. It has always been the aim of Guinness, even if he has not by his own reckoning achieved it. Guinness explains this, according to his colleague Simon Callow, with a complete "lack of self-consciousness and utter dignity":

> Just a *little* more effort, I hope, and I may deny myself that extra pat of butter, the third glass of wine, one lascivious thought, and

achievement when irascibility is controlled, one bitchy remark left unsaid; and more positively, find a way to make some small generous gesture without foresight, and direct a prayer of genuine goodwill towards someone I dislike. It is a fairly pitiful ambition after a quarter of a century of genuflexion.

This ceaseless striving for courtesy and humility has perhaps been at the centre of that quality of intimacy Guinness has always communicated and which, to some, has wrongly seemed innate. Sensitive actresses who were also sensitive women picked up this attractive element at once. Eileen Atkins as a schoolgirl kept a photograph of him as Herbert Pocket under the lid of her desk. Jeanne Moreau reacted to this special quality when she first met him in 1992: "Though I had never met him before it's as if I knew him from all his films."

Observation, too, is the outstanding quality in Guinness, hardly needing any more examples; but so is personality, that instinct and practice of self-projection with which an audience does or does not identify. The following passage from Tyrone Guthrie's *Good Acting* can be seen to refer specifically to the stage acting of Guinness:

> It is only theoretically impossible to separate the actor's skill from his personality. Theoretically, then, the most skilful actor is the most protean, the actor with the widest range. It so happens, however, that the actors with the widest range do not usually go very deep. I have known many protean actors who could achieve startling changes in their appearance, voice and mannerisms, but their performances were apt to be superficial ... Some of the greatest actors have no protean quality at all. In every part, though the make-up and costume may vary, the performance is almost exactly the same. John Gielgud is a case in point; matchless in declamation, with extraordinary intelligence, insight and humour, he commands almost no skill as a character actor. Like many other eminent players, he is "always himself".

Guinness has achieved depth with the range, and this is what has made him unique. While no-one would dispute his astonishing ability to be protean in his disguises, what is truly extraordinary is how he can match the characters he is playing with degrees of profundity and insight to every level, even the very deepest, although, perhaps ultimately, they have to have qualities like his own.

He has never been wholly a comic impersonator, the essence of whose success is that one always knows or is guessing who the actor is behind the impersonation. Peter Sellers was always Peter Sellers the comedian, however exactly he impersonated someone else. Instead, Guinness *loses* himself or disappears totally in the character he is playing. The disguises have always gone so much deeper: they are profound, psychologically secure because the pain underneath that holds them in place has always been so much greater than the disturbance of change into someone else. Yet he has always known he cannot err outside his own range and be successful. An actor, he once said, needs a "slight mystical appearance on stage . . . you can't force a character on yourself".

But the importance of Gielgud for Guinness even so – and it was with this he began, imprisoned in the greater actor's almost stifling shadow – must not be ignored, for it has been a lifelong battle with the influence of Gielgud that Guinness instinctively, and probably never consciously, has fought. He has defined himself as an actor in terms of being different from Gielgud, just as he has defined himself as being different from Olivier. But Gielgud has been much closer to him, and therefore needed a much more tenacious and resistant sense of differentiation. The important thing, however, the most valuable and surprising element about this – and it partly explains why Guinness is one of the greatest actors of his times, together with Olivier, Gielgud and Richardson – is that he never rejected Gielgud. He never denied him his presence in himself, he absorbed him, he assimilated him so that in the end and in one sense he devoured him in such a way that he has interiorised in himself all the qualities that Gielgud has, the essential qualities of the great actor. These have always been at the centre of what he is, his being. The observation, the character skills, these were developed. But the identification with Gielgud, with the pure, untrammelled narcissism of the great actor, always went deeper. As an actor Gielgud always let himself go, he has had to a supreme degree the feminine, exhibitionist streak. Guinness has this only in part, he was encouraged to let go but remained always on his guard. Olivier, the most demonstrably virile of the three, was not afraid of his equivocal sexuality, as Michael Billington interestingly wrote: Olivier was a great actor because he was unafraid to reveal elements in his personality "most of us are trained to keep hidden. Men are taught from childhood to be ashamed of their femininity. Olivier exploits his brilliantly and therefore enables all of us to come to terms with a part of ourselves". But there is a wafer-thin division between coming to terms with oneself and indulging oneself.

Guinness has had a much more cautious, equivocal and uneasy relationship with the feminine side of himself. The mastery over it which he has developed has come from somewhere else, and is perhaps ultimately inexplicable. The most consummate mastery has been that of separating himself from the role he is playing, of impersonating someone and then coming back to himself.

There has always been a life apart. "Otherwise," as he has said, "I love dappled sunlight and being out of doors and meeting one or two chums." It doesn't worry him unduly if no one offers him anything more to act. But he's not going to do something for the cash, or for the sake of working. He had a tough life to begin with, had to work inordinately hard to become the great communicator he has, and has above all tried to give virtue her form. Was le Carré right when he wrote in Guinness's eightieth birthday book, "The deprivals and humiliations of three quarters of a century ago are unresolved. It is as though he were still striving to appease the adult world about him; to winkle love from it, to beg its smile, to deflect or harness its monstrosity"? I would prefer to believe that perhaps it was the darkness in the first place which made him learn to forgive the betrayal he had suffered. And that perhaps he would agree with Antony's forgiveness of Enobarbus for deserting him: "The rarer action is/In virtue than in vengeance."

Appendix

The Career of Alec Guinness

PLAYS

d. = director

1934

April	Non-speaking Junior Counsel in *Libel!* by Edward Woolf (d. Leon M. Lion), Playhouse Theatre
August	Chinese coolie, French pirate, English sailor in *Queer Cargo* by Noël Langley (d. Reginald Bach), Piccadilly Theatre
November	Osric and Third Player in *Hamlet* (d. John Gielgud), New Theatre

1935

July	Wolf in *Noah* by André Obey (d. Michel Saint-Denis), New Theatre
October	Sampson and Apothecary in *Romeo and Juliet* (d. John Gielgud), New Theatre

1936

May	The Workman (and later Yakov) in *The Seagull* by Anton Chekhov (d. Theodore Komisarjevsky), New Theatre
September 1936–April 1937	Season with the Old Vic Company:

Boyet in *Love's Labour's Lost* (d. Tyrone Guthrie)

Le Beau and William in *As You Like It* (d. Tyrone Guthrie)

Old Thorney in *The Witch of Edmonton*, by William Rowley, Thomas Dekker and John Ford (d. Michel Saint-Denis)

Reynaldo and Osric in *Hamlet* (d. Tyrone Guthrie)

Sir Andrew Aguecheek in *Twelfth Night* (d. Tyrone Guthrie)

Exeter in *Henry V* (d. Tyrone Guthrie)

1937
June

Osric, Player Queen and Reynaldo in *Hamlet* (d. Tyrone Guthrie), Old Vic Company at Elsinore

Spetember 1937–May 1938

Season with John Gielgud's Company at the Queen's Theatre:

Aumerle and the Groom in *Richard II* (d. John Gielgud)

Snake in *The School for Scandal* by R.B. Sheridan (d. Tyrone Guthrie)

Fedotik in *The Three Sisters* by Anton Chekhov (d. Michel Saint-Denis)

Lorenzo in *The Merchant of Venice* (d. John Gielgud)

1938
June

Louis Dubedat in *The Doctor's Dilemma* by Bernard Shaw (d. Bernard Miles), Richmond Theatre

September–December:

Season with the Old Vic:

Arthur Gower in *Trelawney of the "Wells"* by A.W. Pinero (d. Tyrone Guthrie)

Hamlet in *Hamlet* (d. Tyrone Guthrie)

Bob Acres in *The Rivals* by R.B. Sheridan (d. Esme Church)

1939
January–April

Tour of Europe and Egypt with the Old Vic Company:

Hamlet in *Hamlet* (d. Tyrone Guthrie)

Chorus in *Henry V* (d. Tyrone Guthrie)

Bob Acres in *The Rivals* (d. Esme Church)

Emile Flordan in *Libel!* (d. Leon M. Lion)

May

Macbeth in *Macbeth* (d. Geoffrey Ost). Playhouse, Sheffield

June

Michael Ransom in *The Ascent of F6* by W.H. Auden and Christopher Isherwood (d. Rupert Doone), Old Vic Theatre

July

Romeo in *Romeo and Juliet* (d. Willard Stoker), Perth Scottish Theatre Festival

December

Herbert Pocket in *Great Expectations*, adapted by Guinness from Charles Dickens (d. George Devine), Rudolf Steiner Hall

1940
March

Richard Meilhac in *Cousin Muriel* by Clemence Dane (d. Norman Marshall), Globe Theatre

The Dauphin in *Saint Joan* by Bernard Shaw (d. Norman Marshall), charity matinée, Palace Theatre

May

Ferdinand in *The Tempest* (ds. George Devine and Marius Goring), Old Vic Theatre

September–December   Charleston in *Thunder Rock* by Robert Ardrey (d. Herbert Marshall), English tour

1942
December   Flight Lieutenant Graham in *Flare Path* by Terence Rattigan (d. Margaret Webster), Henry Miller Theatre, New York

1945
April   Nelson in *Hearts of Oak* pageant by Edward Neil (d. S. Albert Locke), Royal Albert Hall

1946
June   Mitya in *The Brothers Karamazov* adapted by Guinness from Fyodor Dostoievsky (d. Peter Brook), Lyric Theatre, Hammersmith

July   Garcin in *Vicious Circle* (*Huis Clos*) by Jean-Paul Sartre (d. Peter Brook), Arts Theatre

September 1946–May 1947   Season with the Old Vic Company at the New Theatre:
The Fool in *King Lear* (d. Laurence Olivier)
Eric Birling in *An Inspector Calls* by J.B. Priestley (d. Basil Dean)
De Guiche in *Cyrano de Bergerac* by Edmond Rostand (d. Tyrone Guthrie)
Abel Drugger in *The Alchemist* by Ben Jonson (d. John Burrell)

September 1947–May 1948   Season with the Old Vic Company at the New Theatre:
Richard II in *Richard II* (d. Ralph Richardson)

The Dauphin in *Saint Joan* by G.B. Shaw (d. John Burrell)

Menenius Agrippa in *Coriolanus* (d. E. Martin Browne)

1948
September

Directed *Twelfth Night* for Old Vic Company at the New Theatre

1949
February

Dr James Simpson in *The Human Touch* by J. Lee Thompson and Dudley Leslie (d. Peter Ashmore), Savoy Theatre

August

An Unidentified Guest (Sir Henry Harcourt-Reilly) in *The Cocktail Party* by T.S. Eliot (d. E. Martin Browne), Lyceum Theatre, Edinburgh

1950
January

An Unidentified Guest in *The Cocktail Party* (d. E. Martin Browne), Henry Miller Theatre, New York

1951
May

Hamlet in *Hamlet* (ds. Guinness and Frank Hauser), New Theatre

1952
April

The Ant Scientist in *Under the Sycamore Tree* by Sam and Bella Spewack (d. Peter Glenville), Aldwych Theatre

1953
July–September

Season at the Shakespeare Playhouse, Stratford-on-Avon, Ontario:

King of France in *All's Well That Ends Well* (d. Tyrone Guthrie)
Richard III in *Richard III* (d. Tyrone Guthrie)

1954
March   The Cardinal in *The Prisoner* by Bridget Boland (d. Peter Glenville) Globe Theatre

May   Boniface in *Hotel Paradiso* by Georges Feydeau and Maurice Desvallières (d. and translator Peter Glenville), Winter Garden Theatre

1960
May   Aircraftman Ross in *Ross* by Terence Rattigan (d. Glen Byam Shaw), Theatre Royal, Haymarket

1963
August   Bérenger the First in *Exit the King* by Eugène Ionesco (d. George Devine), Royal Lyceum Theatre, Edinburgh

September   Bérenger the First in *Exit the King*, Royal Court Theatre

1964
January   Dylan Thomas in *Dylan* by Sidney Michaels (d. Peter Glenville), Plymouth Theatre, New York

1966
January   Von Berg in *Incident at Vichy* by Arthur Miller (d. Peter Wood), Phoenix Theatre

October   Macbeth in *Macbeth* (d. William Gaskill), Royal Court

1967
October

Mrs Artminster in *Wise Child* by Simon Gray (d. John Dexter), Wyndham's Theatre

1968
May

An Unidentified Guest in *The Cocktail Party* by T.S. Eliot (d. Guinness), Chichester Festival Theatre; Wyndham's Theatre; Haymarket Theatre

1970
July

John in *Time Out of Mind* by Bridget Boland (d. Stephen Barry), Yvonne Arnaud Theatre, Guildford

1971
August

The Father in *A Voyage Round My Father* by John Mortimer (d. Ronald Eyre), Haymarket Theatre

1973
May

Dr Wickstead in *Habeas Corpus* by Alan Bennett (d. Ronald Eyre), Lyric Theatre

1975
April

Dudley in *A Family and a Fortune* adapted by Julian Mitchell from Ivy Compton-Burnett (d. Alan Strachan), Apollo Theatre

1976
October

Dean Swift in *Yahoo* adapted by Guinness and Alan Strachan from the works of Jonathan Swift (d. Alan Strachan), Queen's Theatre

1977
September

Hilary in *The Old Country* by Alan Bennett (d. Clifford Williams), Queen's Theatre

1984
June

Shylock in *The Merchant of Venice* (d. Patrick Garland), Chichester Festival Theatre

1988
October

Andrey Botvinnik in *A Walk in the Woods* (d. Ronald Eyre), Comedy Theatre

FILMS

1933   Walk-on role in *Evensong* (d. Victor Saville)

1946   Herbert Pocket in *Great Expectations* (d. David Lean)

1948   Fagin in *Oliver Twist* (d. David Lean)

1949   The D'Ascoyne family in *Kind Hearts and Coronets* (d. Robert Hamer)
Whimple in *A Run for Your Money* (d. Charles Frend)

1950   George Bird in *Last Holiday* (d. Henry Cass)
Disraeli in *The Mudlark* (d. Jean Negulesco)

1951   Henry Holland in *The Lavender Hill Mob* (d. Charles Crichton)
Sidney Stratton in *The Man in the White Suit* (d. Alexander Mackendrick)

1952   Denry Machin in *The Card* (d. Ronald Neame), released in U.S. as *The Promoter*

1953   Flight Lieutenant Peter Ross in *Malta Story* (d. Brian Desmond Hurst)
Henry St James in *The Captain's Paradise* (d. Anthony Kimmins)
Father Brown in *Father Brown* (d. Robert Hamer), released in the US as *The Detective*

1954   Colonel Sir Edgar Fraser in *To Paris with Love* (d. Robert Hamer)

The Cardinal in *The Prisoner* (d. Peter Glenville)

1955 Professor Marcus in *The Ladykillers* (d. Alexander Mackendrick)

Prince Albert in *The Swan* (d. Charles Vidor)

1957 William Horatio Ambrose in *Barnacle Bill* (d. Charles Frend)

Colonel Nicholson in *The Bridge on the River Kwai* (d. David Lean)

1958 Gulley Jimson in *The Horse's Mouth* (d. Ronald Neame)

1959 John Barrett, Jacques de Gue in *The Scapegoat* (d. Robert Hamer)

Jebal Deeks in *The Wicked Scheme of Jebal Deeks* (d. Franklin Shaffer), for US television

Jim Wormold in *Our Man in Havana* (d. Carol Reed)

1960 Lieutenant-Colonel Jock Sinclair in *Tunes of Glory* (d. Ronald Neame)

1961 Koicho Asano in *Majority of One* (d. Mervyn LeRoy)

1962 Captain Crawford in *HMS Defiant* (d. Lewis Gilbert)

Prince Feisal in *Lawrence of Arabia* (d. David Lean)

1964 Marcus Aurelius in *The Fall of the Roman Empire* (d. Anthony Mann)

1965 Herr Frick in *Situation Hopeless — But Not Serious* (d. Gottfried Reinhardt)

General Yevgraf Zhivago in *Doctor Zhivago* (d. David Lean)

1966 Boniface in *Hotel Paradiso* (d. Peter Glenville)

Pol in *The Quiller Memorandum* (d. Michael Anderson)

1967 Major Jones in *The Comedians* (d. Peter Glenville)

1969 Executioner in *Conversation at Night* (d. Rudolf Cartier) — for television

1970 Charles I in *Cromwell* (d. Ken Hughes)

Marley's Ghost in *Scrooge* (d. Ronald Neame)

Sir Andrew Aguecheek in *Twelfth Night* (ds. John Dexter and John Sichel) for television

1972 Narrator in *Solo* (programme of e.e. cummings's poetry) (d. James Cellan Jones) — for television

Adolf Hitler in *Hitler — The Last Ten Days* (d. Ennio di Concini)

1973 The Pope in *Brother Sun, Sister Moon* (d. Franco Zeffirelli)

1974   Jocelyn Broome in *The Gift of Friendship* (d. Mike Newell)

      Julius Caesar in *Caesar and Cleopatra* (d. James Cellan Jones)

1976   Bensonmum in *Murder by Death* (d. Robert Moore)

1977   Obi-Ben Kenobi in *Star Wars* (d. George Lucas)

1979   George Smiley in *Tinker Tailor Soldier Spy* (d. John Irvin) – for television

1980   Obi-Ben Kenobi in *The Empire Strikes Back* (d. Irvin Kershner)

      Bigalow in *Raise the Titanic* (d. Jerry Jameson)

      The Earl of Dorincourt in *Little Lord Fauntleroy* (d. Jack Gold)

1981   George Smiley in *Smiley's People* (d. Simon Langton) – for television

1982   Sigmund Freud in *Lovesick* (d. Marshall Brickman)

1983   Obi-Ben Kenobi in *Return of the Jedi* (d. Richard Marquand)

1984   Professor Godbole in *A Passage to India* (d. David Lean)

1985   Father Quixote in *Monsignor Quixote* (d. Rodney Bennett)

1986   William Dorrit in *Little Dorrit* (d. Christine Edzard)

1987   Mr Todd in *A Handful of Dust* (d. Charles Sturridge)

1992   Heinrich Mann in *Tales from Hollywood* (d. Howard Davies) – for television

1993   Amos in *A Foreign Field* (d. Charles Sturridge) – for television

Sources

Following are the more important works by Guinness himself, his many published articles and interviews given to press, radio and television, on which I have drawn. I acknowledge with thanks the authors, editors, newspapers, publishers, broadcasting companies, as cited:

(i) *by Alec Guinness*:

"I took my landing craft to the Sicily Beaches", *Daily Telegraph*, 20 August 1943

"Money for Jam", *The Penguin New Writing*, No. 26, 1945

"My Idea of Hamlet", *Spectator*, 6 July 1951

"A Helping Hand From Gielgud", *The Sunday Times*, 22 April 1956

"The 'Horse' and I", *Observer*, 1 February 1959

"Cakes and Ale No More", *Spectator*, 22 October 1983

Essay on Gielgud, *The Ages of Gielgud*, (ed. Ronald Harwood) Hodder and Stoughton, 1984

Blessings in Disguise, Hamish Hamilton, 1985

"Don't Leave Your Fan on the Seat", *Spectator*, 5 September 1987

"Jottings from My Notebook", *Spectator*, 19/26 December 1992

Diary, *Spectator*, 17 July 1993

(ii) by others (for the most part these are interviews with Guinness; the list is by no means comprehensive):

Picture Post, 10 May 1947

Observer, 9 March 1952

Life Magazine, 24 November 1952
Daily Telegraph, 12 April 1953
Daily Telegraph, 30 October 1955
Sunday Times, 19 February 1956
News Chronicle, 31 March 1956
Sunday Times, 22 April 1956
Evening Standard, 2 October 1957
Evening News, 1 January 1958
The Times, 10 February 1958
Daily Mail, 7 March 1958
The Times, 28 March 1958
Everybody's, 23 March 1958
Time, 21 April 1958
Guardian, 10 January 1959
Daily Mail, 3 February 1959
Daily Telegraph, 8 May 1959
Sunday Graphic, 26 July 1959
Evening Standard, 15 January 1960
Daily Telegraph, 22 June 1960
Sunday Express, 7 May 1964
New York Times, 5 February 1965
New York Times, 2 August 1965
Sunday Express, 19 December 1965
Daily Express, 22 October 1966
The Times, 4 December 1967
Daily Mail, 5 May 1968
Evening News, 5 February 1968
Daily Mail, 26 June 1970
Daily Telegraph, 1 August 1971
The Times, 7 August 1971
Daily Mail, 7 August 1971
Sunday Times, 25 August 1971
Evening Standard, 1 September 1972
Daily Mail, 17 December 1972
Daily Telegraph Magazine, 4 May 1973
Guardian, 19 May 1973
Daily Telegraph, 9 December 1974
Evening Standard, 2 February 1975
Daily Telegraph Magazine, 9 September 1975
Evening Standard, 10 September 1976
The Times, 4 October 1976

Sunday Express, 19 February 1977
Evening Standard, 5 August 1977
The Sunday Times Magazine, 2 October 1977
The Times, 8 December 1977
Sunday Express, 17 February 1978
Vogue, September 1979
Guardian, 8 September 1979
The Sunday Times, 8 February 1981
The Times, 30 November 1981
Mail on Sunday, 4 December 1983
The Sunday Times, 29 April 1984
Observer, 9 December 1984
Express Sunday Magazine, 3 July 1985
The Times, 30 September 1985
Guardian, 7 October 1985
Today, 11 May 1987
Observer, 10 January 1988
Independent Magazine, 1 October 1988
The Times, 10 October 1988
Daily Telegraph, 29 October 1992
Spectator, 17 July, 7 August 1993
Telegraph Magazine, 31 July 1993
Independent on Sunday, 20 March 1994

(iii) radio and television broadcasts:

28 February 1942 (*The Rape of the Locks*, BBC)
4 October 1946 (*Huis Clos*, BBC)
4 October 1960 (*Desert Island Discs*, BBC, int. Roy Plomley)
7 October 1971 (BBC, *Tribute to Michel Saint-Denis*
18 March 1974 (BBC, reading and introducing T.S. Eliot's poems)
29 January 1975 (BBC, int. Derek Parker)
6 May 1981 (BBC monologue, Peter Barnes's *People*)
30 September 1982 (BBC, on John le Carré)
10 September 1984 (BBC, on Graham Greene at Eighty)
30 August 1985 (BBC, int. Alan Strachan)
17 February 1985 (LWT, *David Lean: A Life in Film* int. Melvyn Bragg)
6 October 1985 (LWT, *The South Bank Show*, int. Melvyn Bragg)

11 July 1989 (BBC, Funeral of Lord Olivier)

There are hardly any contemporary autobiographies or memoirs
– or books on the British theatre since the mid 1930s or on film
since the late 1940s – that do not contain some reference or
other to Guinness. The following list includes only those works
on which I have drawn most frequently. (The place of publication
is London unless otherwise indicated.)

James Agate, *Ego* (9 vols., 1935–48: vol. I, Hamish Hamilton,
1935; vol.2 Gollancz, 1936; vols. 3–9, Harrap, 1938–48)
—— *Brief Chronicles* (Cape, 1943)
—— *Red Letter Nights* (Cape, 1944)
Alec: A Birthday Present for Alec Guinness (Sinclair-Stevenson,
1994)
Brooks Atkinson, *Broadway, New York* (Macmillan, New
York, 1970)
Enid Bagnold, *Enid Bagnold's Autobiography* (Heinemann,
1969)
Deirdre Bair, *Samuel Beckett* (Cape, 1978)
Michael Balcon, *Michael Balcon Presents . . . A Lifetime of
Films* (Hutchinson, 1969)
Charles Barr, *Ealing Studios* (Cameron and Tayleur/David and
Charles, 1977)
Felix Barker, *The Oliviers* (Hamish Hamilton, 1953)
Wilfred Blunt, *Cockerell* (Hamish Hamilton, 1964)
Michael Billington, *The Modern Actor* (Hamish Hamilton,
1973)
—— *Peggy Ashcroft, 1907–1991* (Mandarin, 1991)
Denys Blakelock, *Advice to a Player* (Heinemann, 1957)
—— *Round the Next Corner* (Gollancz, 1967)
Melvyn Bragg, *Laurence Olivier* (Hutchinson, 1984)
Peter Brook, *The Empty Space* (MacGibbon and Kee, 1968)
Ivor Brown, *The Way of My World* (Collins, 1954)
—— (ed.), *Theatre 1955–6* (Reinhardt, 1956)
Buckle, Richard (ed.), *Cecil Beaton, Self-portrait with Friends:
Diaries 1926–74* (Weidenfeld & Nicolson, 1979)
Peter Bull, *To Sea in a Sieve* (Peter Davies, 1956)
—— *I Know the Face but . . .* (Peter Davies, 1956)
Simon Callow, *On Being an Actor* (Methuen, 1984)
John Casson, *Lewis and Sybil: A Memoir* (Collins, 1954)

T.E.B. Clarke, *This is Where I Came In* (Michael Joseph, 1974)

D. Felicitas Corrigan, *The Nun, the Infidel & the Superman* (John Murray, 1985)

John Cottrell, *Laurence Olivier* (Weidenfeld and Nicolson, 1975)

James Dale, *Pulling Faces for a Living* (Gollancz, 1970)

Monja Danischewsky, *White Russian – Red Face* (Gollancz, 1966)

Peter Daubeny, *My World of Theatre* (Cape, 1971)

Russell Davies (ed.), *The Kenneth Williams Diaries* (Harper Collins, 1993)

Bette Davis, *The Lonely Life* (Alfred Knopf, New York, 1962)

Basil Dean, *The Theatre at War* (Harrap, 1956)

Diana Devlin, *A Speaking Part: Lewis Casson* (Hodder and Stoughton, 1982)

Fabia Drake, *Blind Fortune* (Kimber, 1978)

Daphne du Maurier, *Gerald: A Portrait* (Gollancz, 1934)

Raymond Durgnat: *A Mirror for England: British Movies from Austerity to Affluence* (Faber and Faber, 1970)

T.S. Eliot, *Selected Essays* (Faber and Faber, 1932)

Douglas Fairbanks Jnr. *The Salad Days* (Doubleday, New York, 1985)

Richard Findlater, *Michael Redgrave: Actor* (Heinemann, 1956)

—— *Lilian Baylis: The Lady of the Old Vic* (Allen Lane, 1975)

Bryan Forbes, *Notes for a Life* (Collins, 1974)

—— *Ned's Girl* (Elm Tree, 1977)

Boris Ford (ed.) *The Arts in Britain*, Vol 9 (Cambridge University Press, 1988)

James Forsyth, *Tyrone Guthrie: The Authorized Biography* (Hamish Hamilton, 1976)

Angela Fox, *Slightly Foxed* (Collins, 1986)

—— *Completely Foxed* (Collins, 1989)

James Fox, *Comeback* (Hodder Christian Paperback, 1983)

John French, *Robert Shaw: The Price of Success* (Nick Hern, 1993)

John Gielgud, *Early Stages* (Macmillan, 1939)

—— *Stage Directions* (Heinemann, 1963)

—— *Distinguished Company* (Heinemann Educational, 1972)

—— *An Actor and His Times* (Sidgwick and Jackson, 1979)

Graham Greene, *The Pleasure Dome* (Secker and Warburg, 1972)

Michele Guinness, *The Guinness Legend* (Hodder and Stoughton, 1990)

Tyrone Guthrie, *A Life in the Theatre* (Hamish Hamilton, 1960)

—— *In Various Directions* (Michael Joseph, 1965)

—— *Tyrone Guthrie on Acting* (Studio Vista, 1971)

Peter Hall, *Peter Hall's Diaries* (Hamish Hamilton, 1983)

Cedric Hardwicke, *A Victorian in Orbit* (Methuen, 1961)

Rex Harrison, *Rex* (Macmillan, 1974)

Ronald Harwood, *Sir Donald Wolfit CBE* (Secker and Warburg, 1971)

—— (ed.) *The Ages of Gielgud* (Hodder and Stoughton, 1984)

—— (ed.) *Dear Alec: Guinness at 75* (Hodder and Stoughton, 1989)

Jack Hawkins, *Anything for a Quiet Life* (Elm Tree Books, 1973)

Ronald Hayman, *John Gielgud* (Heinemann Educational, 1971)

Harold Hobson, *Ralph Richardson* (Barrie and Rockliff, 1958)

—— *Unfinished Journey* (Weidenfeld and Nicolson, 1978)

—— *Theatre in Britain* (Phaidon, 1984)

Anthony Holden, *Laurence Olivier: A Biography* (Weidenfeld and Nicolson, 1988)

Allan Hunter: *Alec Guinness on Screen* (Edinburgh, 1982)

Ernest Jones, *Oedipus and Hamlet, Essays in Applied Psychoanalysis* (New York, 1923)

Philip Kemp, *Lethal Innocence: The Cinema of Alexander Mackendrick* (Methuen, 1991)

Michael Korda, *Charmed Lives* (Random House, New York, 1979)

C.A. Lejeune, *Thank You for Having Me* (Hutchinson, 1964)

John le Carré, *A Perfect Spy* (Hodder and Stoughton, 1986)

—— *Tinker Tailor Soldier Spy* (with le Carré's Foreword, Hodder and Stoughton, 1991)

Roger Lewis, *The Life and Death of Peter Sellers* (Century, 1994)

Viola Meynell (ed.), *Further Letters to Sydney Carlyle Cockerell* (Rupert Hart-Davis, 1956)

John Mills, *Up in the Clouds, Gentlemen, Please* (Weidenfeld and Nicolson, 1980)

Sheridan Morley, *Review Copies* (Robson, 1974)

—— *Tales from the Hollywood Raj* (Weidenfeld and Nicolson, 1981)

—— *My Father Robert* (Weidenfeld and Nicolson, 1993)

—— (ed.), *The Theatre Addict's Archive* (Elm Tree Books, 1977)

John Mortimer, *In Character* (Allen Lane, 1983)

Laurence Olivier, *Confessions of an Actor* (Weidenfeld and Nicolson, (1982)

—— *On Acting* (Weidenfeld and Nicolson, 1986)

Graham Payn and Sheridan Morley (eds.), *The Noël Coward Diaries* (Weidenfeld and Nicolson, 1982)

George Perry (ed.), *Forever Ealing* (Pavilion, 1981)

J.B. Priestley, *Particular Pleasures* (Stein and Day, New York, 1975)

Anthony Quayle, *A Time to Speak* (Century, 1990)

Michael Redgrave, *In My Mind's Eye* (Weidenfeld and Nicolson, 1983)

Andrew Sinclair, *Spiegel: The Man Behind the Pictures* (Weidenfeld and Nicolson, 1987)

Donald Sinden, *A Touch of the Memoirs* (Hodder and Stoughton, 1982)

Robert Speaight, *The Property Basket* (Collins, 1970)

Anthony Storr, *The School of Genius* (André Deutsch, 1988)

John Russell Taylor, *Alec Guinness: A Celebration* (Pavilion, 1985)

J.C. Trewin, *Edith Evans* (Rockliff, 1964)

—— *Drama in Britain 1951–64* (Longman, 1965)

—— *Five & Eighty Hamlets* (Hutchinson, 1987)

Kathleen Tynan, *The Life of Kenneth Tynan* (Weidenfeld and Nicolson, 1987)

—— (ed.) *The Letters of Kenneth Tynan* (Weidenfeld and Nicolson, 1994)

Kenneth Tynan, *Alec Guinness* (Rockliff, 1953)

—— *Curtains* (Longman, 1961)

—— *A View of the English Stage* (Davis-Poynter, 1975)

Peter Ustinov, *Dear Me* (Heinemann, 1977)

John Vickers, *The Old Vic in Photographs* (Saturn, 1947)

—— *Five Seasons* (Saturn, 1950)

Hugo Vickers, *Vivien Leigh* (Hamish Hamilton, 1988)

Alexander Walker, *Hollywood, England* (Michael Joseph, 1974)

Irving Wardle, *The Theatres of George Devine* (Cape, 1978)

Michael Warre, *Designing and Making Stage Scenery* (Studio Vista, 1966)

Margaret Webster, *The Same Only Different* (Gollancz, 1969)

Herbert Wilcox, *Twenty-five Thousand Sunsets* (Bodley Head, 1967)

E.G. Harcourt Williams, *Old Vic Saga* (Winchester, 1949)

Audrey Williamson, *Old Vic Drama* (Rockliff, 1951)

Kenneth Williams, *Just William: An Autobiography* (Harper Collins, 1993)

B.A. Young, *The Rattigan Version* (Hamish Hamilton, 1986)

Acknowledgements

This book owes much to the effort and encouragement of Ion Trewin, who originally commissioned it, Deborah Rogers, Richard Cohen, and, in its final stages, to the dedicated participation of Carole Welch and of John Bright-Holmes, whom I thank warmly for his careful editing. To Barbara Everett I must express my gratitude for comments on the typescript and for pointing out many errors, while I am grateful to John Tydeman, Kevin Brownlow, and Claire Trocmé for reading through the proofs. I have been forbidden to quote from unpublished letters, however I wish to thank those who have lent me such material, or made it available, as well as all those many colleagues, friends, admirers, critics and interviewers of Guinness who have either consented to be interviewed, or helped the completion of this book in some way or another. I must also thank those who have contributed to my previous books on Ralph Richardson, Laurence Olivier, Peter Brook, and Shakespeare for much material on Guinness that I did not use at the time – as well as for some that I did – and which has now proved invaluable.

The following is a list, by no means complete, of those who have helped the book either by consenting to be interviewed, or in some other way, and towards whom I must express my gratitude: the late Dame Peggy Ashcroft; the late Harry Andrews; Clare Astor; Eileen Atkins; Jill Balcon; Michael Billington; Melvyn Bragg; the late Coral Browne; Kevin Brownlow; Elaine Burrows; Simon Callow; Father Philip Caraman; Betty Coxon; Charles Crichton; Michael Codron; Peter Copley; Anthony Daniels; Alexander Davion; Frank Delaney; David Drummond; Elaine Dundy; Christine Edzard; Charlotte Elson; Martin Esslin; Barbara Everett; Clive Francis; Angela Fox; Edward Fox; Stuart Freeborn; Andrew Geddes; Lord Geddes; Sir John Gielgud; David Gothard; Simon Gough; Simon Gray; the late Graham Greene; Kate Griffin; Margaret

Harris; Ronald Harwood; Frank Hauser; Nick Hern; Michael Holroyd; Nigel Horne; Nicholas Hunter; Miles Hutchinson; Emrys Jones; James Cellan Jones; Dominic Lawson; the late Sir David Lean; George Lucas; the late Leueen MacGrath; the late Alexander Mackendrick; Sir John Mills; Sheridan Morley; John Mortimer; Michael Meyer; David Miller; Margaret Philipsborn; Michael Pickwoad; the late J.B. Priestley; the late Sir Anthony Quayle; Corin Redgrave; Michael Relph; Simon Relph; George Rylands; Rosemary Say; Andrew Sinclair; Donald Sinden; Douglas Slocombe; The Earl of Snowdon; Oliver Stockman; Alix Stone; Anthony Storr; Alan Strachan; Father Roderick Strange; John Swanzy; the late J.C. Trewin; Wendy Trewin; John Tydeman; Kathleen Tynan (to whom I am grateful for permission to quote copyright material); Gore Vidal; Alexander Walker; John Walsh; Irving Wardle; Michael Warre; Sue Westwood; Clifford Williams; Irene Worth; Franco Zeffirelli. Thanks also are due to Faber and Faber Ltd, for permission to quote from T.S. Eliot's *Murder in the Cathedral* and *The Cocktail Party*.

I must again emphasise this is not an authorised biography, and that the interpretation or construction I have brought to Guinness's life, his family and his career is entirely my own, should be so judged, and not be imputed to him or to anyone else. Finally I must make a plea that this portrait is of a living person, and should be considered as a whole, not blown up or distorted through undue emphasis placed upon some of its detail or colour.

G.O'C.
Oxford, May 1994

Index

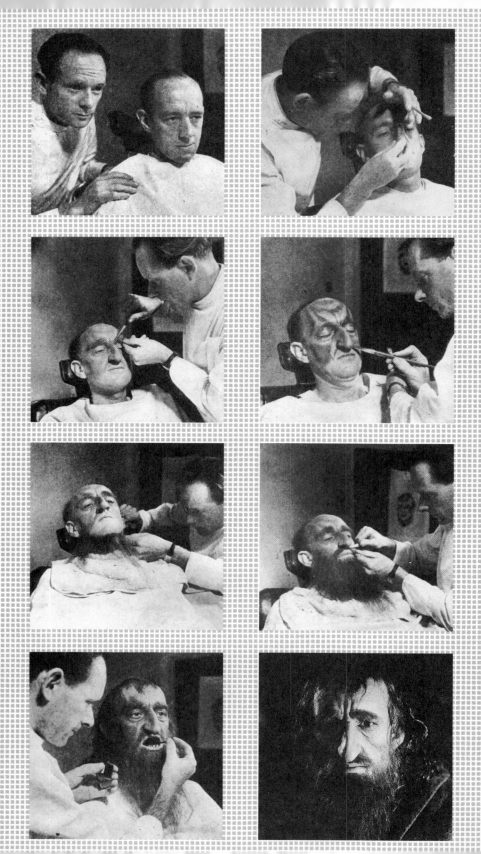